THE PLAYERS

As nations cannot be rewarded or punished in the next world, they must be in this. By an inevitable chain of causes and effects, Providence punishes national sins by national calamities.
　　　　　—Colonel Mason (Constitutional Convention, 1787)

We must not interfere with the institution of slavery in the states where it exists because the Constitution forbids it and the general welfare does not require us to do so.
　　　　　—Abraham Lincoln

[Slavery is] a moral and political evil in any country. I think it, however, a greater evil to the white than to the black race.
　　　　　—Robert E. Lee

[Slavery] was in no wise the cause of the conflict [Civil War].
　　　　　—Jefferson Davis

We hold these truths to be self evident, that all men are created equal.
　　　　　—Thomas Jefferson (The Declaration of Independence)

The South was fighting to take slavery out of the Union and the North was fighting to keep it in the Union...both despising the Negro, both insulting the Negro.
　　　　　—Frederick Douglass

The framers of the Constitution had not regarded Negroes as citizens, and the present condition of that race warranted no change in their legal status.
　　　　　—Chief Justice Roger B. Taney

I shudder when I think of the calamities which slavery is likely to produce in this country. The whites will be exasperated to madness—shall be wicked enough to exterminate the Negroes.
　　　　　—John Quincy Adams

FROM SLAVE TO UNTOUCHABLE

LINCOLN'S SOLUTION

by Paul Kalra

Foreword by Congressman Jesse L. Jackson, Jr.

Antenna Publishing Co.
Pleasant Hill, California

Published by: **Antenna Publishing Co**.
Post Office Box 23826
Pleasant Hill, CA 94523, USA
www.SlaveToUntouchable.com

Copyright ©2011 by Paul Kalra

ISBN 978-0-9647173-6-7 hardback
ISBN 978-0-9647173-7-4 paperback
ISBN 978-0-9647173-8-1 ebook

LCCN: 2011902568   Call #973.711 KALRA

1 3 5 7 9 10 8 6 4 2

Publisher's Cataloging in Publication Data
Kalra, Paul S.
From Slave To Untouchable: Lincoln's Solution / by Paul Kalra

Includes bibliographical references and index
1. United States—History—Civil War—Causes.
2. Lincoln, Abraham—Political and social views.
3. Slaves—United States—Social conditions.
4. United States—Constitution.
5. Presidents—United States
6. Catholic Church—Louisiana—History.
7. Social classes—United States.
8. Equality—United States.
9. United States—Economic conditions.
10. America—Race relations.

Printed in the United States of America

To the 620,000 Americans who perished in the Civil War
to remove the sin of
Protestant slavery from the slaveholders' Constitution,

and

To Mother Teresa, my hometown saint for her blessing:

Only in heaven will we see how much we owe to the poor for
helping us to love God better because of them.
Do not allow anyone to feel unloved, neglected or unwanted.
Do to them what you would want someone to do for you.
Be God's love and bring His light into their lives.

Also by Paul Kalra

The American Class System: Divide and Rule

Contents

FOREWORD

By Congressman Jesse Jackson, Jr.

The United States operates under an illusion that has a profound impact on everything from how we as individuals view each other to what we expect from our government. The illusion is simply this: the Civil War is over. Certainly it is true that the fighting from 1861 to 1865, which threatened to irreparably shred the fabric of our national union, has ended; but its central questions remain. As a result, our nation exists in various states of perpetual unrest within the confines of those unanswered questions: how does the nation politically enfranchise those once viewed as three-fifths of a human being, and how will these newly freed slaves be brought into the economic mainstream? We must look to the war itself for those answers. Scholars such as Paul Kalra provide vital information on slavery during the Civil War era, which helps light our path toward the necessary solutions to the war's unanswered questions.

Radical Republicans of the Civil War era wanted immediate emancipation, and proposed the "liberal" solution of the government by providing the freed slaves with housing, education, and health care. The defeated Democrats of the Confederacy put forth the "conservative" remedy of having the freed slaves pick themselves up by their own bootstraps and move on. The "moderate" plan of helping the freed slaves for a short time was chosen. We now know that plan as Reconstruction.

The history, and to some extent the current status, of those of African descent in America shows that having constitutional *rights* to live as full citizens and having the *ability* to do so are two separate issues. Slaves living in states engaged in the Civil War were freed when the Emancipation Proclamation took effect on January 1, 1863. The institution of slavery in the United States was abolished in 1865 by the Thirteenth Amendment to the Constitution. The newly freed slaves were formally granted United States citizenship after passage of the Fourteenth Amendment in 1868. Two years later, the

Fifteenth Amendment was passed, granting them the right to vote. However, the descendants of slaves and others of African descent in America did not enjoy the full freedom of American citizenship until well into the twentieth century. That ability was underscored by the 1954 *Brown v. Board of Education of Topeka, Kansas* Supreme Court Ruling, the 1964 Civil Rights Act, the 1965 Voting Rights Act, affirmative action, and, other initiatives.

Standing at the dawn of the twenty-first century, we see that emancipation and more than a century of legal and political advancement have yet to produce racial equality and social justice. That is because the war defeated the Confederate troops, but not the Confederate way of perceiving slaves and non-slaveholding whites. Those who were of African descent—and later a range of non-whites—were considered "less than" those who were white. Among whites, those who were not wealthy, non-slaveholding landowners were considered "less than" those who were.

Many students of Civil War history have long held that wealthy, Southern whites who wanted to maintain economic supremacy—and the political power that came with it—fueled views of white racial superiority to keep poor whites and white yeoman farmers emotionally committed to their side. The powerful whites advanced the states rights' premise to give their effort to maintain political power cover. Confederate leaders needed this one-two punch to counter Abraham Lincoln and the Republicans' political motive of preserving the Union, and the moral imperative of abolishing slavery.

The descendants of slaves, and those who looked like them, were labeled "uncivilized," "criminal in orientation," "shiftless," and "incapable of governing." Groups such as the Ku Klux Klan sprang up to violently repress African Americans. Political repression was even more rampant. Many Southern states had Black Codes that restored many of the same social and work conditions of slavery. Among Mississippi's Black Codes, for example, was a provision making it illegal to preach the Gospel without a state license. The Black Codes were to mature into the Jim Crow laws that followed the Supreme Court's *Plessy v. Ferguson* decision of 1896. That decision put forth the concept of "separate but equal."

Racism and classism, already comfortably nestled into the fabric of the national consciousness, found political expression during the Civil War. The war's race and race-generated economic concerns trimmed our political parties down to the Democrats and Republicans who wield power today. The twists and turns about economically enfranchising the freed slaves gave us our concepts of 'liberal," "moderate," and "conservative." Like the yeoman farmers and poor whites of the old South, many Americans still feel wealth has an inordinate amount of power over the political process. The Confederate battle flag is just losing its place of prominence atop the State House domes of South Carolina, Georgia, Florida, and Mississippi. Even much of the common language of political debate today remains informed by the slavery-based divide that was supposed to have been bridged at the conclusion of the Civil War: "tax and spend liberal," "the other side of the aisle," and calls for states' rights to be protected when the federal government moves to ensure equal protection under the law for all Americans.

So you see, the Civil War is far from over in the hearts and minds of many Americans—even if they are not consciously aware of it. The way to *really* put an end to the Civil War is to advance rights for *all* Americans, rights that address fundamental issues our present two-party–dominated political system is incapable of addressing. We must constitutionally guarantee every American new rights. Among them: a public education of equal high quality; access to health care of equal high quality; a clean, safe and sustainable environment; and the right to vote.

In order to successfully advance new rights, it is imperative that we understand the slavery-based history that created the need for them. Paul Kalra's scholarship regarding the racial and political implications of the Civil War is indispensable. He explores rarely detailed aspects of the race question, including laws limiting the liberties of free African Americans in what is often believed to be the "liberal" North. The history detailed in *From Slave to Untouchable:*

Lincoln's Solution not only augments our understanding of slavery, but deepens our understanding of slavery's impact on the racial divide that still exists in America. All serious students of the Civil War, race relations, and public policy will benefit greatly from Paul Kalra's work.

Preface

In the fall of 1990, like millions of Americans, I watched with great fascination Ken Burns' story of the Civil War, the bloodiest war in American History. More Americans died in the Civil War than all the other wars combined—including World Wars I and II, Korea, and Vietnam. The 620,000 dead in a population of 30 million was equivalent to more than 6 million dead in twenty-first–century America. I wondered what these Americans had been fighting for; whether the war could have been avoided; and if not, why not. Burns referred to his television series as "a chronicle of making permanent that which was promised, but not delivered, in the Declaration of Independence and the Constitution." This created my intense curiosity to understand the reasons for the Civil War; for surely part of the story was being withheld from the public.

The first episode of the story began with a searing indictment of slavery. Black slaves, I learned, could not marry each other, though some went through mock ceremonies by "jumping the broom." Their children, born and unborn, were owned by the slaveholder. These were shocking revelations for me, though I had lived in the U.S. for twenty-five years. I asked a native-born American what Americans had been fighting and dying for in the Civil War. His answer: they were fighting to free the slaves. I then asked why blacks had not been allowed to marry each other. Although my friend had gone through school and college in America, he was unaware that black people were not allowed to marry before the Civil War. I realized then I was not alone in my ignorance of American history. Still, because I could not imagine why more than a half-million whites would die to free the slaves, I made it my mission to find answers to this enigma of slavery and the Civil War.

In 1965, I had come from India to the United States to pursue my Masters in Electrical Engineering at the Illinois Institute of Technology in Chicago. Because I believed the United States to be a classless, democratic society, I chose to come here rather than go to the United Kingdom, which I knew to be a colonial power that had committed many atrocities in India for more than two hundred years. Shortly after I arrived, the foreign student advisor took us on a bus tour of Washington D.C. where I visited the Lincoln Memorial, a tribute to the "Great Emancipator"; the Washington Monument, commemorating the first U.S. president; the White House; and the John F. Kennedy Eternal Flame in the Arlington Cemetery. The guide told us about the separate bathrooms and drinking fountains for blacks and whites that had once been required by the segregation laws of the land. It occurred to me at the time that blacks were the untouchables of America, much like the Indian untouchables who cleaned the toilets and cremated the dead.

Back in Chicago, I got my first taste of prejudice when some dark-skinned Indian students were called "niggers," an experience that frightened all of us. What I saw as the American version of untouchability had first come to my attention through the story of Satish Kumar, a Nuclear Disarmament and world peace activist in India in Mahatma Gandhi's tradition. In 1962 he decided to undertake a peace walk to the nuclear world capitals—Moscow, Paris, London, and finally Washington, D.C., where he intended to present a petition to John F. Kennedy.

After much planning and help from world peace American activists, Kumar began the last leg of the journey from New York to Washington D.C. On the way he and his friend stopped at a café and ordered tea and cheese sandwiches. The waitress told them, "Sorry, we have no tea and cheese sandwiches and nothing else" before she quickly disappeared. They went to the manager, who stood at the cash register. "Can't we have a cup of tea?" Kumar asked. "No you can't. Please leave immediately," he replied. "Isn't this a café to serve public?" Kumar then asked, only to be told, "It is my café, and I serve whom I like." When Kumar did not move fast enough, the manager opened a drawer, took out a pistol, pointed it at Kumar's chest, and said, "Are you getting out, or should I teach you a lesson?" Soon café employees and customers gathered around and pushed both Kumar and his friend out of the café.

The "untouchability" Kumar experienced due to the color of his skin was different in character from that practiced in India.

In the context of traditional Indian caste system, untouchable status (outside the four castes or occupations) has been historically associated with occupations regarded as ritually impure, such as any involving leatherwork, butchering, or removal of rubbish, animal carcasses, and waste. Untouchables work as manual laborers cleaning streets, latrines, and sewers. Engaging in these activities was considered polluting to the individual as well as contagious to others. As a result, untouchables were commonly segregated and banned from full participation in Hindu social life. For example, they could not enter a temple or school and were required to stay outside the village.

The importance of untouchables in daily life became clear during the partition of India and creation of Pakistan in 1947. About 150,000 Delhi Muslims who wanted to move to Pakistan were assembled in a refugee camp set up at the "Old Fort" (Purana Quila) waiting for safe transportation. These refugees had to live without shelter from sun or monsoons and in conditions of indescribable filth, with sanitation by open latrine. Although the Muslim refugees did not have a caste system, they believed they were *not* untouchables; and so, despite the increasing filth, they refused to clean the latrines. At the height of Delhi's troubles, the Emergency Committee sent scores of Hindu sweeper untouchables under armed guard into the fort to clean the latrines.

Similar situations occurred in the refugee camps in Pakistan where Sikhs and Hindus were crowded like sardines, waiting for safe transportation to India. They complained bitterly to their Muslim guards that they were forced to live in filth because no untouchables were available to clean latrines. In Karachi, the new capital of Pakistan, the street-cleaning services began to collapse because Hindu untouchables had fled. To save the situation and prevent chaos, the Muslim administrators proclaimed a special status for Hindu untouchables. Instead of making them pariahs, administrators made them a privileged sect distinguished by wearing green and white armbands similar to those of the Muslim National Guard and permitted them to stay as citizens of Pakistan.

Although American blacks had separate drinking fountains and could not piss in the same pot as whites, the character and legal basis for American untouchability was different. Before the Civil War, blacks were considered neither human nor citizens of the United States. After the Civil War, the citizenship of the blacks was recognized through Constitution amendments; however, the Supreme Court's "separate but equal" doctrine became the law of the land, essentially creating two classes of citizenship. Blacks, prohibited from using the same public facilities as whites, became veritable untouchables in the American Legal System. Skin color became their badge of untouchability and justification for second-class citizenship in America.

According to Warren Buffet, who lived in Washington D.C. as a teenager, the nation's capital was the most segregated city in the United States. Blacks could not work as streetcar conductors, motor men, or in any but the most menial jobs. They could not enter the YMCA, eat in most restaurants, rent hotel rooms, or buy theater tickets. A prominent black man who experienced Jim Crow laws noted, "Blacks had to carry their urine bottles with them because there were no public facilities available to relieve themselves." Even dark-skinned diplomats, embarrassed and scandalized by this provincialism encountered nowhere else in the world, had to be chaperoned. One foreign visitor said, "I would rather be an untouchable in the Hindu caste system than a Negro in Washington."

The word "untouchable" is deeply offensive to blacks in the United States. Orlando Patterson of Harvard University's Sociology Department wrote to me: "African Americans were never an untouchable group in this country and your attempt to impose this perspective on their past is wide of the mark. It is also offensive, however well-meaning you may be." He further noted, "The very shadow of Indian untouchables desecrates African Americans, both during and after the period of slavery, were so regarded. To the contrary, they had strong ties of intimacy with the dominant white group—as surrogate mothers, as lovers, as playmates, as cooks and nursemaids and numerous other occupations that brought them close and continuous contact with whites. Segregation laws in the south applied only to public places, not to private quarters. The same woman who would not ride in the public carriage with an African American would go home and gladly hand over her baby to be suckled by an African American nurse." Apparently the half-million mulattos in the United States before the Civil War provided ample proof that blacks were not untouchable in America.

When I was completing my MBA at the University of Pittsburg, reading *The Autobiography of Malcolm X* was a course requirement. In 1998 *Time* magazine named it one of the ten most influential nonfiction books of the twentieth century. Malcolm X, a mulatto born as Malcolm Little to a black mother and white father, changed his name because it constantly reminded him of white Americans whom he indicted in the harshest terms for their crimes against black Americans. While serving an eight-to-ten-year prison sentence for a number of criminal activities, he became a member of the Nation of Islam because of its message of equality of all men before God, whether rich or poor, and independent of skin color—a belief that directly contradicted the Constitution of the United States.

After earning my MBA, I was sponsored for the green card by Westinghouse Electric Corporation and had to register for the Selective Service draft. As a research engineer, I was routinely eligible for draft deferment during the Vietnam War; but just a month before my twenty-sixth birthday, my deferment was revoked and I was called to take a physical exam. I not only feared being sent to Vietnam because of war's death and destruction, but I had never touched a gun and believed in the non-violence principle of Mahatma Gandhi. Colleagues at work advised me to submit an appeal to the draft board.

It became obvious that getting a draft deferment, especially for whites in colleges, was a routine affair without negative consequences (as would be confirmed when both Bill Clinton and the Junior George Bush escaped the draft yet went on to be elected President). But the rules for blacks were different. For example, World Heavyweight Champion and Olympic gold medalist Muhammad Ali, born Cassius Clay, Jr. refused to be conscripted into the U.S. military, based on his religious beliefs and opposition to the Vietnam War. His conversion to Islam so angered the military establishment and the government that he was arrested and found guilty on draft evasion charges, stripped of his boxing title, had his boxing license suspended, and was barred from boxing for nearly four years while his appeal worked its way to the U.S. Supreme Court. Although his appeal was successful, the message for the blacks was clear: in spite of the Supreme Court's Brown v Board of Education and the Civil Rights Act of 1964, blacks would remain second-class citizens of America.

In the 1970s I was sent to Brazil as a consultant to the Sao Paulo Metro system, which has a carbon copy of the San Francisco Bay Area Rapid Transit control system. While living there for seven years, I married a Brazilian girl whose parents owned three coffee farms and came to understand a bit about the history and social life in Brazil. As a colony, Brazil achieved independence from Portugal in 1822. Slavery in Brazil shaped the country's social structure and ethnic landscape. During the colonial epoch and for over six decades after the 1822 independence, slavery was a mainstay of the Brazilian economy, especially in mining and sugar cane production. Brazil obtained thirty-five percent of all enslaved Africans traded in the Atlantic Slave trade.

Although slavery in mainland Portugal was abolished in 1761, it continued in Brazil until its final abolition in 1888. From the late eighteenth century to the 1830s, slaves were owned by the upper and middle classes, by the poor, and even by other slaves. The foreign slave trade was abolished by 1850, and new laws controlled slave traffickers and speculators. Then, by 1871, the sons of the slaves were freed. The Paraguayan War contributed to end slavery, since slaves enlisted in exchange for freedom. The point is that Catholic Brazil could abolish slavery gradually without a violent and bloody Civil War. Also Brazil had no need for separate but equal laws because slaves of various shades of black and white were always considered human beings and citizens entitled to the equal protection of laws. During the Carnival every February, for example, I witnessed this mixing of the races with no boundaries. My experience in Brazil confirmed that even though whites controlled the power structure and the economy, there was no need for separate public facilities for the races thus no "untouchability."

My experience in America was completely different, and I was even more certain that 620,000 white Americans did not give their lives in the Civil War just to free the slaves. My mission and obsession was to find verifiable answers to this enigma of slavery and the Civil War. To do so, I first became a member of all the public libraries in the San Francisco Bay Area and began checking out history books related to slavery and the Civil War. I soon came across Frank Tannenbaum's *Slave and Citizen*, which suggested that American Protestant Slavery was unique because it denied the humanity of the black slaves and asserted that they could never be freed. In contrast, Catholic slavery implemented in South American countries such as Brazil acknowledged the humanity of the slaves. Although Catholic slavery could be as brutal as Protestant slavery, because it defined slaves as citizens included in the legal structure of the state, it could be abolished gradually—without Civil War. My experience in Brazil led me to accept Tannenbaum's interpretation as a reasonable hypothesis. To investigate this theory, I followed every lead applicable by taking full advantage of the interlibrary loan system. At first, I got more questions than answers. Once the puzzle pieces began to connect, I decided to put what I discovered into writing to benefit others interested in American history and affected by the Constitution of the United States.

My major insight was the discovery of the American class system, which became the slave capitalism paradigm of the Constitution. Once the legal status of slaves was defined by skin color, the white race automatically divided into slaveholders, non-slaveholders, and poor whites. The slaveholder was, of course, the beneficiary of Black Protestant Slavery; but because he could never free his slaves, he was obligated to feed and shelter them, even in sickness and old age. On the other hand, the white non-slaveholder became a victim of slavery because he had to compete with the slaves in commodity markets, which often reduced his economic status to the level of a black slave. The condition of the poor white or "white trash" was even worse because his food and shelter were not guaranteed. This class system created dilemmas for the races that are examined and documented extensively in the book.

Once the precedent of Black Protestant Slavery was set after a century of experience, the Southern slaveholder–dominated governing body wrote the Constitution of the United States, including in it that blacks were not human therefore were denied citizenship. This was a Constitution of, by, and for the slaveholders, who failed to understand that they could not sustain this lie forever. By excluding blacks from the U.S. Constitution, the North and South also excluded blacks from their state constitutions, leaving freed black slaves nowhere to go. (The only apparent solution to this dilemma—to send the blacks back to Africa—was clearly not a practical proposition.) The slavery paradigm of the Constitution violated the "one man, one vote" principle for whites by mandating two senators per state, whatever its size, and by excluding blacks altogether. It followed that the problems facing the country could not be resolved with elections. Lincoln's election triggered the South's secession, which in turn triggered the Civil War.

Another way to find answers to the slavery enigma and the Civil War is to follow the actions and speeches of the participants at the Constitutional Convention in 1787, as well as Presidents, members of Congress, Governors, and Supreme Court Justices during the seventy-year period leading up to the Civil War. At the constitutional Convention, for example, Colonel Mason warned that slavery was a national sin and would lead to national calamities such as a Civil War, but his warning was ignored and the slaveholders successfully enshrined slavery into the Constitution. In addition, writings and actions of Presidents Thomas Jefferson, George Washington, John Quincy Adams, James Buchanan, and Supreme Court Justice Roger Taney illuminate the issues in a straightforward manner.

Finally, to get to the bottom of the issues and controversies of slavery and the Civil War, it is only necessary to follow Abraham Lincoln's articulate speeches and debates, and his writings leading to his election as President of the United States. Although he is remembered as the Great Emancipator, Boston abolitionist

Wendell Phillips called him "the slave hound of Illinois" for his public support of the Fugitive Slave Law. Because Lincoln made his position crystal clear, the South announced in advance that they would secede from the Union if Lincoln was elected, a threat they promptly acted upon.

In the end, 150 years after the Civil War, all the dots have been identified in thousands of books examining these subjects from every angle. My effort was to connect the dots and follow leads provided by the Constitution and the players in the greatest drama of American History. My objective in writing this book is to inform and promote understanding of why the South seceded from the Union, why Lincoln did not let them get away with it, and why 620,000 Americans died in the Civil War. By reading on, you will learn why the Civil War was inevitable and why ordinary Americans were ready to fight and die to protect their rights under the decidedly undemocratic slaveholders' Constitution. You will get answers for frequently asked questions about slavery and the Civil War—questions and answers that Ken Burns omitted in his series.

Acknowledgements

With a problem-solving and commonsense approach to this book, I want to acknowledge my special debt to the writings of Kenneth M. Stampp, John Hope Franklin, Leon F. Litwack, James M. McPherson, and Frank Tannenbaum. Their perspectives provided the leading questions that had to be answered by my study.

I owe a special debt of gratitude to Kenneth M. Stampp, William L. Barney, Kenneth B. Clark, Ellis Cose, David F. Dorsey, Jude P. Dougherty, Eric Foner, Tony P. Hall, Percy C. Hintzen, Harold Holzer, John Y. Simon, Charles B. Stozier, and Virgil W. Woolbright, who read the entire manuscript and offered advice, observations, and suggestions.

Parts of the manuscript were reviewed by Eduardo Bodipo-Malumba, Jack Chatfield, Adelaide M. Cromwell, David Brion Davis, Carl N. Degler, John A. Dennis Jr., Robin Einhorn, Stanley M. Elkins, John Hope Franklin, George M. Fredrickson, Nathan Glazer, Carl Guarneri, Charles P. Henry, and Orlando Patterson. Their comments were very much appreciated even if they did not agree with every interpretation in the manuscript.

Congressman Jesse L. Jackson, Jr. and his assistant Theresa Caldwell, and Congressman Tony Hall and his assistant Max Finberg were very generous with their time and cooperated beyond the call of duty.

Thanks are due to Mario Cuomo, Colin L. Powell, and Arthur M. Schlesinger, Jr. for their attention and letters of encouragement.

Staff members of the Contra Costa County Library in California have my gratitude because I would have been unable to obtain hundreds of books through interlibrary loan facilities from all over the United States without their help.

Perceptive editing and assistance from Joan Brookbank, Sanjukta Banerjee, Neil O'Brien, Ruben Israel, and Leslie Keenan was indispensable for the publication of this manuscript. Double thanks to editor-in-chief Ruth Younger for guidance and judgment in keeping me focused on the reader and to Pete Masterson for bringing this twenty-year effort to fruition.

Chapter 1
The Moral Setting

What you sow is what you reap.
                    —The Bible, Galatians 6:7

Come, saints and sinners, hear me tell
How pious priests whip Jack and Nell,
And women buy and children sell,
And preach all sinners down to hell,
And sing of heavenly union

                    —Frederick Douglass, "The Parody," 1854

Abraham Lincoln had a secret. During the election campaign for the Senate in 1858 he made his famous speech on slavery in the Union: "A house divided against itself cannot stand. I believe this government cannot endure, permanently half slave and half free. I do not expect the Union to be dissolved—I do not expect the house to fall—but I do expect it will cease to be divided. It will become all one thing, or the other."[1]

In the presidential campaign of 1860, Lincoln changed tack: "I have no purpose directly or indirectly to interfere with the institution of slavery in the States where it exists. I believe I have no lawful right to do so, and I have no inclination to do so." Such contradictions defined the dilemma of Lincoln's supporters and opponents because he never provided a direct answer even when the issue was repeatedly debated with his opponent Stephen A. Douglas. How did Lincoln intend to abolish slavery in the South without interfering with it? "Lincoln never poured out his soul to any mortal creature at any time …. He was the most secretive, reticent, shut mouthed man that ever existed." This studied opinion from his former law partner, William H. Herndon, defined the enigmatic characteristic of Abraham Lincoln's personality. An understanding of Lincoln's ambiguity provides the key to understanding the crisis of the Civil War and the lessons to be learned from it.[2]

Lincoln said slavery was morally wrong. So did some Southerners. Robert E. Lee, the Commander-in-Chief of the army of Northern Virginia, described it in 1856 as "a moral and political evil in any country. I think it, however, a greater evil to the white than to the black race." Slavery had existed in one form or another long before biblical times. There was no agreement on why slavery was morally wrong or a moral and political evil. Nor did Lee elaborate why slavery was a greater evil for the white race. Historians have suggested that if slavery were immoral, it had to have adverse consequences. To prove it, they have attempted to establish a cause-and-effect relationship between immoral acts and historical consequences; particularly, the relationship between slavery and secession on the one hand, and the Civil War on the other. They have had their work cut out for them, as the journey from the advent of slavery to its demise in the USA, following the Civil War, does not represent the triumph of human rights over human wrongs.[3]

Looked at another way, slavery may be seen largely as a story of man's inhumanity towards man, fueled by a lust for wealth that prompted a denial of the basic catholicity of mankind. Slavery also created a tumultuous relationship between two geographical regions with different economic fundamentals: Each region's wealthy few had an overwhelming desire for social control in order to amass wealth. Enormous duplicity informed the interactions between one white man and another within each region and among them. The inclusion of slavery and its institutionalization in the Constitution to satisfy greed were the principal outcomes. While much has apparently changed in the social structures since the war, there is reason to ask whether even today there has been a fundamental shift in the unfairness of American society.

Morality Tests

A universal test of political morality is whether it provides good over a long period of time for the greatest number of people. Usually it takes several generations for the cause-and-effect relationships of a set of actions to work out in a specific setting. Lincoln observed that morality required faith that right begets might. Immorality assumed might was right and looked for immediate rewards without regard to long-term consequences. Usually politically immoral action is guided by the time frame of an election or term of office.

Yet again, the political test for moral action may lie in whether it results in more good than evil. Lincoln explained the moral way of arriving at decisions:

> The true rule, in determining to embrace or reject anything, is not whether it have any evil in it, but whether it have more of evil than of good. There are few things wholly evil or wholly good. Almost everything, especially of governmental policy, is an inseparable compound of the two; so that our best judgment of the preponderance between them is continually demanded.

A general test for morality in a democracy is whether it is good for the majority of the population over a period extended to generations. Lincoln related the morality of slavery to the history of all mankind in the following way:

> There are two principles that have stood face to face from the beginning of time; and will ever continue to struggle. The one is the common right of humanity and the other the divine right of kings. It is the same spirit that says, you work and toil and earn bread, and I'll eat it. No matter in what shape it comes, whether from the mouth of a king who seeks to bestride the people of his own nation and live by the fruit of their labor, or from one race of men as an apology for enslaving another race, it is the same tyrannical principle.[4]

Evaluating the political morality of slavery requires an understanding of how it affected different population segments in the North and South for over two centuries. It is also necessary to take into account the relationships of the institutions in control, such as the monarchy or the church, and their representatives in a distant colony. The early colonists made choices regarding slavery based on historical precedent and available experience with far-reaching consequences for whites and blacks. Understanding the cause and effect of their choices is essential to see how the dominant groups deceived the majority of their people in order to garner support for their own self-serving objectives.

The early Southern colonies had built-in segmentation for at least three economic classes: the slaveholders, the slaves, and the non-slaveholders. Their mutual relationship is germane to any evaluation of the morality of slavery. The slaveholders were a minority who benefited from slavery because they initiated and controlled the institution. The slaves, victims of the institution, had to be a minority, lest they seize any opportunity to overpower the slaveholders and free themselves. In the majority were the non-slaveholders, who did not benefit from slavery but whose cooperation was essential in controlling the economy and protecting slaveholders from the slaves.

Slavery also divided the country into two sections, the North and the South, based not only on geography but also on the proportion of blacks in the population. The Southern economy was based on black slave labor and whites had to live with them. The North, with a tiny black population of around two percent, was not economically dependent on black labor and was largely indifferent to what Southerners did with their blacks so long as they kept them in the South.

The other interesting influences around the issue of the morality of slavery were the church and king of England. He did not care what the slaveholders did in his faraway colonies so long as he received his profits, nor had he any experience with black slavery. After the Revolution, the slaveholders, rid of the king, wrote a Constitution that preserved their peculiar institution. Most slaveholders were Protestants and did not have to comply with the Pope's directives on slavery, as did the Catholics. From the outset, Protestants assumed the authority of the king in interpreting the Bible for their own convenience, eliminating the role of the church in questions of slavery and morality.

The final influence on this socio-economic phenomenon was the white indentured servant who worked on the cash crop, tobacco. As an extension of an English custom, young men and women bound themselves to a master for between four and seven years in exchange for a passage to America, food, and shelter. White indentured servants were considered by Southern colonists to be more difficult to handle than the slaves and had to be kept at bay with slave power. Therefore, the slaveholders installed a legal infrastructure permitting permanent control over black slaves through generations. To prevent any interference by the church, they passed laws that the baptism of a black as a Christian would not affect his status as a slave.

Evolution of Slavery

Perhaps the most dominating influence in the process was the Protestant faith of the early colonists in the South. As the South set out its own slave legislation agenda, it selected as its model English Protestant slavery as developed in the West Indies. This could be compared with the French Catholic slavery of Louisiana. The two systems were based on different relationships between the slaveholder, the slave, the non-slaveholder, the king, and the church.

The code of Protestant slavery was first defined by legislation in Barbados, among the earliest British settlements in the tropics with a plantation system dependent on black slaves. Following a dozen minor laws to control the blacks since 1644, Barbados adopted a comprehensive slavery statute that came into force in 1688. When South Carolina needed a general statute in 1712, the assembly virtually copied the Barbadian Act of 1688. Later, Georgia in 1770 and Florida in 1822 based their laws on the South Carolina code. A similar set of laws was adopted by Virginia and passed on to Maryland, Delaware, and North Carolina, making the Protestant slave code the law of the South.

The preamble to the general statute of 1688 points out that the plantation industry was dependent upon great numbers of Negro slaves whose "barbarous, wild and savage nature ... renders them wholly unqualified to be governed by the laws, customs and practices of our nation," and the need for separate laws and orders to "restrain the disorders, rapines and inhumanities to which they are naturally prone and inclined." Because Protestant slavery codes denied the humanity of blacks, laws applicable to the white slaveholders, yeoman farmers, and indentured servants were not applicable to them. For black men, the slaveholder would be the accuser, the judge, and the executioner; and he would countenance no interference in the management of his slave property from other citizens, black or white. Indeed, the Protestant slavery laws prevented blacks from entering into contracts of any nature, even marriage.[5]

The Protestant slavery codes defined all blacks as slaves, with the color of their skin providing the necessary evidence. A Maryland law of 1663 said, "All Negroes or other slaves within the provinces, and all Negroes and other slaves to be hereafter imported into the province, shall serve *durante vita*; and all children born of any Negro or other slave, shall be slaves as their fathers were, for the term of their lives."[6]

The Catholic slavery code, the *Code Noir*, was promulgated by the French State in 1685, and an improved version was decreed by Louis XV for the colony of Louisiana in 1724. In 1763, the French colony was transferred to Spain and returned to the France of Napoleon I in 1801. It became a part of the United States with the Louisiana Purchase of 1803. Originally the purchased territory was set up as the Territory of Orleans, becoming a state in 1812 under the old name of Louisiana. After Louisiana entered the United States, the Catholic slavery code was gradually replaced by its Protestant counterpart, so that by the time of the Civil War, Louisiana was almost indistinguishable from the other Southern states in its treatment of blacks.[7]

According to the *Code Noir*, blacks were human beings and subject to the same law as whites; slavery was not a condition defined by color; a black man could be a slave or he could be free. Indeed, in the absence of proof to the contrary, a black man was assumed to be free just as in the case of a white man. The *Code Noir*, decreed by the king in France, treated slaveholders, slaves, and non-slaveholders as the subjects of the king, with rights and responsibilities. Blacks—whether slave or free—had a legal right to marry, a right to life, and to safeguards against abuse while fulfilling their contracts as slaves. They could be baptized, become Christians, and stand on an equal footing with whites in the sight of God and the Church. A black man was a member of the community, and the non-slaveholders and the Church had a say in his treatment. Having made a provision for free blacks, Catholic slavery provided an infrastructure for the gradual abolition of slavery if the circumstances required it.

The roots of the variance lay in the Catholics' and Protestants' historical experience. Negroes had been brought to the Iberian Peninsula as slaves in the mid-fifteenth century. Slavery, which had ended in the rest of Western Europe, survived there because the continuing wars with the Moors provided war captives as slaves. At the end of the fifteenth century, Portugal and Spain had numerous slaves, including Negroes, Moors, Jews, and Spaniards. By the mid-sixteenth century, Negroes outnumbered whites in Lisbon. As late as 1616, the law speaks of baptized Moorish slaves. Catholic slavery had a long tradition of slave law that had come down from the Justinian Code. By the time the Catholics came to America, they had over two hundred years of experience and a body of slave laws to guide their actions. When black men were brought to the new continent, a slave slot previously filled by Moors or Jews was available to them.[8]

In contrast, Protestant slavery in the Americas was a novel phenomenon for the British, who had no previous experience with blacks. British common law had a written contract for indentured servants, but long-term slavery for life was unknown to them. As land was scarce and the number of paupers abundant, the British could not imagine why anybody would want to accept the responsibility of feeding another person for life. Therefore, slavery was not only inconceivable in law but also in thought. Because of the remote nature of the American colony, the king and parliament allowed the slaveholders total freedom to maximize profits. In defining the Protestant slavery code, the slaveholders maximized profits by eliminating interference from non-slaveholders and the church, and by ignoring considerations of morality and precedents for the future.

Cause and Effect

Lincoln hinted that the Civil War was the day of reckoning for the misdeeds of the slaveholders. In his Second Inaugural Address, he prayed that the War might quickly end:

> Yet, if God wills that it continue, until all the wealth piled by the bondman's two hundred and fifty years of unrequited toil shall be sunk, and until every drop of blood drawn by the lash, shall be paid by another drawn with the sword, as was said three thousand years ago, so still it must be said, "the judgments of the Lord, are true and righteous altogether."[9]

In a democracy, ballots are supposed to substitute for bullets to resolve differences between different classes of people. Yet Lincoln's victory in the 1860 presidential election caused the Southern states to secede from the union. Why did the South believe that it could win with bullets what they had lost at the ballot box? Was the Constitution, the handiwork of the slaveholders which dictated the rules of the election, rigged? Obviously, the slaveholders controlled the federal government, including the presidency, for over two-thirds of the time before the Civil War. Clearly they understood the rules of the game. Why were the Southern states so alarmed by the election of Abraham Lincoln, and why did the slaveholders feel they had no option other than to secede?

After the end of the Civil War, Jefferson Davis, the president of the Confederate States, insisted that slavery "was in no wise the cause of the conflict," without offering any specific explanation for his statement. That is why it is necessary to clearly establish the cause-and-effect relationship between slavery and the Civil War.[10]

The same Constitution—whose checks and balances of freedom of the press and the independence of the legislative, judicial, and executive branches, was thwarted by the slaveholders—that was in force before the Civil War, was in effect *with amendments* after the war. It was not meant to guarantee the rule of the people, for the people, and by the people because it was written by the slaveholders to closely protect their interests. Constitutional checks and balances were bound to be historically circumvented. Abraham Lincoln noted this wide gap between the principles of the Declaration of Independence and the actual operation of the Constitution in his Peoria speech of 1854:

> This declared indifference, but as I must think, covert real zeal for the spread of slavery, I cannot but hate. I hate it because of the monstrous injustice of slavery itself. I hate it because it deprives our republican example of its just influence in the world—enables the enemies of free institutions, with plausibility, to taunt us as hypocrites—causes the real friends of freedom to doubt our sincerity, and especially because it forces so many really good men amongst ourselves into an open war with the very fundamental principles of civil liberty—criticizing the Declaration of Independence, and insisting that there is no right principle of action but self interest.[11]

Historian Charles A. Beard observed that slavery was "no simple, isolated phenomenon. It was a labor system, the foundation of the Southern aristocracy. It took more than a finite eye to discern where slavery as an ethical question left off and economics—the struggle over the distribution of wealth—began." If the Civil War was in reality a war over the distribution of wealth, that is, the class system, it has important lessons to offer. Some Southerners have pointed out that the North had a white "wage slavery" system before the Civil War. The Civil War and the Thirteenth Amendment to the Constitution abolished only the black Protestant slavery of the South and acknowledged the humanity of the blacks, but "wage slavery" as practiced in the North has continued. Abraham Lincoln, who realized the dangers of wage slavery, thought a class of yeoman farmers, who would be the foundation of the Republican form of government, would check its abuses. It is therefore possible to see the Civil War as an economic class war and a second American Revolution. Learning these lessons about balance in the economic class system for political stability may prevent other social upheavals in the future.[12]

One historian has suggested:

> That the Lord seems to have worked back to his Old Testament phase, bent on an eye for an eye and the wiping out of armies. For every Negro slave hustled ashore filthy and naked in North America, a white man was to die in fratricidal violence; for every misbegotten excuse for treating men like things, a white man would lie festering in a fly-fetid hospital; for every free Negro treated as subhuman by Northerners reproaching the South for the crime of slavery, a Yankee would succumb to some foul camp disease; for every mulatto sold to strangers by his own cousins, a white child would be orphaned. The score had long accumulated, and compounding interest had long since dwarfed the principal.

About the morality of slavery, Thomas Jefferson said: "I tremble for my country when I reflect that God is just: that this justice cannot sleep for ever: that considering numbers, nature and natural means only, a revolution of the wheel of fortune, an exchange of situation is among possible events: that it may become probable by supernatural interference!" We shall also see how numbers, nature, and natural means combined in the American setting to make the Civil War as inevitable as the day of reckoning.[13]

Chapter 2

The Economic Class System

Mankind is divisible into two great classes:
Hosts and Guests

> —Max Beerbohm

They'll raise tobacco, corn, and rye,
And drive, and thieve, and cheat, and lie,
And lay up treasures in the sky,
By making switch and cowskin fly,
In hope of heavenly Union.

> —Frederick Douglass, "The Parody," 1854

Prior to the Civil War, John Randolph, a Southerner, taunted: "Northern gentlemen think to govern us by our black slaves; but let me tell them, we intend to govern them by their white slaves." The significance of "white slaves" was also noted by Senator James Hammond of South Carolina, who expounded his doctrine of the economic class system:

> In all social systems there must be a class to do the mean duties, to perform the drudgery of life …. Such a class you must have or you would not have that other class which leads to progress, refinement and civilization … we call them slaves. We are old fashioned at the South yet; it is a word discarded not by ears polite; I will not characterize that class at the North by that term; but you have it; it is there; it is everywhere; it is eternal …. The

difference between us is that our slaves are hired for life and well compensated; there is no starvation, no begging, no want of employment among our people, and not too much employment either. Yours are hired by the day, not cared for, and scantily compensated, which may be proved in the most deplorable manner, at any hour in any street of your large towns …. Our slaves do not vote. We give them no political power. Yours do vote and being the majority, they are the depositories of all your political power. If they knew the tremendous secret that the ballot box is stronger than an army with bayonets, and could combine, where would you be? Your society would be reconstructed, your government reconstructed, your property divided … [1]

Both the South with black slaves and the North with white slaves were part of the four-tiered economic class system.

Four-Tiered Society

Randolph and Hammond referred to basic differences in the economic class systems of the North and South before the Civil War that had evolved over two hundred years. Each had its limitations, the balance being maintained by the prevalent class system that shaped the Constitution of the United States, democracy and liberty in America. We can view this structure in broad terms to gain insight into the system, understanding that individuals at the time acted in self-interest, and may not have been conscious of the role they played.

From colonial times, property ownership has been the principal class determinant in America: those who owned property, primarily land, and those who did not. Ideally, in a democracy, all citizens would own property; historically, however, distribution of wealth in which half the citizens owned property has been sufficient for political stability. In a system in which only property holders are allowed to vote, as in pre-Revolution America, property ownership tended to be concentrated in the hands of the most powerful.

Property-owners themselves could be divided into two major groups: employer-controllers and yeoman farmers who owned and worked small pieces of land. Similarly, non-owners were divided into two classes: slaves or wage workers; and unemployed paupers who were supported by welfare or held in prisons. These four population classes were identifiable at all times in both the North and South.

The employer-controllers were the leaders and most powerful members of the class system. Their numbers were usually limited to less than ten percent of the total population, but they owned over sixty percent of the nation's wealth. During the colonial period this group consisted of plantation owners in the South and owners of lumbering, mining, and trading operations in the North. After the Revolution, the cotton plantation owners became the employer-controllers of the South while the owners of textile mills, ironworks, and other industry were the employer-controllers of the North. Corporate ownership to share risk was popular in the North, and those who controlled the corporations were members of this class even though they were not direct employers.

Small property-owners or yeoman farmers made up the second tier of the economic class system. Again, in an ideal democracy where voting is not restricted to property owners, they usually constitute around forty percent of the population. In a direct contest of numbers, this group would be the most important class, outnumbering the employer-controllers by at least four to one though the employer-controllers were more powerful. During the colonial period, Southern yeoman farmers grew cash crops while Northern yeoman farmers typically produced food crops. After the Revolution, Southern yeoman farmers switched to growing cotton while the Northern property-owning class expanded to include skilled craftsmen and traders with some capital.

The next tier of the economic class system consisted of slaves and wage workers, or "wage slaves," who formed the bulk of the non-property owning class. These usually comprised about forty percent of the population. Since they owned no property, they had no assets or savings to cushion their lives. In the South, this class consisted of black slaves who had to work or be flogged. In the North, the white "wage slaves" had to work or starve. White "wage slavery" became more common in the North after the Revolution with the growth of industry and increased immigration from Europe. While it's clear that black slavery was profoundly different in its effect on the mind, economically the effect of "wage slavery" was the same. For convenience, both groups are referred to as "slaves" within the context of this model.

Paupers and criminals formed the bottom tier of the economic class system. In Great Britain and Europe, where land was limited and population pressures great, paupers and criminals were a common part of the landscape. America had an abundance of land and a labor shortage, so this class should have been non-existent. In a capitalist, cash-crop economy, albeit subject to booms and busts, these unemployed and unemployables were usually the last to be hired and the first to be fired. This class, which comprised about ten percent of the population, had to be fed, either on public welfare or in prisons where they often conveniently ended up in order to avoid starvation.

In the South, where black slaves were fixed costs for slave-owners, this unemployables slot was filled by poor whites or "white trash." As the North geared to a system of white wage slavery, free blacks were subjected to segregation that categorized them as untouchables and restricted them to menial jobs, forcing them into this bottom tier.

The four classes of employers, property owners, slaves, and paupers were held in a stable class system for generations through balancing societal forces. In order to be elected to seats of power and control, the employers allowed forty percent of the country's wealth to go to the property owners who constituted about forty percent of the population. This was considered fair because forty percent of the population received forty percent of the national wealth. The employers, only ten percent of the population, divided sixty percent of the nation's wealth amongst themselves. As employers and property owners together constituted a majority, slaves and paupers were not permitted any share of the national wealth. It was only considered necessary to keep slaves well fed and motivated for maximum productivity with minimum consumption, as the nation depended on them for labor and to fight wars. Property-less workers filled the ranks of common soldiers and constituted cannon fodder in the Civil War as well as in other conflicts.

Each productive class had slightly different motivations for fulfilling its role in society. Employers were driven by a thirst for power, wealth, and status. Property owners worked to accumulate wealth and property for themselves and their children. Property-less workers had to be threatened to work or face starvation, which thus became their primary motivator. The growing economy, however, provided wage workers with an opportunity to limit family size, imbibe education and vocational skills, and acquire property over a generation or two. For wage slaves, the dream that their children or grandchildren might be able to acquire property was a secondary motivator.

The threat of starvation was made credible by the existence of the class of paupers. A welfare system ensured that their women and children did not die, since keeping them alive and visible motivated wage slaves to continue working. As paupers and their offspring were only for display and not engaged in productive work, their numbers too had to be limited.

With the practice of hire and fire providing flexibility in coping with business cycles or even seasonal demand, labor had to be mobile for interstate or inter-industry transfer. Property owners, small traders, and skilled craftsmen could be controlled by employers because of their dependence on wages, markets, or loans, including mortgages. Their skill, education, and savings gave property owners some flexibility in decision-making. They normally rode through boom-bust cycles because their property appreciated during rising business cycles, giving them a cushion to fall back upon during recessions. Meanwhile, in the North, an excess supply of labor gained through controlled new immigration served as a weapon to control wage slaves by increasing the leverage in favor of employers. Wage slaves could be hired and fired by the day and moved from city to city or from one state to another, and were not allowed to unionize. The easiest to control were the paupers, who were forced to enter prisons in order to eat, while their women and children had to submit to the welfare system to avoid starvation.

The entry of blacks into a white population meant special problems in motivating and controlling the economic classes. White yeoman farmers had to compete against black slaves owned by white slaveholders. Black slaves, better fed and cared for than white paupers, added to the dilemma of the class system in the South.

A stable class structure demanded that free blacks in the North be relegated to pauper or untouchable status and restricted to menial jobs to eliminate competition. Blacks doing menial and domestic work would not require close supervision; and since they did no productive work, motivating them became unimportant. They could remain permanent paupers down the generations provided their numbers were limited to about ten percent of the population, which could be achieved by increasing white immigration.

Alternative Slave Systems

The Southern Protestant slavery code had reserved a permanent slave status for blacks, to be controlled by slaveholders without any interference from non-slaveholders or the church. Indeed, no economic opportunity could be provided for a slave to buy his freedom or be freed. Under the Act of 1740, South Carolina made it illegal for any slave to "raise and breed for the benefit of such slave, any horses, mares, cattle, sheep or hogs under pain of forfeiture of all such goods, etc." Slaveholders who allowed their slaves such benefits would be punished. For example, a master in Georgia permitting his slave to hire himself out to another for personal benefit was fined thirty dollars for every weekly offense.[2]

All mulattos, including those with only a trace of Negro blood, were defined by law as Negroes to prevent any movement up the class system. Southern laws denied the right of a slave to property even with a master's consent to prevent rich planters who had fathered mulatto children from freeing them or giving them property and upsetting the basic assumptions of the Protestant system of slavery.

Since black slaves could not be freed, slaveholders needed an escape route if the slaves' utility declined due to crop failure, reduction in cash crop prices or soil exhaustion, or increases in the slave population. The slaveholder having unconditional rights of sale and the slave being denied all rights to a contract, including marriage, meant that the slave was transferable. If the black population increased, excess slaves were shifted, preferably at a profit, to new territory with untapped markets.

The operational rule for controlling the black under the Protestant system of slavery was that the slave must work or be flogged. This meant slaveholders had to maintain close supervision at all times. The system could only work with cash crops and economies of scale, using overseers to supervise the workers constantly and inflict pain when necessary. The Protestant system of slavery would not work in a factory system that required workers to think and where constant supervision was impractical.

While guaranteeing fixed slave status to blacks, the Protestant system of slavery also forced whites into the class system's pauper category. For dangerous tasks where a slave's life was too valuable, as investment to risk, slaveholders hired white workers at higher wages to avoid the prospective financial loss of a slave's death. Frederic Law Olmsted, who visited the South in 1850, recorded this conversation with a planter on the Virginia seaboard, who hired an Irish gang to drain swamps on contract. When asked why he employed Irishmen in preference to organizing the work himself and using his own slaves, he responded: "It's dangerous work . . . A Negro's life is too valuable to be risked at it. If a Negro dies, it is a considerable loss you know." A major weakness of the Protestant system of slavery was in making the whites in the pauper class worse off than slaves and their lives more expendable.[3]

The majority of whites under Protestant system of slavery were yeoman farmers engaged in growing cash crops, competing with slaveholders because their crop's price was determined in distant markets. Yeoman farmers depended on planters to market their crops but typically owned the worst land and no slaves. This forced them to limit their consumption and lifestyles to slave level in order to minimize costs and compete. Thus, by forcing yeoman farmers and white wage workers into direct competition with black slaves, the Protestant system of slavery victimized both non-slaveholding whites and black slaves in what was to prove its fatal flaw.

In contrast to the Protestant system of slavery, its Catholic counterpart assumed slavery to be a long-term apprenticeship contract between slave and slaveholder, with the king and church ensuring that slaves' rights were respected. Indeed, under the Catholic system, slaves were to be provided every opportunity to hone their skills and abilities to win their freedom and become part of the community. Slaves between fourteen and sixty years old could not be seized for debt unless their master's plantation was also seized, nor could there be any judicial seizure or sale of any real estate without including the slaves attached to them. The Catholic system of slavery tied slaves to the land, like real estate, and restricted labor mobility. Thus, in 1836, when George W. Grove of Concordia Parish offered to sell one thousand acres of land, he included two hundred and fifty cleared acres, ten good field hands, cattle, hogs, farming equipment, and a year's supply of corn.[4]

The Catholic system of slavery, the *Code Noir,* also encouraged freeing slaves and allowing them to hire out their own time with their masters' permission. A slave was required to turn over some portion of the money earned to his master as "wages," but could retain any surplus earnings. This enabled him to save enough to buy his freedom. A slave could have his price declared so that he might, if able to accumulate the necessary resources, buy his freedom.[5]

The *Code Noir* further provided that slaves should not be required to work on Sundays and feast days without compensation. In their spare time they could work on plots allocated to them and sell the produce with their masters' permission. To facilitate slaves' transition to freedom, it encouraged educating and baptizing slaves into Christianity.[6]

Catholic slavery assumed the formation of a free black population which was granted "the same rights, privileges and immunities which free persons enjoyed." Although it prohibited marriages between whites and blacks, it included an escape clause that enabled white fathers to acknowledge and provide for mulatto children. Free mulattos could obtain education, skills, and even property through their blood connections with rich whites. This allowed many mulattos a higher standard of living than that of poor whites.[7]

Given the liberty contained within the Catholic slavery code, the slaveholder had no reason to prefer a black man to a white man, thereby avoiding the fatal flaw of the Protestant system. Priorities were clear-cut: whites were given top priority, then mulattos, and then blacks. Even among mulattos, priority was determined by their proportion of white blood. Whiteness could also be purchased for a consideration. Whites and mulattos were given preference in hiring, dictated by circumstances and employers' convenience. Under the law all free people were considered equal, whatever their color. Their economic status determined their class. Color was taken into account in everyday life but operated at an individual level. The most important feature of the Catholic system of slavery lay in its permitting a gradual transition from long-term slavery to wage slavery without creating social control problems based on color.

A third alternative to the Protestant or Catholic systems of slavery, when job seekers exceeded the available jobs, was wage slavery. John C. Calhoun of South Carolina saw the social order as inevitably based on arrangements between an owning class and a property-less working class, in which the former utilized a variety of coercive devices to compel the latter to labor for it. He wrote: "there never has existed a wealthy and civilized society in which one portion of the community did not, in point of fact, live on the labor of the other. The devices to accomplish this are almost innumerable, from the brute force and gross superstition of ancient times to the subtle and artful contrivances of modern times." A wage slave was distinguished from a wage worker in owning no property, having no savings, and having only limited choices; but calling a wage slave a free worker was deception because he was only free to starve. Thomas Carlyle succinctly said: "Free labor means work or starve." Dependence on wages robbed a man of his independence and, therefore, his liberty. The employer was similar to a slaveholder. He determined the hours of toil, the pace of work, the division of labor, the level of wages; he could hire and fire at will.[8]

Even children were not exempt from the reach of wage slavery. Alexander Hamilton championed child labor as a means of keeping minors out of mischief and ordered small looms from England for the use of child workers. In the Providence area, entire families of children above the age of five often worked twelve to fourteen hours a day in the mills. England, according to Lord Ashley's 1842 report, worked five thousand white women underground in coal mines where, half-naked and in rags, they were harnessed with leather straps to coal cars, which they dragged all day for a starvation wage, crawling on all fours. Wage slavery could reduce consumption to even lower levels than that prevalent under Protestant system of slavery by committing workers to the streets or the almshouse during sickness or old age. It also absolved employers from responsibility for the wage slaves' children.[9]

Notwithstanding this, wage slavery encapsulated a positive motivation for workers to work hard and better themselves. There was always a slim chance of an education, training, expertise, experience, or savings to improve one's condition and eventually have the vote and a voice in influencing the future. Horatio Alger stories of successes and dreams-come-true motivated the wage slave, who hoped his children or grandchildren would, with hard work and a little luck, acquire property and improve their condition.

As an economic fact of life, lifelong slavery was viable only while there was plenty of land and few people to work it. In the long run, a population multiplies until it exceeds the available stock of land. When land as a resource became more important than the people who worked it, wage slavery became the preferred labor control system. Achille Loria explained in *The Economic Synthesis:*

> When the growth of population has made land so dear
> that common laborers in freedom cannot save enough
> to buy farms, the occasion for slavery serfdom lapses.
> Laborers may now be freed to become a wage-earning
> proletariat, to take their own risks. An automatic coercion
> replaces the systematic; the labor stimulus is intensified,
> but the stress of the employers is diminished. The laborer
> does not escape coercion, but merely exchanges one of its
> forms for another.[10]

Thus, it was only a matter of time before long-term slavery came to an end and wage slavery took over. The speed of conversion from body slavery to wage slavery was influenced by the labor force's racial mix, soil exhaustion, industrialization, credit availability, and the political control system, whether democratic or autocratic. These factors changed continually over a two-hundred–year period.

Colonial Period

In the early colonial days in the South, a pauper class barely existed. Land was abundant, labor scarce, and labor requirements were met by white indentured servants. At least three-fourths of immigrants in the Southern colonies were indentured servants. When they had completed their indenture, males, who constituted the vast majority, could expect to receive such benefits as tools, clothing, and sometimes land to start a new life as free workers or independent farmers. Females were largely employed as domestics and were expected to marry after completing their contracts. This was never a problem because males in the colonies outnumbered females three to one during the seventeenth century.

However, white indentured servants included convicts and criminals who were auctioned off. Others were prisoners of war taken in battles with the Scots and Irish. The demand for labor was so high that orphans, vagrants, and paupers in Great Britain were fair game. No questions were asked if pirates sold kidnapped people. White indentured servants, because of their backgrounds and the treatment they received in the colonies, were more trouble than they were worth to Southern tobacco planters. These servants had written indentures and could theoretically appeal to their home countries if maltreated. They could easily escape and mingle with the local population in another town without being caught. Worst of all, they had to be released when their term was up, and all the time and energy that had gone into training them was lost.

The situation was ripe for Bacon's Rebellion in 1676. On the surface this was a conflict between small white landowners on the western frontier and the large landed aristocracy in the east. In reality it revealed the instability caused by a large landless population of white former indentured servants with no employment and no families. Nathaniel Bacon convinced the landless whites to support him by taking advantage of their intense hatred for the frontier Indians. The landowners felt that the landless whites, if unchecked, could well start a revolution in the colonies.

One alternative was Indian slave labor that had been tried in the West Indies' sugar plantations. Indians, however, lacked sufficient stamina and did not survive diseases and severe working conditions. In the South, Indian slaves could always escape along forest trails to the protection of their own people. Moreover, the colonists valued their friendship, as the Indians had helped them survive when they had come as early settlers. As early as 1656, the Virginia Assembly passed laws prohibiting Indian enslavement. In the eighteenth century, the Virginia courts accepted Indian descent as proof when deciding questions of freedom.

Around the 1670s, economic conditions in Great Britain improved and the availability of indentured servants declined while their prices increased. A solution to the labor shortage was present in the colonial population, though to a limited degree. The first blacks were brought to Jamestown in 1619; and the colonists, familiar with white indentured servants, treated the blacks as servants to be freed after the expiration of a certain term. It was now only necessary to consign blacks to slave status. According to the state constitution, "Every freeman of Carolina shall have absolute power and authority over his Negro slaves of what opinion or religion so ever." Enslaving blacks had several advantages in that they had no legal rights, no written indentures, nor any problematic ideas of liberty. They could easily be identified and captured if they tried to escape and could be held for generations. Moreover, they could be used to get rid of the dangerous poor landless whites. Most white indentured servants avoided going South after this period.[11]

Black slavery was encouraged in Carolina by early settlers from Barbados who had previous experience with it and had brought their slaves with them. The proprietors of Carolina also had a financial interest in the African slave trade. Therefore all forces—primarily the greed of uncompromising profit-seekers of Barbados and the Carolina proprietors—combined to make black slavery a successful venture. By the end of the seventeenth century, black slaves comprised about ten percent of the Southern population.

Tobacco and black slavery were ideally suited to each other. A ready market for tobacco was provided when the king banned all production of tobacco in England and Wales around 1619. It was an ideal cash crop because it had a high value-to-weight ratio and could be exported to Europe in the small ships available at the time. Its cultivation did not entail much skill or capital and was therefore suitable for the generation of quick profits. Slave energies had to be consumed throughout the year because the investment in labor was fixed. The operation was dispersed across large tracts of land, which isolated the laborers, thereby reducing control and discipline problems. Growing tobacco with slave labor was such a specialized and profitable operation that plantation owners would rather buy corn and pork to feed slaves than grow it.

Indeed, the returns from slave labor were far higher than the whites could possibly achieve with their own. Virginia was established to generate profits for a company based in London and for its agents in America. Thus this man-made institution served both the slaveholders and British shareholders, who never paused to consider that the logic of their course forced them toward the conclusion that slavery must go on forever.[12]

From the outset, Virginia, Maryland, and the Carolinas had large landholdings for proprietors, first operated by indentured servants and later by black slaves. Virginia was a royal colony; its governor appointed by the king since 1624. One of those royal governors, Sir William Berkeley, dominated the colony's policy for over thirty years. He defeated the Indians in 1644, forcing them to cede all the land between the York and James Rivers. This territorial expansion continued whenever new settlers needed new land. In Maryland, the proprietor retained absolute authority to distribute land as he wished, and Lord Baltimore initially granted large estates to his relatives and other British aristocrats so that a distinct class of landed slaveholders could be established.

In 1669, the Constitution of Carolina provided for the territory to be divided into counties of equal size, with each county divided into equal parcels. The largest number of parcels was distributed amongst the proprietors themselves, a local aristocracy received fewer parcels, and ordinary settlers received still less. At the bottom of this stratified society were poor whites with no political rights and black slaves whose subjugation was complete. By the end of the seventeenth century, all government power and control was consolidated in slaveholders' hands.

When the first burgesses were elected in Virginia in 1619, all men aged seventeen or more were entitled to vote. By 1670, the vote was restricted to landowners, and elections were rare. The same burgesses, loyal and subservient to the governor, remained in office year after year. Each county continued to have only two representatives, even though some new counties in the interior were inhabited by many more people than the old counties of the tidewater area. Thus the more recent settlers were underrepresented or not represented at all. A pattern was emerging in Virginia that would repeat itself time and again in other parts of America.

In Maryland, the proprietor retained absolute authority to distribute land as he wished. A representative assembly, the House of Delegates, was established at the insistence of the first settlers in 1635. Its proceedings were based on the rules of Parliament. By 1650, the colony had a bicameral legislature in which the upper house consisted of the governor and his council who held controlling power. According to the Constitution for Carolina in 1669, the proprietors, nobles, and other landholders would have a voice in the colonial parliament in proportion to the size of their landholdings.

It was clear to the proprietors and the king that the colonies could not be successful if they were populated only with slaveholders, indentured servants, and black slaves. A class of white yeoman farmers was needed for economic and political stability. To attract this class of people, both Virginia and Maryland adopted a head right system: a grant of one hundred acres to each male settler, another hundred acres to his wife and each servant, and fifty acres to each of his children. In the Carolina territory, ordinary settlers would also be given land to attract them. Nevertheless, the great landlords and slaveholders of the colony's earliest years always retained control of government even as the population grew larger and more diverse. The foundation of the American class system, based on property ownership and control by slaveholders, with black slaves at the bottom, was laid in the South in the seventeenth century.

In the North, the immigrants could not aspire to rich farms but developed a profitable trade in fish and furs. Since commercial farming was impossible for them due to poor soil and weather conditions, the settlers cultivated small areas of land, growing food, raising animals, and in general attempting to become self-sufficient. Most Northern settlers came in family groups, so the male to female ratio was sixty to forty, resulting in more stable relationships and family life.

The Yankees, without rich farmlands, applied their ingenuity to developing a flourishing three-way trade between New England, Europe, and Africa. When the slave monopoly of the Royal African Trade Company was terminated in 1697, they moved in to satisfy the increased demand for slaves. Around this time, the New England Puritans began distilling rum from West Indian molasses. Ships sailed from New England to Europe with cargoes of rum and Southern tobacco. When they reached Great Britain, they exchanged rum and tobacco for manufactured goods and headed for the West African coast. There they exchanged more rum for slaves and set sail for the West Indies island of Barbados and the

French colonies of Martinique and Guadalupe. In the West Indies, some slaves and manufactured goods were exchanged for molasses, which was brought back to New England to be distilled into rum. On the way back to New England, the ships stopped in the South to exchange manufactured goods and slaves for tobacco. The Yankees both profited greatly from the black slave trade and supplied slaves to the South. In the process, some black slaves were introduced into the middle colonies of New York and New Jersey.

The German immigrants who arrived in the North were unwilling to work as tenants in the large estates of New York and moved to Pennsylvania. Here they applied intensive farming methods learned in Europe to increase production. Most German men came with women who worked alongside them on the farms, forming the yeoman farmer class that was part of the small-property owner class in the North.

To augment their agricultural economy, New England entrepreneurs in New Jersey and Pennsylvania started industrial enterprises such as spinning, weaving, carpentry, rifle-making, and cabinet-making. Water power from the many streams and rivers ran mills for grinding grain, processing cloth, milling lumber and serving the ship-building industry. British capital and German know-how founded several flourishing ironworks in the North. The vast forests for lumber and mines for iron and other minerals provided the base for a diversified, self-sufficient economy based on trade and processed raw materials. Those who owned and controlled mills, mines, iron works, and ships, together with merchants and traders, formed the North's employer class.

It cost the British government only about one pound five shillings to pay for an individual's passage to North America. This was such a bargain price that about fifty thousand white indentured workers, including many convicts and criminals, were dumped on the North American mainland between 1717 and 1775. Benjamin Franklin protested that these scum were being sent to America. New England, being choosy, received the smallest number of them. They served as wage workers in Pennsylvanian mines and lumbering operations. Those who escaped went South to become "white trash."

The growing Northern colonial cities made urbanization a visible phenomenon. The cities served as trading centers for local farmers and international trade marts. Rich merchants with conspicuous estates and wealth provided leadership. All the schools and cultural centers were located in cities, as were rum distilleries. On the flip side were a large population of wage slaves, living in crowded and filthy conditions, and urban problems such as crime, pollution, and traffic congestion. Police forces and fire departments had to be established and provisions made to prevent paupers and the unemployed from starving. Therefore, even before the Revolution, the framework of the Northern economic class system was in place with rich controller-employers, yeomen farmers, wage slaves, and paupers.

Southern Class System

Matters were different in states such as South Carolina and Georgia, which could grow no tobacco. The black slaves served a different purpose there as they produced rice in knee-deep mud and malarial swamps, where white workers refused to venture. White planters depended on black slaves in this region more than anywhere else. In consequence, by the time the Revolution started, South Carolina's black slave population exceeded that of whites.

Indigo, in great demand, was a complementary cash crop for rice. It grew on higher ground and slaves could harvest it while the rice was growing. Between 1740 and 1776 rice exports to Europe grew threefold while indigo exports grew fourfold, bringing prosperity to the region. By 1776, the elite of Charleston, the capital of South Carolina, were the richest in North America.

Although individual planters from the South were the richest in the country, all tobacco, rice, and indigo exports were handled by Yankees in the North. They also supplied slaves, food, and other manufactured goods to the South. The yeoman farmers and white wage workers of the South were reduced to the same economic level as black slaves by direct competition. In consequence, the South was unable to develop even a small commercial or industrial economy and became totally dependent on, and a virtual colony of, the North.

Then came the developments around cotton, the driving force in the Southern economy during the evolution of slavery. Southern farmers were faced with the challenge of meeting the cotton needs of the post-Revolution textile industry in Great Britain. Long staple cotton with easily removable seeds, which grew well only along the coast or on the offshore islands of Georgia and South Carolina, was the most economical crop. Short staple cotton, which could grow anywhere in the South, had sticky green seeds that were difficult to remove manually and required several slaves to produce just a few pounds of cotton a day. Matters changed around 1793, when Whitney invented the cotton gin to remove seeds from short staple cotton, increasing a slave's efficiency tenfold. A single slave could produce more cotton in a few hours than several slaves had previously produced in a day, making it economical to grow cotton anywhere in the South and ushering in a new era in the South's economic history.

Revolution injected new fears in this class system. The British army tried to recruit blacks with promises of freedom. This frightened whites, prompting every state in the South, except Georgia and South Carolina, to prohibit slave imports to keep their numbers down. Georgia and South Carolina instituted a temporary war-time ban for economic reasons. Trade disruptions due to the war sent the demand and prices for tobacco and rice plummeting, leading in turn to a decline in the demand and prices for slaves. The South did not want to further reduce the value of their slaves by importing new ones. Moreover, in 1789 in Santo Domingo, blacks revolted and took over the island, killing whites and creating the republic of Haiti. These developments made both the North and the South agree in Congress to ban the slave trade on January 1, 1808. From the standpoint of security, the United States had reached black slavery's natural limit by the end of the eighteenth century. Future population growth would have to be achieved with white immigrants. The question of dealing with the existing blacks persisted. Without the cotton gin, this would have been a good time to abolish slavery to spare slaveholders the responsibility of feeding them.

Thomas Jefferson's embargo to force the British and French to the negotiating table created a depression in 1807. All American ships were prohibited from leaving the United States for any foreign port, and Southern planters were deprived of foreign markets. Yet the slaves had to be fed and the financiers were ever ready to foreclose on farms and slaves if loans were not repaid on time. The cotton gin saved the day for slavery. The war with the British from 1812 to 1815 led to the opening up of new Southern territories for black slavery on cotton plantations and boom times.

After the war, the demand for cotton revived. Many Southern lands had been depleted by erosion and overplanting, and virgin land was in demand to keep the slaves in work. The following years saw one of the largest land booms in the nation's history. In 1815, government land offices sold a million acres; this figure rose to five million acres in 1819. Credit helped the boom along. Land could be purchased with an eighty-dollar down payment and three subsequent installments payable over four years. Settlers hoped to earn their installment payments by farming the land. Speculators bought choice tracts, hoping to sell them to incoming settlers at a profit. At land auctions, bidding became so spirited that some land in Alabama and Mississippi sold for a hundred dollars per acre when the minimum reserved price was two dollars per acre.

There was no lack of ambitious farmers seeking to cultivate new land in central Alabama and Mississippi. The first arrivals were usually frontiersmen and small farmers who made rough clearings in the forest. Then came the wealthier planters, who bought the cleared land, while the original settlers moved farther west to start the process afresh. The wealthy planters were followed by the aristocracy, who came in large caravans consisting of herds of livestock and wagonloads of household goods. Eventually, the small clearings grew into vast cotton fields and log cabins were replaced by imposing mansions that signaled the rise of the new wealthy class. The rapid expansion to the west resulted in Mississippi and Alabama being admitted into the Union in 1817 and 1819 respectively.

The growing demand for cotton and the availability of virgin land created a demand for more slaves, since cotton cultivation was impractical without them. Since slave importation had been banned by Congress in 1808, half a million black slaves were moved from the South to the Southwestern states of Mississippi and Alabama. This massive shift was accomplished through the offices of speculators and agents who bought slaves in Virginia and the upper Southern states and transported them to the new states for sale. None of the existing laws against interstate slave commerce were enforced. The upper South was ready, willing, and able to sell their slaves because prices were high and the tobacco economy was depressed and was to remain so for a long time. Demand for slaves was so great that Yankee merchants continued to smuggle in blacks from abroad despite the ban.

This speculative boom and revival and expansion of the Southern slave plantation economy would have been impossible had Catholic slavery restraints on slave mobility been enforced. Failure to enforce laws against interstate slave commerce and the slave importation ban postponed the solution of America's black problem by fifty years.

The Southern cash crop economy initially saw the Indians moved to reservations in the West. These were encroached on for more land. Eventually the Indians were reduced to such straits of poverty and desolation that they had little strength to resist. The westward expansion progressed with the admission of Texas, Iowa, and Missouri into statehood and continued until the Civil War.

In the South, industry remained an insignificant force in comparison to the cash crop agricultural economy. At the time of the Civil War, textile manufacture accounted for only two percent of the value of cotton exports. The South's financial infrastructure was rudimentary. Planters depended on financiers to market their crops. In turn, Southern financiers were totally dependent on Yankee merchants, financiers, and professionals. Some scholars claim that the Southern industrial and commercial economy failed to develop because most of their capital was invested in land and slaves. However, the competition from black slavery possibly hurt non-slaveholders, the South's white majority, even more. The colonization of the South by the North that had evolved earlier with tobacco, rice, and indigo, continued with cotton. Although Southern cotton accounted for two-thirds of the United States' export trade, it was controlled by Northern merchants and financiers.

Just before the Civil War, there were around four million slaves in the total population of twelve million in the slave states. Among one and a half million free families, only 385,000 were slaveholders. This meant that three-fourths of Southern whites had no connection with slavery through direct ownership or family ties. The typical Southern white was a yeoman farmer and non-slaveholder. The planter aristocracy consisted of about ten thousand families who owned about two million slaves amongst them. If the planter class is defined as ownership of at least twenty slaves, the typical slaveholder did not belong to that class, since 88 percent of slaveholders owned fewer than twenty.[13]

The planter aristocracy was at society's apex, determining the South's political, economic, and social life. Even though the black slaves were not citizens and could not vote, they counted as three-fifths of a white man for Congressional representation. This leverage gave slaveholding aristocrats total political control of the South and provided them with bargaining power in Congress against the North out of proportion to their numbers.

The slaveholder aristocracy also controlled the South's yeoman farmers by forcing them to depend upon the aristocrat planters to market their crops and for finances to deal with the boom and bust cycles. The cash crop's cost was minimized through economies of scale when thirty slaves and an overseer were used to work the land. The overseer ensured maximal output from the slaves, who at the same time were fed at subsistence level. To compete in the same market, yeoman farmers had to minimize their costs, limiting their consumption to slave level. M. Traver of Missouri, in a paper on "Domestic Manufactures in the South and West" described the situation as follows:

The non-slaveholders possess, generally, but very small means, and the land which they possess is almost universally poor, and so sterile that a scanty subsistence is all that can be derived from its cultivation; and the more fertile soil, being in the possession of the slaveholders, must ever remain out of the power of those who have none. This state of things is a great drawback, and bears heavily upon and depresses the moral energies of the poor classes. The acquisition of a respectable position in the scale of wealth appears so difficult, that they decline the hopeless pursuit, and many of them settle down into habits of idleness, and become the almost passive subjects of all its consequences.[14]

At the bottom of the Southern economy were the half million "white trash," also called "crackers" or "sandhillers." They occupied the infertile pine barrens, red hills, and swamps in miserable cabins and squalor. No matter how hungry they were, they did not want to work beside the blacks or do any work that was done by blacks. So sapped were they by poverty that they did not have the strength to protest. Frederic Olmsted, noted: "From childhood the one thing in their condition which had made life invaluable to the mass of whites has been that the niggers are yet their inferiors." They existed on dreams of racial supremacy and went along with the other Southern whites.[15]

The testimony of Governor Hammond of South Carolina is revealing:

Of the three hundred thousand white inhabitants of South Carolina, there are not less than fifty thousand, in the present condition of things, adequate to procure them, honestly, such a support as every white person is, and feels himself entitled to. And this, next to emigration, is perhaps, the heaviest of the weights that press upon the springs of our prosperity. Most of these now follow agricultural pursuits, in feeble, yet injurious competition with slave labor. Some, perhaps, not more from inclination, than from want of due encouragement, can scarcely be said to work at all. They obtain a precarious subsistence, by occasional jobs, by hunting, by fishing, sometimes by plundering fields or folds, and too often by what is, in its effects, far worse—trading with slaves, and reducing them to plunder for their benefit.[16]

Thus the Civil War was preceded by an extreme economic class structure in the South that economically enslaved both black slaves and white non-slaveholders while most Southern wealth and political power was concentrated in slaveholders' hands. This system was politically and economically unstable because white non-slaveholders always had a theoretical option of moving into free states. The Civil War evolved as a contest for the hearts and minds of Southern white non-slaveholders.

Northern Class System

In the North, the economic pattern during slavery's period of maturity was controlled by three forces: industrialization and urbanization in the Northeast, increased white immigration, and growing numbers of yeoman farmers in the new Northwestern territories. After the steam engine was patented in England in 1769, industrialists built factories to house textile machinery to make cloth. Despite attempts by the British government to prevent both the export of textile machinery and the emigration of skilled mechanics, some immigrants arrived in the United States with advanced knowledge of British technology and a willingness to introduce the new machines into America.

The first spinning mill in America was set up in Rhode Island in 1790, laying the foundation of a large textile industry in the North to process Southern cotton. By 1810, there were 15,000 distilleries, and the textile industry went through a spectacular period of growth from 1840 to 1860 when the canal and railroad network expanded and telegraph lines spread rapidly.

The European immigrant supplied the labor for industry. To attract white labor, all the Northern states abolished slavery by legislative or judicial means, either gradually or abruptly. All new states prohibited black immigration. They used fugitive slave laws and harassment or mob violence to rid themselves of the existing blacks, forcing most to leave the North or agree to segregation and restriction to menial jobs. The North thus provided for white wage slaves by eliminating direct competition from the blacks. Since America exported more goods to Europe than it imported, its trading ships brought back new immigrants on the return trip. From 1820 to 1860, the population of the North increased fourfold, from five million to twenty million. After 1820, the indentured labor system became a thing of the past. Most immigrants were Catholics, escaping from European famines, who had to adjust to the factory system's harsh realities and become wage slaves.

To meet the initial labor demands of the textile factory system, whole families had been enticed from farms to the mills in the mid-Atlantic states and New England. Farmers' daughters in their late teens and twenties, especially in Massachusetts, were enlisted for such work. They worked in the mills for a number of years, saved money, and returned to the farms to marry. The Northeast's agricultural farm economy was on the decline, so these females contributed to their families' maintenance. The competitive textile markets of the 1830s and 1840s saw frequent booms and busts. Wages were reduced, work hours lengthened, and conditions in female boardinghouses deteriorated. A strike organized by the factory females' union protested a twenty-five percent wage cut. During the recession of 1837, the union was destroyed and the textile factories came to rely for labor on immigrants who had less leverage because they were unfamiliar with the country.

Irish immigrants were used in construction gangs for heavy, unskilled work on turnpikes, canals, and railroads. Without marketable skills, they received low wages, intermittently got seasonal jobs, and had trouble feeding their families. By 1840, Irish workers predominated in the New England textile mills, worsening working conditions. Employers paid piece-rates rather than daily wages and used other strategies to increase production and exploit workers. By the mid-1840s, working class neighborhoods in Northeastern cities were squalid slums. Modern manufacturing factories also threatened the existence of skilled artisans. To protect themselves from competition, craftsmen organized themselves into unions. Carpenters, masons, plasterers, shipbuilders, and other skilled craftsmen formed unions, first by city and later on a regional basis, only to succumb to the 1837 depression.

By 1840, a large permanent labor class was emerging in urban areas and had to find whatever accommodations it could in crowded conditions. Factories were becoming large, noisy, and unsanitary. The average workday extended from twelve to fourteen hours. Skilled workers earned about seven dollars a week, the unskilled made half that, and women and children even less. Many states tried to protect workers with ten-hour workday laws, but employers evaded them by making workers sign "express contracts" as a condition for hiring.

All efforts by skilled and unskilled workers to protect themselves were doomed by a flood of immigrants. Ethnic divisions and tensions between natives and immigrants kept them at each other's throats rather than directing their energies against employers' maltreatment. The industrial capitalists used their substantial economic, political, and social power to resist all challenges from laborers.

A very small number of workers, however, raised themselves from this morass of poverty to riches through hard work, ingenuity, and luck. Their example provided hope to the multitudes, and it was not unrealistic for a dedicated worker to move one step up in the economic class system in a generation. An unskilled worker could become a skilled craftsman. A field hand could hope to buy a small farm. The other avenue was to travel west, though most workers lacked the savings and expertise required to move to the frontier. Instead, they moved from town to town because of layoffs, in search of better opportunities, their rootlessness depriving them of any savings or political power.

Women, for whom all work outside the household save teaching or nursing, was considered derogatory, had to work at whatever they could to help feed their families. They worked in factories and mills or as domestics, which became one of their most frequent forms of employment. Abortions were legal in some states and birth-control methods were available before the Civil War. However, many immigrants were Catholic and did not use birth control to limit family size. Large families headed by underpaid parents afforded each member less opportunity to acquire education or accumulate savings, and their children continued to fill the class system's wage slave niche for generations.

Meanwhile, the Northern industrialists and capitalists used corporate organization to spread their risks and control the region's resources and infrastructure. Just before the Civil War, there were thirty thousand miles of railroad and fifty thousand miles of telegraphic wire services for communications. The Northeast produced two-thirds of the country's manufactured goods. Coal, the new energy source, was mined in Pennsylvania and controlled by the corporations. Before the Civil War, five percent of the population, the employer-controller aristocracy, owned fifty percent of the regional wealth; the Northern employer-controller aristocrats having access to their own slaves: white and bodily free.

Some skilled Germans came between 1820 and 1860 with some savings and traveled west, where land was available by expelling the Indians. As beer drinkers, the Germans created a brewing industry; and hard work by the German men and their wives enabled them to raise reasonably prosperous family farms. An average farm during that time consisted of about two hundred acres and was owned by the people working it. Increased demand for farm produce in Europe and rising prices enhanced the prosperity of these family farms.

Much of the prosperity of the Northwestern German was due to their Protestant faith, which allowed them to use birth control to limit family size. However, the growth of this economic class depended on land availability and homestead policies that allowed people to purchase land for a small fee after living on it for a number of years. The importance of this property owner class to the country's political stability became apparent in 1860, just prior to the Civil War. Thomas Jefferson, himself a farmer, opposed extensive factory development because it would lead to the growth of cities full of property-less wage slaves. He believed America's abundant land was its greatest economic resource.

Following the increase in white immigration from 1820 to 1860, the proportion of blacks in the North declined sharply. The number was small to begin with because most Northern states had abolished slavery and did not want blacks among them. After the panic of 1837, and with the increase in Irish immigrants, the blacks' position in the Northeast went from bad to worse. Between 1840 and 1860, unskilled Irish laborers took menial jobs, depressing wages and driving out blacks. Railroad and canal construction projects were soon dominated by the Irish, who also broke the blacks' monopoly of service occupations. A Philadelphia newspaper remarked that "within a few years the blacks have ceased to be hackney men and draymen, and now they are almost displaced as stevedores. They are rapidly losing their place as barbers and servants. Ten families employ white servants now, where one did 20 years ago." In 1830, blacks constituted a majority of New York City's servants. Twenty years later, Irish servants outnumbered the black population ten to one. Blacks were being forced into the unemployed untouchable class in the North.[17]

Even so, the black man had his uses. The capitalists used blacks to control Irish wage slaves and break their strikes. In 1842, Irish coal miners in Pennsylvania battled with blacks for jobs. In 1853, armed blacks replaced striking Irishmen on the Erie Railroads. Two years later the Irish and blacks battled it out on the New York docks when the Irish longshoremen struck against wage cuts and blacks replaced them. Confronted with this economic reality, the Irish soon channeled their frustration and anger into a hatred for the blacks and began to find what comfort they could in white supremacy doctrines. To prevent economic competition, they took recourse to mob violence and restricted blacks to slums in urban areas. Before the Civil War, the North had twenty million people, included about half a million employer-controllers and no more than half a million blacks.[18]

The Northern economic prosperity was thus in no way directly dependent on the blacks. The Irish Catholic wage slaves hated blacks, felt superior to them, and blamed them for their own miserable condition. Just before the Civil War, the classic American class system pattern had evolved in the North. The employer-controllers of the Northeast, the German family-owned farms of the Northwest, the Irish wage slaves of the Northeast, and black untouchables of the North provided all four classes in the right proportions for economic and political stability.

The Northern industry, however, also needed Southern raw materials and Southern markets for its products. It could not simply allow the South to secede. However, it cared little what the South did to blacks, so long as they were kept out of the North and the new territories. New territories, exclusively for the whites, had to be found to attract yeoman farmers who would counterbalance the number of white wage slaves necessary for continued industrial expansion. This was in direct opposition to the interests of the Southern slaveholders who needed the new territories to sustain the institution of slavery.

Before the Civil War the country was divided into the North, which was ninety-five percent white, and the South, which was one-third black. The slaveholders, though a minority, controlled the government at the state and federal levels and had brainwashed the white non-slaveholders on their side, stopping them from leaving the south to avoid competing with slaves. One possible solution to the slaveholders' dilemma was to free their black slaves gradually, but why would the slaveholder, who had had it his way all along, do so without compensation or, for that matter, without a fight?

In the following chapters we shall see how the Protestant slavery code as practiced in the South had forever eliminated the possibility of freeing the slaves.

Chapter 3

Law and Order

Presumed guilty unless proven innocent
> —The Protestant Slavery Code

They'll crack old Tony on the skull,
And preach and roar like Bashan bull,
Or braying ass, of mischief full,
Then seize old Jacob by the wool,
And pull for heavenly Union.
> —Frederick Douglas, "The Parody," 1854

A slave, prized by his owner for intelligence, seized an axe and killed the overseer who was beating him. Prosecutor Henry Clay, the Secretary of State under John Quincy Adams, argued that a free man could have pleaded self-defense, but since the defendant was a slave, the act was murder. Clay secured a conviction and the slave was hanged. The Negro's conduct at the trial, however, so impressed Clay that he resigned as prosecutor and "never failed to express his sorrow at the part he had played in this case."[1]

The Constitution of the United States made law and order the responsibility of individual states, and most states adopted the Protestant slavery code to deal with the slaves. There were two sets of laws and courts: one for whites and another for blacks, including mulattos, who were defined as blacks. For blacks the slaveholders were the law and, indeed, God. The black man's color was proof of his guilt. For whites the law was "presumed innocent unless found guilty," for blacks the law was "presumed guilty unless found innocent."

Southern Legal Framework

In virtually all colonial communities, slavery was established by custom alone, as the first blacks brought to the colonies in the seventeenth century were treated as indentured servants. With accumulated experience, the slaveholders realized the advantages of black slavery and legislated to define slave status, regulations, and the machinery to police them. Barbados, which used black plantation labor, enacted a dozen minor laws beginning in 1644 for controlling and recapturing runaways, passing a general statute in 1688. The black code of Barbados, with minor modifications, would be the source of the black slave code or the Protestant slavery code to be adopted by other British colonies. Adopting this model was no accident, but a deliberate choice by Southern slaveholders.

The Barbados statute gave masters claims for pecuniary compensation for black slaves stolen or illegally killed by other freemen, though the principal concern of the statute was controlling and punishing slave malfeasance. Slaves were not to leave their masters' premises at any time unless in the company of whites or when wearing servants' livery or carrying written passes. Offenders might be whipped and taken into custody by any white person who encountered them. A black man striking a white person, except in lawful defense of his master's person, family, or goods, was criminally punishable, though only with lashes for a first offense. Thefts to the value of more than a shilling, along with other serious infractions, were capital crimes. Black transgressors were to be summarily tried by courts comprised of two justices of the peace and three freeholders from the area nearest the crime and were to be punished immediately upon conviction.

To dissuade masters from concealing crimes committed by their black slaves, magistrates were to appraise each slave convicted of capital offence, within a limit of $25, and to estimate also the extent of damage to the person or property caused by the crime. The colonial treasurer was then required to take the amount assessed from public funds and, after making reimbursements for the injury done, pay the remainder, if any, to the criminal's owner. If, however, it appeared to the magistrate that the crime had been prompted by the master's neglect, the treasurer was to pay the master nothing. A master who wantonly killed his own slave was to be fined $15. Any other person who killed a slave illegally was to pay the master double the slave's value, be fined $25, and give a bond for subsequent good behavior. The destruction of a slave's life or limb in the course of punishment by his master constituted no legal offense, nor did the killing of one by any person when found stealing or attempting a theft by night. This act henceforward served as the basic law so long as slavery survived in the island.[2]

The Barbados Act was copied by South Carolina with additions from other sources in 1712. As a consequence of numerous revolts that followed, by 1739 the legislature had enacted new restraints on black slaves: no slaves were to be sold liquor without their masters' approval, none were to be taught to write, no more than seven men in a group were permitted to travel on the high roads unless in company of white persons, no houses or lands were to be rented to slaves, and no slaves were to be kept on any plantation where no white person was resident. This Act was supplemented by curfew and patrol laws and amended in later years by the enhancement of penalties for blacks convicted of striking white persons.[3]

Most Southern states adopted the South Carolina law with minor modifications. Meanwhile, complementary legislation in all these jurisdictions recognized slaves as personal property with children always following the mother's condition and declared their judicial incapacity to enter into contracts. Blacks were debarred from giving testimony in courts in all cases involving white persons.

The principles of local self-government and states' rights enabled the states to choose the Protestant slavery code. Locally elected Southern assemblies were controlled by slaveholders, whose greed and desire for social control made them err on the side of safety and flexibility for themselves. The basic issue around slave law and order was to extract the maximum labor out of slaves. As blacks were slaves forever, their only motivation under the Protestant slavery code was to minimize pain. Slaveholders had full liberty to inflict any punishment, including death. A North Carolina planter wrote: "Its a pity that, agreeable to nature of things slavery and tyranny must go together and that there is no such thing as having an obedient and useful slave without the painful exercise of undue and tyrannical authority." The slaveholders passed laws accordingly. As a Southern judge said, "The power of the master must be absolute, to render the submission of the slave perfect." Fear and violence were the means of settling the terms between acceptable and unacceptable productivity and other control techniques were of secondary importance.[4]

In order to keep black slaves working, masters used the carrot and the stick—the stick constantly, in the form of a whip standardized to avoid serious injury so that slaves could continue to work after being beaten. To make the lashes more effective, black males and females were stripped in front of others, including visitors, and whipped. Physical pain was enhanced by psychological pain as the slave lost face in front of his co-workers. Sometimes the master used a black overseer to keep production high. This created divisions between slaves, making the black overseer distance himself from other slaves and identify with his master's interests.

The proverbial carrots were harder to provide and were only possible on small farms where the master came into regular contact with his slaves. He could allow slaves to work in small gardens growing food for themselves or for sale, give a male slave traveling passes to a neighboring plantation to visit his "broad wife," or reward them with choice assignments such as working in the house or driving the carriage.

Laws, however, prohibited slaves from acquiring goods and trading with other slaves to discourage them from stealing. Cash was not allowed, therefore slaveowners would market whatever their slaves produced, paying them with orders on the store. Field hands clandestinely patronized small stores set up at the roadside by poor whites or recently landed immigrants who had progressed from peddling and were trying to accumulate capital for storekeeping in town. Neither asked questions of a slave who was swapping food or other stolen goods for whiskey or a few yards of calico. These traders knew how to advance a slave some enticing item on credit and then threaten to denounce him for previous pilferage, forcing him into further thieving to cover the debt. If the slave was caught stealing, the lashes followed and he could be placed in solitary confinement on his day off.

Runaway slaves were the master's biggest problem. He had to find ways to discourage this, apprehend them, and bring them back. A slave could not leave his master's land without a written piece of paper giving his name, identification marks, destination, and the route to be taken. Without this, he was considered a runaway, and the patrol was likely to whip him on the spot or take him home for the master to punish. Repeated attempts to run away were punishable by branding, maiming, and dismemberment. This became useful because the master advertising the runaway slaves could describe scars and brands for easy identification. As late as 1838, a North Carolinian advertised that Betty, a fugitive, was recently "burnt with a hot iron on the left side of her face, I tried to make the letter M."[5]

The murder of a black implied loss of slaveholder property and had to be covered by appropriate laws because slaveholders had to be compensated even if the killer was another black. Giving black criminals long prison sentences did slaveholders no good. Nor did imposing large fines, since slaves had no money. The court's only purpose was to determine if a black criminal was more useful to whites dead or alive. If it was more useful to execute a black criminal to set an example, it would be done publicly, and in the most horrible way imaginable. The only decision left was to compensate the masters so that they did not suffer financial loss and did not try to protect slaves by concealing their crimes. Blacks were then tried in special courts that did not concern themselves with the formalities of traditional British justice but relied on speedy verdicts and certain punishments.

According to the South Carolina code of 1740, a slave accused of a capital offense was to be tried "in the most summary and expeditious manner." These courts were comprised of a justice and one to five slaveholders. Capital cases could be tried before two justices and ten slaveholders. When white passions ran high and tension was great, it did not matter which court tried the black slave. In any case, a black trial was not a trial before peers. It was a trial in which someone with inferior rights was judged by his superiors. Questions of justice were unimportant. What was important to judges and jurors was arriving at a quick conviction that stressed the discipline and control whites exercised over blacks; this helped ensure that slaves knew their place.

In reality, no court proceedings were necessary if a black man killed a white man, attempted to rape a white woman, or revolt; even black courts were not speedy enough for white justice. White mobs frequently lynched blacks. A Georgia newspaper reported in 1860 that Mr. Williams Smith was killed by a Negro on Saturday evening. The Negro made his escape but was arrested on Sunday. On Monday morning, a number of citizens who had investigated the case burned him at the stake.[6]

The quickest way to see a black man lynched was to accuse him of attempting to rape a white woman. A slave named Ben was sentenced to death for attempted rape upon a white woman in Mobile, Alabama, in 1849. Also in Alabama, at the same time, a large number of people took a black man accused of raping a white woman out of prison before his trial, chained him to a stake, and burned him alive. An 1858 case in White County, Tennessee, known through the court record, featured a suit brought by a slave's owners to recover monetary damages from those who had lynched him. The record shows that the black man was in legal custody under a charge of rape and murder when certain citizens, some of whom had signed a written agreement to "stand by each other," broke into the jail and hanged the prisoner.[7]

A black had a better chance of getting a fair trial in a Negro court when accused of killing another black. In such cases, the court could hear the case without confusing issues of racial discipline and control. The black accused of murdering another black was rarely punished since this would result in additional financial loss to another white man. A black slave in Rapid Parish, Louisiana, accused of beating another slave to death, was found guilty of misdemeanor and sentenced to receive one hundred lashes on four successive days and to wear a ball and chain for three months. A slave in Clay County, Missouri, convicted of murdering another slave, received thirty-nine lashes and was sold out of state. Southern codes provided the same penalties for blacks or whites who murdered slaves. The theory was that one offense was as serious as the other, but the white men who applied the law usually came to think otherwise.[8]

In most Southern states, a black slave's death "under correction" was of no legal consequence. The logical principle was laid down in a Virginia colonial statute: "Since it cannot be prepoised malice (which alone makes a murder a felony) should induce a man to destroy his own estate." An Alabama slaveholder was convicted of whipping a slave to death in spite of protests from an uncomfortable neighbor; the verdict was manslaughter, with a penalty of two months in prison and a $500 fine.[9]

Whites could kill blacks whenever they wanted so long as there were no white witnesses because no black could appear as a witness against a white person in court. Most Southern states made it legal to kill runaways on sight to protect whites from other litigious owners. These laws were pointless, since the odds were a hundred to one against indicting a white man for killing a known runaway, outlaw or not, anywhere in the South. Given the manner in which the laws were enforced, whites did not have to worry about legality when killing blacks. Those whites who were indicted were usually acquitted or never brought to trial.

A slave placed in opposition to his master was in a helpless position; he had to depend on other whites to testify on his behalf. White witnesses were reluctant to testify against white offenders, so obsessed were they with the need for racial solidarity and fear that the whole system of control might fall apart if the master's authority was even questioned. Frederick Douglass cited the case of a Maryland woman who murdered a slave with a piece of firewood. A warrant for her arrest was issued but never served. Even if whites could be found to testify, it was a problem to get a white jury to convict. The foreman of a South Carolina jury declared frankly the feelings of most white jurymen that he "would not convict the defendant or any other white person for murdering a slave."[10]

In Maryland, Frederick Douglass remembered hearing white men say that it was "worth but half a cent to kill a nigger, and half a cent to bury him." A Mississippi editor explained: "There are many persons who think they have the same right to shoot a Negro that they have to shoot down a dog."[11]

The Protestant slavery codes institutionalized a double standard in that the whites believed that blacks would be the only victims, and all rewards would accrue to the whites who supported this system. This was the short-term viewpoint. In the long term, once an economic justification had been found to kill or maltreat a black man, the same principal could be used to justify a rich white man killing a poor white man. This did happen when a black slave killed a white man in self-defense and the case was tried in a black court. He had the benefit of two mistrials. An overseer wrote in disgust, "There are some slaveowners who think that a white man's life is worth nothing in comparison with a slave."

Some means were necessary to control black slaves when they ran errands for the master away from the farm or plantation. A mechanism was also needed to detect, catch, and return runaway slaves to their owners. This function was filled by the patrol. Theoretically, all whites performed rotational service in the patrol, which was often tied to the militia system. Usually the well-to-do found ways of buying their way out of patrol duty, and the responsibility fell on overseers as the patrolling system's backbone. In other places, regular patrols were hired from poor whites and small white farmers, who were given special training in abusing blacks that they put to use during lynch-mob duty. These ill-disciplined parties of whites, organized under community sanction, and often passing the bottle freely on their rounds, were the root of the Ku Klux Klan.

Complaints about patrols abusing their powers were as common as complaints about their failing to function. The poor whites who formed the major part of the patrols disliked the masters almost as intensely as they hated the blacks and, as patrollers, they were in a position to vent their feelings toward both. Slaveholders repeatedly went to the courts with complaints that patrollers had invaded their premises and whipped their slaves excessively or illegally. The black slaves in turn hated and feared the patrollers and tried to get even with them when they could. The masters were, however, stuck with the patrol system.

Hinton Rowan Helper, a Southern nonslaveholder and author before the Civil War, summarized the Protestant slavery code as follows:

> All slaveholders are under the shield of a perpetual license to murder. This license they have issued to themselves. According to their own infamous statutes, if the slave raises his hand to ward off an unmerited blow, they are permitted to take his life with impunity. We are personally acquainted with three ruffians who have become actual murderers under circumstances of this nature. One of them killed two negroes on one occasion; the other two have murdered but one each. Neither of them has ever been subjected to even the preliminaries of a trial; not one of them has ever been arrested; their own private explanations of the homicides exculpated them from all manner of blame to the premises. They had done nothing wrong in the eyes of the community. The negroes made an effort to shield themselves from the tortures of a merciless flagellation and were shot dead on the spot. Their murderers still live, and are treated as honorable members of society! No matter how many slaves or free negroes may witness the perpetration of these atrocious homicides, not one of them is ever allowed to lift up his voice in behalf of his murdered brother. In the South negroes, whether bond or free, are never, under any circumstances, permitted to utter a syllable under oath, except for or against persons of their own color; their testimony against white persons is of no more consequence than the idle zephyr of the summer.[12]

Patrolling and compensation for dead blacks was the only interference slaveholders tolerated from non-slave-holders. A non-slaveholding Southerner wrote:

> We are taxed to support slavery. The clean cash goes out of our own pockets into the pockets of the slaveholder, and this in many ways. I will now allude to but two. If a slave, for crime, is put to death or transported, the owner is paid for him out of the public treasury, and under this law thousands are paid out every year. Again, a standing army is kept up in the city of Richmond for no other purpose than to be ready to quell insurrection among slaves; this is paid for out of the public treasury annually. This standing army is called the public guard, but it is no less a standing army always kept up.

Another non-slaveholder had the following thoughts about his patrolling responsibilities:

> Here I am, a poor but sober and industrious man, with a family dependent on me for support, and after I have finished my day's labor, I am compelled to walk the streets from nine in the evening till three in the morning, to restrain the roving propensities of other people's "property"—niggers. Why should I thus be deprived of sleep that the slaveholder may slumber? I am becoming restless, and have been debating within my own mind whether I had not better emigrate to a free State.[13]

Louisiana's Legal Framework

The only exception to this Protestant code was Louisiana, because of its origin as a Latin colony. Louisiana's Catholic slavery code gave slaves some of the characteristics of real estate. Blacks, whether slave or free, were to be tried by the same courts and with the same procedures as white persons. When Louisiana became a territory and then a state, the Catholic slavery code was discarded and gradually replaced by the Protestant slavery code.

The *Code Noir* continued to be in effect in Louisiana until 1806, after American administration began, until the first legislature of the Territory of Orleans turned its attention to slavery legislation. It had unique features for dealing with runaway slaves and their capture, jailing slaves, control and murder of slaves, and miscegenation (marriage or cohabitation between races). It provided that a runaway slave who remained at large a month or more should have his ears cropped and be branded on one shoulder. For a second offence he was to be hamstrung (crippled by cutting leg tendons) and branded on the other shoulder. Should he manage to escape a third time, he was to suffer death. However, an appeal to the province's superior court was permitted before a sentence of hamstringing or death was carried out. Although branding was not uncommon, hamstringing and death were rare because of the due process provided for the slaves' protection. Free Negroes who concealed fugitives were to be fined thirty livres (a French monetary unit) for each day a runaway was harbored in their homes. Runaways' owners were empowered to seek them out or to have them sought out in any way they might think proper.[14]

The Catholic slavery code also held the masters responsible for the slave's treatment in such a manner as to discourage flight. Masters of slaves who fled were required to inform a magistrate, who officially recorded this. The magistrate was also required to be informed when the fugitive returned. Whoever captured an absconding slave was entitled to ten dollars for the capture and fifty cents per league for the distance the prisoner was transported to jail. Since the master had to pay these costs when claiming his property, he was likely to do all he could to keep his slaves from running away. In the event that a master neglected to inform a magistrate when one of his slaves fled, he was responsible for any damage to property caused by the slave before this formality was observed.

When an absconding slave was lodged in jail, his master was responsible for maintenance costs and for the cost of advertising his detention. If the imprisoned slave was not claimed within two years, he was to be sold to the highest bidder and the costs of his capture and captivity recovered from the sale proceeds. Any surplus was to be held for a year and a day, and if still not claimed by the slave's former owner, the money was to be devoted to public use.[15]

Holding slaveholders responsible for slaves' treatment created an unusual situation in Louisiana, where runaway slaves would go unclaimed in jail for years. Some slaveholders had decided it was not worth paying the costs as well as another dollar to the magistrate for receiving proof of ownership, and left their slaves unclaimed.

Since all blacks were not slaves, in contrast to the Protestant slave code, a runaway slave who was not apprehended by the slaveholder would only be caught and jailed when he committed a crime. This encouraged skilled slaves who could support themselves to run away. The intelligent slaves made good their escape or traveled far enough to add greatly to the expense of securing their return. Above-average slaves ran away with striking regularity. Alfred, captured at Donaldsonville in July 1850, was a bricklayer. Tom Anderson, a carpenter who escaped from Robert Barrow in 1855, could "read and write, though not very well." A fiddler carried his instrument with him when he ran away from a St Mary plantation in 1831.[16]

Another problem for Louisiana was recovering costs for taking care of unclaimed slaves in jail. Legislative Acts concerning runaways during the 1820s and 1830s were primarily devoted to establishing central depots to which runaways unclaimed for two months or longer were to be transported. Parishes where depots were located could use the prisoners on public works but had to maintain them while doing so. In 1845, the legislature ordered keepers of three municipal jails to advertise slaves confined as runways once a week for three months. At the end of three months, any unclaimed slave imprisoned for as long as twelve months prior to March 10, 1845, was to be sold at auction. In 1855, new legislation was passed whereby any slave not claimed within twelve months was to be turned over to the supervisor of slaves owned by the state and worked as one of the state hands; his master could still claim him by submitting proof of ownership and paying all accrued expenses.[17]

At least officially, slaves in Louisiana were subject to a single set of laws as dictated by the Catholic slavery code. New Orleans slaveholders who lacked the weight or inclination to administer corporal punishment with their own hands could write a note setting forth the number of lashes to be administered and make the culprit carry the note to the municipal jail. There the jailor meted out the blows and sent back a note attesting the fact. Presumably this was a convenience offered to the city's citizens rather than a public function.

Crimes punished at the court's discretion included threatening an overseer and revolting against an overseer while being punished. The penalty usually amounted to a severe lashing. The law specifically provided that a slave who stole wood from the land of a person other than his master was to receive thirty-nine lashes. Minor slave crime was handled by parish or municipal ordinances. Slaves found drinking or gaming or guilty of disturbing or disorderly conduct within the town limits were to receive thirty-nine lashes. The slave's owner was required to bear the costs of this. If he did not, the costs and a fine exceeding twenty dollars were to be worked out by the unhappy slave at the rate of thirty cents a day.[18]

According to Louisiana's Catholic slavery code, a slave was subject to accusation by any free person under oath, including free blacks. The justice of the peace before whom the accusation was made then ordered the slave arrested and confined in jail. If the crime was capital, the trial was held before two justices of the peace and ten slaveholders who lived in the parish. Non-capital cases were tried before one justice of the peace and four resident slaveholders. The justice before whom the accusation was made called on another magistrate to aid him in selecting a jury and regular summonses were issued to those selected.

Prosecuting capital cases was the district attorney's responsibility, but if he failed to appear the court could appoint any licensed attorney to act as prosecutor. Testimony from other slaves under oath was admissible in a slave's trial. All members of the court, including the presiding justices, had a voice in determining guilt or innocence, and a unanimous vote was required either to acquit or convict. If the court was unable to agree on a verdict, it had "the power to decree the infliction of such corporeal punishment as it may consider deserved." The court also had the authority to sentence a slave to life imprisonment if a unanimous verdict was not attainable. Of ninety-four slaves confined in 1856, thirty had been guilty of murder, eleven of arson, five of attempted poisoning, two of attempted rape, one of assisting in a rape, and the rest were imprisoned for various kinds of attempts to kill and assault. Under the Protestant slavery code prevalent in other states, which made no provision for imprisonment or trials, these blacks would have been lynched or burnt at the stake without a second thought.[19]

Under Louisiana's Catholic slavery code, a person who willfully killed a slave belonging to himself or to another was guilty of murder, and cruel punishment "except flogging, or striking with a whip, leather thong, switch, or light stick" could be fined between $200 and $500. When a slave was abused without witnesses, the person in charge was held responsible. Any non-slaveholder was entitled to bring action on behalf of a slave who was not properly cared for. If the charges were proved true, the justice who heard the case could take such action as he saw fit for the slave's relief. An overseer who killed a slave for outright defiance was subject to a coroner's court which held an inquest over the slave's body. This was a sharp contrast to the Protestant slavery code, under which killing a slave was the slaveholder's private affair and, if questioned, the slaveholder's explanation was sufficient.[20]

The dangers of rebellion were recognized in the *Code Noir* of 1724, which forbade slaves carrying arms except when sent hunting by their masters. Slaves belonging to different masters were forbidden to gather under any pretext, and disregard for this ban was to be punished with branding or death. In 1806, an Act on slave crimes made rebellion punishable by death and provided that any bondsmen who revealed "any plot, rebellion, raising in arms, or mutinous assemblies" should be set free and given further rewards which the legislature might see fit to grant. To protect slaves against false accusation, the Louisiana code reiterated the principle that slaves executed for insurrection should be the loss of the owner alone. Slaves sentenced for striking master, mistress, or overseer were placed in the same category.

This was again in sharp contrast to the Protestant slavery code, under which slaves were lynched on suspicion of rebellion and the slaveholder compensated from the public purse. Also, setting a black free, even if he was an informant, was out of the question in a Protestant slavery setting. In 1837, Lewis, a slave belonging to David Cheyney, informed his master of a massacre plot. Contrary to the Catholic slavery law, two conspirators were hanged by a citizens' lynching committee; the masters of those two slaves and Lewis were given compensation and $500 was appropriated for Lewis to aid him to leave the state. This shows, once again, that in spite of the Catholic slavery code, Louisiana operated more and more by the South's Protestant slavery code during the period preceding the Civil War.[21]

Free Blacks' Legal Framework

One of the Protestant slavery code's fatal flaws was that it made no provision for free blacks, and hence there were no specific prisons for those who committed crimes. Lack of prison facilities for free blacks meant that only two options were available: they could receive either physical punishment such as flogging or a death sentence—without regard to the seriousness of their crimes. Enticing a slave to run away was a capital felony under the law. In Pitt County, Dorset Wiggins was tried for his life on charges of "enticing Bill, a slave belonging to Isaiah Repess ... to run away .... " Although Wiggins won his case, many were satisfied that he was guilty and that his exoneration was the result of the jury's unwillingness to send a man to the gallows for any offense short of murder. The editor of one paper remarked that Wiggins' acquittal showed the need for a penitentiary. If North Carolina had a prison, the journalist asserted, Wiggins would not go unpunished.[22]

A free black's fate in court was sealed by the Protestant slavery code, resulting in entrapment from all sides. Although the free Negro enjoyed the right to sue, the rug was pulled from under his feet by eliminating most of his rights—the right to secure witnesses among lawful and truthful men, the right to offer testimony on his own behalf, and the guarantee of immunity against incompetent witnesses. In 1777, the General Assembly of North Carolina passed an Act establishing free blacks' incompetence as witnesses once and for all: "All Negroes and all Persons of Mixed Blood descended from Negro and Indian Ancestors, to the fourth generation inclusive whether bond or free, shall be deemed and taken to be incapable in Law to be witnesses in any case whatsoever, except against each other." This Act prevented free blacks from testifying in any case against a white and made it impossible to gather testimony in such a case from anyone but white persons, which in itself was a nearly impossible task. The free black's prospect for justice was practically nonexistent.[23]

Free blacks were brought completely under slaveholders' control through an Act that validated the testimony of slaves against free blacks in 1821 as follows:

> In all pleas of the State, where the defendant may be a negro, Indian, or person of mixed blood … whether such person be bond or free, the evidence of a negro and of all persons of mixed blood … whether the person or persons whose evidence is offered be bond or free, shall be admissible and the witnesses competent.

By the Act of 1821, North Carolina fell into line with action being taken in other states of the South, such as Maryland and Virginia. This law perfectly met the requirements of slaveholders who wanted to rid their communities of free Negroes. Slaveholders could force a slave to offer testimony against a free Negro that might lead to the latter's conviction.[24]

Lack of prison facilities for free blacks required unique punishments at the court's discretion. A free Negro who preached or exhorted in public was to receive "upon conviction before a single magistrate … not exceeding thirty-nine lashes on his bare back." The same punishment was meted out to free Negroes found guilty of gaming with slaves. Any black who gave false testimony against a slave charged with a capital crime was to have one ear nailed to the pillory and stand there for one hour, when the said ear was to be cut off. In 1830, a free Negro found guilty of manslaughter was "burnt in the hand." Sylvester Chavers, a free woman of color, was found guilty of fatally stabbing her husband with a "dirk knife" and sentenced to be branded.[25]

Free blacks found guilty of murder or rape were to be hanged. The general assembly passed an Act in 1823 whereby "any person of color convicted of assault with attempt to commit a rape upon the body of a white female, shall suffer death without benefit of clergy." However, free Negroes were also tried for raping women of their own color. In 1836, Jones Kiff was tried on an indictment of rape committed on a free Negro woman "supposed to be 80 years of age." William Haywood, Jr., counsel for the defendant, secured an acquittal verdict. Evidently, no efforts were spared to get rid of blacks under any pretext.[26]

Theoretically, Northern blacks were free though subject to various laws. They had no masters to protect them from harm and injury, nor any guarantee that food and shelter would be provided to them. They were restricted to the most menial jobs, subject to mob violence, and often forced to engage in petty theft and crime to avoid starvation. In urban areas, this led to arrest and imprisonment. Official statistics documented more crime among blacks in the North than in the South. Northern prejudice against blacks was greater than in the South. This was confirmed by an observation by the French political thinker and writer Alexis de Tocqueville when he visited America:

> The prejudice which repels the Negroes seems to increase in proportion as they are emancipated. Northern blacks were victimized by mob violence and had virtually no access to education and could not vote and were barred from all but the menial occupations. Most worked as domestic servants or sailors in the American merchant marine and their wages were such that they lived in squalor.[27]

The North passed separate laws for blacks. Five states—Illinois, Ohio, Iowa, Indiana, and California—prohibited black testimony in cases where a white man was a party and Oregon forbade blacks to hold real estate, make contracts, or maintain lawsuits. The California Supreme Court ruled that in a criminal action against a white man, no black, not even if he were the injured party, could testify. Where courts refused to admit black testimony, legal protection for blacks was limited. A white man could assault, rob, or even murder a black amidst a number of black witnesses and escape prosecution unless another white man had been present and had agreed to testify.[28]

To feed themselves in the absence of jobs, blacks often engaged in theft and other petty crimes or fought whites in self-defense. Hopelessly outnumbered by whites—who were the constables, magistrates, and jurors—black convictions and jailings increased manifold. Jails were the North's preferred solution for blacks and the prospects of a black man being convicted and jailed for crime in the North were eleven times greater than for a white man. From many a black man's point of view, jail meant he would not go hungry. A Pennsylvania state senate committee reported in 1836:

> Already our prisons and poorhouses are crowded with blacks. The disparity of crime between the whites and the blacks, which is at present so distressing to every friend of humanity and virtue, and so burdensome to the community, will become absolutely intolerable in a few years: and the danger to be apprehended is, that if not removed, they will be exterminated.[29]

Religion as a Control Weapon

Religion was another instrument used to control slaves for maximal productivity. It provided black slaves with hope for the next world. Slaveowners were initially opposed to converting slaves to Christianity lest baptism gave blacks a claim to future freedom. This was resolved by a directive from the Bishop in London and an Act from the colonial legislature stating that conversion or baptism to Christianity would have no affect on blacks' status as slaves. Thereafter most masters encouraged the preaching of Christianity among black slaves, and prior to the Civil War virtually all slaves had become Christians.

Slaves learned through religious instruction that slavery had divine sanction and that an insolent act against the master was equivalent to an insolent act against God. They received the biblical command that servants should obey their masters and were made aware that punishments for disobedience awaited them in the hereafter. Eternal salvation would be their reward for faithful service and, on the day of judgment, "God would deal impartially with the poor and rich, the black man and the white man."

Fanny Kemble noted that white preachers jumped the present life and furnished black slaves with all the requisite conveniences for the next. Frederick Douglass explained the slaveholders' rationale as follows: "I was told by some one very early that 'God up in the sky' had made all things, and had made black people to be slaves and white people to be masters. I was told too that God was good and that he knew what was best for everybody."[30]

In regions with small slaveholdings, whites and blacks commonly belonged to the same churches. On large plantations, only household slaves accompanied their masters to worship. When there were mixed congregations, the slaves sat in the galleries or were bunched together in the rear. Sometimes special Sunday afternoon services were held for black slaves. With the increase in the black population, this brotherhood in Christ between blacks and whites ended, and it was agreed that whites and blacks would be better brothers in the next world than in this one. A Wayne County slave remonstrated with a white preacher for his attitude toward black spiritual lives as follows:

> Master John, I want permition if you pleas to speak a word to you … in the first place I want you to tell me the reson you always preach to the white folks and keep your back to us. Is it because they sit upon the hill. We have no chance among them. Then must we be forgotten because we cant get near nough without geting in the edg of the Swamp behind you …. If I should ask you what must I do

to be saved perhaps you would tell me pray let the bible be my gide, this would do very well if we could read. I do not think there is one in fifty that can read. I have been more fortunate than the most of the black people. I can read and write in my way as to be understood …. If God sent you to preach to siners did he direct you to keep your face to the white peoples constantly or is it because they give you money … did God tell you to have your meeting houses just large enough to hold the white folks and let the black people stand in the sone and rain as the broks in the field.[31]

The whites were in a quandary. They did not want their churches integrated with blacks, but were even more uneasy about separate black churches. After the Denmark Vesey conspiracy, which came close to insurrection in 1822, the African Church in Charleston was outlawed. Slave owners felt that religious meetings among slaves could easily be converted into conspiracies and black preachers could become provocateurs. Thus, in Richmond in 1826, when some Negroes petitioned the Virginia legislature, citing that white Baptist churches did not have enough room to permit black attendance and asking sanction for the creation of a Baptist African Church, the legislature withheld its permission. In 1841, a solution was found: a black church would not violate the law provided it had a white preacher.

In the North, where blacks were theoretically free, integrated churches were unacceptable to whites. Initially, when attending services in white churches, the blacks found themselves segregated either in an "African Corner," a "Nigger Pew," seats marked "B. M." (Black members), or aloft in "Nigger Heaven." Property-minded whites generally deeded their pews on condition that no black be permitted to purchase them, for this would reduce the value of nearby pews. Churches protected themselves against such incidents by inserting into all pew deeds a restriction that confined any transfer to "respectable white persons." Northern whites did not need black workers to provide food or shelter, so they felt it only appropriate that blacks stay out of white churches. Blacks had no choice but to start their own churches if they were to attend at all.

In colonial Louisiana, Catholicism was the state religion and masters were required by law to instruct their slaves in its rites and doctrines. The Catholic religion protected slaves by reminding slaveholders that slave and owner were equals in the eyes of the church and God. Slaveholders took an interest in their slaves' religious training, and men and women of high estate often served as godparents when adult Negroes were baptized.[32]

Blacks and whites never ceased worshipping side by side in Catholic churches. Many travelers noted the contrast between the joint prayer of masters and slaves in St Louis Cathedral in New Orleans and the practice in Protestant churches where blacks were either excluded or "mewed up in some remote corner, separated by barriers from the body of the church." Some white Catholics objected to this state of affairs. At St. Martinville, masters sought to drive slaves away from the Holy Table, but the pastor promptly stopped this abuse.[33]

After Louisiana became a territory and later a state, the Hephzibah Baptist Church, located in East Feliciana Parish, tried to operate in accordance with the Catholic Church's guidelines. It sought to admit and dismiss slaves in exactly the same manner as whites, subjected slaves to the same discipline as whites, and furnished them with some protection against abuse. To protect a slave member from abuse, in 1820, the congregation "took up the conduct of Br Wilm. West for whipping his black brother; the church considered there was no cause for his doing so and he was excluded for the same by the church."[34]

The Black Man Revolts

As Protestant slavery placed blacks completely at the slaveholders' mercy, there were several attempts at revolts and insurrections both in the South and North. Retribution against blacks was swift and overwhelming because slaveholders had nothing to lose. Compensation from the public treasury to slaveholders for slaves killed, as noted, was guaranteed by Protestant slavery code.

As early as 1689, on a plantation at Stono, outside Charleston, South Carolina, slaves secured arms and ammunition by killing two guards in a warehouse. They proceeded to escape toward Florida and freedom. Marching to the beat of drums, they were joined by other blacks and killed all whites in their way. The whites soon armed themselves and captured or killed all but ten of the blacks. About 30 whites and 44 blacks were killed in this incident. To teach the black slaves a lesson, 150 unarmed blacks were attacked by whites and 50 were captured and hanged at the rate of 10 a day.

Around 1741, when slavery was legal in the middle colonies, New York City plunged into a hysteria of black persecutions based on fears of slave uprisings caused by a series of fires. The winter was severe and Britain was at war with Spain; whites feared that blacks might help the enemy if the Spanish entered New York. There were rumors that blacks and poor whites were conspiring to destroy law and order in the city and seize control. The city council offered generous rewards for information leading to the conspirators' arrest and promised informers immunity from prosecution. Mary Burton, an indentured servant, came forward with a series of sensational revelations that surpassed the wildest imaginings of most whites; she claimed to know about three blacks who intended to kill all whites and establish a monarchy.

In the excitement of the moment and with the help of confessions, 154 blacks and 25 whites were tried. Convictions were secured for 101 blacks, of whom 18 were hanged, 13 burnt alive, and 70 banished. Four poor whites, including two women, were also hanged. At the rate of two every week, one hanged and one burnt alive, the victims were executed amidst prayers and shrieks of agony in a public display while all other business was suspended. The blacks got the message loud and clear; no more problems were caused by blacks in New York. By the time of the Revolution, New Yorkers had decided blacks were undesirable in the population and turned to white immigrants for their labor.

When the French Revolution started in 1789, blacks on the West Indies island of Santo Domingo, a French colony, wanted the same freedoms for themselves as white Frenchmen received at home.

Losing patience with whites who refused to recognize their rights, the blacks, led by Toussant l'Ouverture, started a violent uprising in 1791, with blacks ruthlessly killing their white masters and forcing the French assembly to send troops to quell the disturbance. A bitter struggle ensued and lasted for over two years, resulting in the French Republic granting freedom to all black slaves. Santo Domingo eventually achieved freedom from the French and was renamed Haiti.[35]

Around 1800, some blacks realized that the white man's revolution against the British had passed them by and decided to force some liberty for themselves by breaking away from slavery. Some Virginia blacks revolted under the leadership of Gabriel Prosser and Jack Bowler. For months they planned the desperate move, collecting clubs, swords, and other arms; and then one thousand slaves met six miles outside Richmond to march on the city. Two slaves had already informed the whites, and the governor had called in the troops and notified every militia commander in the state. Scores of slaves were arrested. Thirty-five were executed and four escaped, one of whom committed suicide. Gabriel was captured later but refused to talk and was executed. For the white man, the total disregard the slaves had for their own lives and their stony silence were cause for terror. The purpose of the entire exercise was revealed in a statement made by one black who was later executed:

> I have nothing more to offer than what General Washington would have had to offer, had he been taken by the British officers and put to trial by them. I have ventured my life in endeavoring to obtain the liberty of my countrymen, and am a willing sacrifice to their cause, and I beg, as a favor, that I may be immediately led to execution. I know that you have predetermined to shed my blood, why then all this mockery of a trial?[35]

The developments in Haiti terrified the whites. Despite the profitability of slave labor, the South realized that a large black population could be dangerous therefore banned further importation. In 1792, South Carolina prohibited importation of slaves for two years and North Carolina passed a law to the same effect in 1794. Virginia and Maryland strengthened their non-importation laws. The activities of blacks in Haiti during the next ten years convinced the United States Congress in 1808 of the necessity of banning the importation of any more slaves into the country.

Perhaps the most elaborately planned revolt, though not the most effective, was the Denmark Vesey insurrection. Vesey had purchased his freedom in 1800 and made a comfortable living as a carpenter in Charleston, South Carolina. Over several years he planned his revolt, chose his assistants, and collected weapons. He set the second Sunday in July 1822 for the revolt. When word leaked out, he shifted the date forward one month, but not all his assistants, who were scattered for miles around Charleston, got the message. Meanwhile, whites had learned of the plan through informers and rounded up suspects. At least 139 blacks were arrested, 47 of whom were executed.

Jack Purcell, a Vesey accomplice, weakened in the crisis and confessed. He said that Vesey was in the habit of reading to him all passages in the newspapers that related to Santo Domingo and apparently every accessible pamphlet that had any connection with slavery. From the white point of view, the connection between the ability to read and write and revolts was clear. Educated blacks were muddling their minds with newspapers, reading about the French revolution and events in Haiti. State after state in the South passed new laws to make it impossible for black slaves to read or write or assemble for this purpose.

The increasing number of revolts during this period culminated with the Nat Turner insurrection in 1831. This Virginian black was a mystic and rebellious slave who had run away several times and then returned to his master. He believed that God had selected him to free his people and decided that the solar eclipse in February 1831 was his signal to prepare. He selected the fourth of July to start the revolt but fell ill and postponed it. On August 21, he and his followers killed several white families, starting with the family of Turner's master, Joseph Travise. Within twenty-four hours sixty whites had been killed, and the revolt was spreading rapidly when the main groups of blacks were met and overpowered by state and federal troops. Over a hundred blacks were killed in the encounter and thirteen slaves and three free blacks were immediately hanged. Turner was captured and executed within two weeks. It became known that Turner had acquired his education in Sunday schools, reading the Bible, and from his indulgent young master. Also, Nat Turner, acting as a slave preacher, had used religious meetings to plan his revolt in secret. The South, dazed by Turner's revolt, passed special legislative statutes to prevent blacks from assembling for religious purposes or otherwise without proper white supervision.

John Brown was a white man who wanted to free Southern blacks, set up a black republic, and eventually force the South to free their slaves. In October 1859, with eighteen followers, several of them black, he seized the federal arsenal at Harper's Ferry, Virginia, in the hope of securing sufficient ammunition to carry out a large-scale operation against Virginia slaveholders. Almost immediately he was attacked by the citizens and a detachment of U.S. Marines. After ten of John Brown's men were killed, he was forced to surrender, was tried in a Virginia court for treason, and hanged.

This raid provided a perfect opportunity for Southern slaveholders to prepare the South for secession. Since slaveholders controlled the press and state governments throughout the South, they used the raid to convince non-slaveholders that the Yankees would stop at nothing to wipe out slavery in the South. All Northern disclaimers and actions contrary to this opinion, showing that John Brown was a fanatic without popular backing, were suppressed by the slaveholders. Instead, they used the raid as an excuse to put the whole of the South on a semi-war footing, and militia commanders of most states increased demands for arms and ammunition, almost as if in preparation of a Southern secession, which would come a year later.

Some conclusions can be drawn from the black revolts over the one hundred and fifty years that ended with the Civil War. There was never a remote prospect of any revolt succeeding. They did not solve any problems for blacks and were lost causes before they even began. They all ended with massacres of blacks. After each revolt, slaveholders took new steps to further tighten slavery's noose around black necks. Revolts could only be used to make a statement. Not only were blacks outnumbered by the whites, but they did not have the education, arms, or community structure to make their statement credible.

By providing two sets of standards, one for blacks and another for whites, Southern slaveholders were asking for trouble. It became clear to Southern non-slaveholders that there were as many kinds of law as the circumstances required. There was one set of laws for non-slaveholders, another set for slave owners, and separate sets for slaves and free blacks. This essentially meant that there was no law at all. Mob justice and lynch law ruled the South. The slaveholders had pushed themselves into a corner with choices disregarding long-term consequences that demanded a day of reckoning.

CHAPTER 4

FAMILY VALUES

Till death or distance do you part
                    —Kentucky minister before the Civil War

The daughter of Jefferson sold for a slave!
The child of a freeman for dollars and francs!
The roar of applause, when your orators rave,
Is lost in the sound of her chain, as it clanks.[1]
                    —Merrill D. Peterson, "Jeffersonian Image"

In 1802, James T. Callender attacked Thomas Jefferson in the columns of the *Richmond Recorder* for keeping a slave concubine named Sally Hemings and fathering children by her. Sally was described as unusually pretty and "mighty near white." When Jefferson, a widower, was United States Minister in France, the teenaged Sally was sent to join him there, ostensibly to serve as maid to Jefferson's daughter Polly. Sally eventually had five children. The eldest had features that were "said to bear a striking resemblance to those of the president himself." Another son, Madison Hemings, was named after Jefferson's closest colleague and "learned to be a great fiddler."[2]

To provide further credibility to this story, historians have noted that the Hemings family received favored treatment at Jefferson's hands, and in his will three of them were given their freedom. DNA studies done in 1998 seemed to have removed all reasonable doubt that Jefferson was their father. Jefferson persuaded the Virginia legislature to introduce a stricter definition of a mulatto from one-eighth to one-quarter Negro, a standard by which Sally Heming's children should have been adjudged white. In his *Notes*, Jefferson asserted that interbreeding with whites produced "the improvement of the blacks in body and mind." Since the Negro population's presence in the United States was a fait accompli, Jefferson may well have considered that in siring Sally's children he was improving the colored population. This view would certainly have accorded with theories he approved of, namely eugenics and supplying superior men with harems for breeding purposes. Jefferson was plagued in later years by denunciations from abolitionists and white supremacy advocates alike who wrote of Jefferson's "African brothel" and of the "sooty charms" of "Black Sal."[3]

This story illustrates some of the Protestant slavery code's important features as it applied both to marriages and families of both blacks and whites. It is an indisputable fact that Sally Hemings had five children; but because her blood was one-fourth Negro, legally she was not allowed to marry either a black or white man; therefore the father of her children was "unknown" in the law's eyes. Further, the president of the United States, one of the authors of the Declaration of Independence, could not legally marry the mother of his children by Hemings or acknowledge their paternity. His own flesh and blood were born into slavery, and even when freed were denied United States citizenship and treated as "untouchables."

Destruction of the family was a natural consequence of the Protestant slavery code that refused to recognize black marriages and permitted mothers to be separated from their children and husbands from their wives without restriction. By the time of the Revolution it was too late to make changes; state rights and state laws were firmly entrenched and the precedents had already been set.

Evolution of Family Codes

In the seventeenth-century South, most work was done by white indentured servants who formed a major part of the labor force. At that time, the male population outnumbered females three to one. There was also an acute shortage of labor. To ensure a regular and secure labor force, the slaveholders first passed legislation defining the status of blacks as slaves. They then passed laws against miscegenation to control sexual relations between blacks and whites to prevent a population of free mulattos. Thus a Virginia law of 1662 imposed twice as large a fine on fornication between blacks and whites as on fornication between two whites.

Controlling relations between the races was difficult. The Assembly had imposed punishments for miscegenation long before this, but the Virginia law of 1662 had nothing to do with morality or Christianity. If a white male indentured servant fornicated with a black female slave, slaveholders did not want any interference from non-slaveholders regarding the child's paternity. Also, if a white female indentured servant fornicated with a black slave, slaveholders wanted to control her and her mulatto child in order to prevent a population of free mulattos. A Maryland statute of 1664 made white women servants who fornicated with black slaves serve the slave's master for life and declared their union's issue slaves for life.[4]

Passing laws to prevent miscegenation was easy. However, passing laws to prevent marriages between blacks, in order to have greater control over slaves, required slaveholders to show greater ingenuity. Protestant slaveholders interpreted the *Bible* themselves, stating that since the Holy Ghost resides in each individual, they needed no outside help in interpreting the *Bible* or God's word. The law passed by them said: "The relation of master and slave is wholly incompatible with even the qualified relation of husband and wife, as it is supposed to exist among slaves." This ensured that no aspect of the slave's life was independent from his owner's power. Through this law, slaveholders succeeded in preventing any interference in their affairs by non-slaveholders and the church.[5]

Since the law did not recognize black marriage contracts, none of marriage's usual consequences followed for slaves. Slaveholders had given themselves power to separate offspring from parents indiscriminately. Slaveholders could also rape black slaves with impunity because Southern jurists' universal understanding was that, "the father of a slave is unknown to our law," and there was no law against fornicating with black females. Control over black children passed into the slaveholders' hands after the mother had given birth and successfully completed her breeding function.[6]

Slaveholders defined their priorities clearly. If it was necessary to destroy families for colonial America's progress, then so be it. Colonial America had abundant land, with the frontier constantly moving west, and slave labor was necessary to clear forests. Cleared land was sold and the process repeated. Therefore, tying slaves to the land they worked on was too restrictive. Laws binding serfs to the land were practical in Europe where land was limited and serfs unlimited. In America it was just the opposite. Slaveholders sought to maximize the mobility and flexibility of their slave labor. By legislating the invalidity of black marriages, slaveholders disowned moral responsibility for destroying black families and created a totally mobile labor force.

The Catholic *Code Noir* also prohibited marriage between the races, but required that slaves be married by a priest, granting slave marriages the same standing in the eyes of the law and church as white marriages. In Louisiana's Catholic parishes, marriage rites between slaves were often performed by priests, especially on plantations whose owners were Catholic. Bishop Polk always married his slaves with a religious ceremony and made it an occasion for pomp and celebration unless the couple had "misbehaved" before the wedding. In the latter case the wedding was short and private. Sometimes Negro preachers tied the marital bonds. A Baptist church in the Florida parishes expelled white and black members for adultery. After Louisiana became a territory of the United States, the Protestant slavery code came into effect and the legality of black marriages was abandoned.[7]

According to the Catholic slavery code the master could not deny his slaves permission to marry. When slaves on different plantations married, it was customary to allow the husband to visit his wife on Wednesdays and Saturdays after he had completed his work. On Comite Plantation, for instance, an entry was made in the overseer's diary almost every Wednesday and Saturday that "Jourdan, Simon and Lewis goes to see their wives." Passes for such visits were often good for a month at a time. When husbands and wives were located too far apart to see each other regularly, they often tried to persuade the master of one to become the owner of both.[8]

Although the *Code Noir* prohibited marriages between whites and Negroes, it also protected slaves from the lust of slaveholders. A white master whose slave woman bore a child by him could lose both mother and child. The slave woman could appeal for justice to the church or the Superior Council if she had been raped by a master. There are records of a mulatto woman, suing for the right to her freedom, who testified that "her master bought her when he was a bachelor and that she had served him as his only household slave." Since marriage with slaves was legally binding, a white master could also marry a slave, because the definition of a Negro was not clear-cut. Early in the Spanish period, in 1769, a marriage contract was made between a white man and "Charlotte, natural daughter of … a free mulatress, and the late Roy Villeray," the father of the bride having been a white man. In 1723, a couple accused of theft was identified as a white locksmith and his wife, "a negress." Even if the slaveholder did not want to marry his slave, he could always become his child's godfather at the baptism or free his child and provide him or her with an education and property. A slaveholder named Trumbull acknowledged five children by his slave Rachael, emancipated the mother and children, and left them one-third of his property.[9]

The *Code Noir* protected black families by forbidding separation of husbands and wives, or of children under fourteen from their parents, whether by legal seizure or voluntary sale. Therefore ownership changes had to occur for the complete slave family as a unit. This meant the slaves were essentially tied to the land. Any seizure or judicial sale of real estate had to include the slaves attached to it. After his crop had been gathered, R. B. Lynch offered to sell fifteen hundred and forty-four acres, three hundred of which were cultivated, a cotton gin, Negro quarters, and forty Negroes, of whom thirty were working hands.[10]

The principle that the institutions of slavery and family were incompatible was the invention of Protestant slaveholders. This concept, which led to the undermining of the family unit, had dire consequences for black men, women and children, including mulattos. There were also unintended consequences for white males, females, and children, and most importantly, for non-slaveholders that would fuel the Civil War.

Destroying Black Families

Since the Protestant slavery code did not recognize black marriages, these were perceived by whites as occasions for mockery and the cause of amusement. Some generous masters provided food and drink, helped the couple with special clothing, opened the big house for the ceremony, and heard the vows themselves. More often, slave weddings consisted of jumping over the broom before witnesses. The white man received God's blessing on his marriage; for the black man, the master's blessing sufficed. Masters could join slaves in marriage and then break them apart. The slaves also knew that no black woman was safe from the master's sons, the white overseer, or even the master himself. With both realism and irony, a Kentucky minister conducted slave marriages with the revised proviso, "till death or distance do you part."[11]

Most white boys experienced their first sexual encounter with a black woman. Bragging Southern men asserted it as fact. A modern Southerner said, "the slave woman was to be had for the taking. Boys on and about the plantation inevitably learnt to use her, and having acquired the habit, often continued it into manhood or even after marriage ... efforts to build up a taboo against miscegenation made little progress." James Madison said that in Virginia, slave girls were expected to become mothers by the age of fifteen; how they arranged impregnation was apparently their own affair. When miscegenation was detected, it carried no penalties. There was some talk and sometimes a few crude jokes, but most often it was forgotten. Besides, if practiced with caution, the chances of detection were slim.[12]

Poor whites frequently raped black women. Masters often complained about poor neighborhood whites troubling their slave women. A Virginian noted in his records "Cato born of Dinah, by some white chap on the commons." Another Virginian affirmed that one of his slave women had all of her children "by whoredom most of them gotten by white men" at a neighbor's house. For years, he wrote, these men had been sending for his slave women "to whore it with" whenever he was away. Female slaves were quite accessible to both rural and urban non-slaveholders who desired casual sexual partners.[13]

Overseers could take their pick of black slave women. Most masters were indifferent to this, but some complained that the tendency of the overseers to "equalize" with slave women resulted in "evils too numerous to be mentioned." One master clarified this when he noted that his overseer was causing his "Negro men to run away by interfering with their wives." In his instructions to overseers, a Louisiana planter warned that: "Intercourse with Negro woman would not be tolerated because it bred more trouble on a plantation then all else put together." The author of an essay on selecting an overseer advised that he should preferably be a married man. On a Louisiana plantation, an overseer named Patrick caused his employer a lot of trouble by his habit of "sneaking about after Negro girls," and when he was fired he left behind a brood of mulatto children. The new overseer, named Mulkey, was a married man who proved to be nearly as bad as Patrick. Mulkey's dismissal came after a "great fuss" that occurred when a slave told Mrs. Mulkey about her husband's escapades in the quarters.[14]

Most of the males of the slaveholding class viewed these relationships with black females as casual adventures by adolescents engaging in sexual experimentation, college students having fun, and older bachelors or widowers forcing themselves on their female slaves. Some of the relationships developed into a form of concubinage that lasted until marriage or occasionally throughout life.

Once Protestant slaveowners decided there was no need to tie black slaves to the land or to keep black families together, opportunities for abuse became widespread. In a cash crop economy black families were broken by selling individual members to satisfy creditor claims, or by shifting slaves from one crop-growing area to another.

Slaveowners had the right to deed their slaves in any manner they pleased. In preparing his will, a white man often separated individual black family members to provide equitable distribution amongst his heirs. Sometimes will probates or claims by heirs of slaveholders who died intestate could not be settled without selling slaves. In such cases, Southern courts did not worry about breaking up slave families. The estate's executor was expected to dispose of slaves and other property in the way that most profited the heirs. The North Carolina Supreme Court said: "It may be harsh to separate members of families, yet it must be done, if the executor discovers that the interest of the estate required it, for he is not to indulge his charities at the expense of others." Masters often specifically authorized or ordered slave sales in their wills.[15]

Black slaves' offspring were sometimes designated as gifts before they were born, and occasionally before they were conceived. In Fairfield District, South Carolina, in 1830, Mary Kincaid gave a slave woman named Sillar to a grandchild and Sillar's two children to other grandchildren. It was stated that if Sillar should have a third child, it was to go to yet another grandchild. If not, "I will that two children now living be sold at twelve years of age and the proceeds equally divided among my said grandchildren." In Mechlenbury County, North Carolina in 1839, George Houston willed to one daughter a slave named Charity and to another daughter "the first child that … Charity shall have."[16]

Since slaves were sold on credit and used as security for loans, they were subject to seizure. Family ties were ignored for these "execution sales" in favor of maximum benefits to the debtor. As a witness testified before the Georgia Supreme Court: "It is not usual to put up Negroes in families at Sheriff sales." A typical Sheriff's notice in the town of Covington, Newton County, Georgia, read as follows:

> Within the usual hours of sale, on the first Tuesday in February next, the following property to wit: three Negroes, John, a boy about 16 years old; Ann, a girl about 4 years old; Riley, a boy about 3 years old, all levied on as

the property of Burwel Moss, to satisfy a mortgage—in favor of Alfred M. Ramsey.[17]

The insensitive role of legal codes and court records, of sheriffs' notices and administrators' accounts, was an indication of slaveholders' attitudes. The laws were written by practical men who expected them to be applied to real situations. Breaking up slave families was not a consideration when slaves were awarded as prizes in lotteries and raffles or wagered at gaming tables and horse races.

In the new regions of Alabama and Mississippi during the 1830s, buying and selling slaves and plantations was a favored occupation for speculators. People invested cash in slaves just as Northern capitalists invested in stocks and bonds. A Virginia judge said, "With us nothing is so usual as to advance children by gifts of slaves. They stand with us instead of money." A Kentuckian in easy circumstances was in the habit of presenting a slave to each of his grandchildren. A Tennessee planter wrote, "I buy ... Negro boy Jessee and sent him as a gift to my daughter Eva and the heirs of her boy."[18]

Since titles to slaves were transferable, blacks represented a mobile labor supply and slaves were moved to new areas as they opened for settlement. As the demand for cotton increased and tobacco prices fell, about a million blacks were transferred from the upper Southern states of Virginia, Maryland, Kentucky, North Carolina, and South Carolina to the Southwestern territories from the Georgia Piedmont to the Texas prairies. This had a devastating affect on black families, since individuals were sold indiscriminately to speculators and traders for maximum profit. During economic depressions, many slaves were hired out by owners to work in quarries, in iron milling and manufacturing, in textile mills, on railroads, for clearing forests, and as lumbermen. These slaves had to leave the farm, and their women were provided with alternative stud service to allow the breeding operation to proceed unabated.

Discarding Family Values

The most obvious victims of the white man's slave-breeding program were black women. Promiscuity was encouraged and black women were rewarded for it. They were forced to accept rape as a normal event in their lives. In addition, they had to work full time at productive labor, along with the black men, to pay for their upkeep. Black women were not supposed to be bothered by values relating to virginity or problems of widowhood the way white women were. All the experience female slaves gained through producing children was considered an asset and increased their resale value. Large families brought female slaves no increased responsibilities, and if anything, resulted in less work on the plantation. Fanny Kemble observed that on her husband's Georgia plantation, slave women understood clearly what gave them value as property: "This was perfectly evident to me from the meritous air with which the women always made haste to inform me of the number of children they had borne exclaiming—look missis little niggers for you and massa, plenty little niggers for you and little missis."[19]

Some owners tempted their slave women to produce more children by rewarding them for each baby they bore. In an essay on plantation management, one master recommended this policy to others:

> No inconsiderable part of a farmers profits being in little Negroes he succeeds in raising; the breeding women, when lusty, are allowed a great many privileges and required to work pretty much as they please. When they come out of the straw, a nice calico dress is presented to each one as a reward and inducement to produce more children.

The mistress of a Louisiana plantation ordered some gay calico from her business agent, saying, "I have always given a dress to every women after having a young child—they do much better, by being encouraged a little—and I have every thought they deserve it."[20]

Black women clearly understood their position in white men's eyes. A Kentucky slave woman who had each of her seven children by a different father was by no means unique. Frederick Olmsted cited numerous instances of masters who regarded the whole matter with complete unconcern and were pleased when slave women became pregnant. A Virginia planter kept a record of the fathers of his slaves' children when he knew who the fathers were, but often he could only guess, and sometimes he suggested that the child was sired "by the Commonwealth" or by the "Universe" or "God knows who by." Overseers were generally even less concerned. As one overseer explained, slaves' morals were "no business of his, and he did not care what they did." When a Mississippi male slave was indicted for raping a female slave, the State Supreme Court dismissed the case on the ground that it was not an offense known to common or statute law.[21]

Black females quickly learned the advantages of submitting to white males' advances. Black women who normally rejected most whites submitted to their master or overseer in the hope that their reward might be special privileges and perhaps freedom. Most submitted under coercion, which was little less than rape, though no such offense against a black woman was recognized by law. The Louisiana Supreme Court regretfully confessed that the female slave was "peculiarly exposed ... to the seductions of an unprincipled master."[22]

There is no way of gauging the psychological consequences of repeated rape of black women, but it is certain that they did not escape without serious damage to their psyches. They were aware that white women were respected and treated like goddesses and knew the double standards surrounding them. It was common for them to develop a destructive attitude towards their children, not caring whether they lived or died. They also came to regard black men as useless and good for nothing because they could not protect their women.

Black men were also victims of slaveholder breeding policies and the resulting destruction of the black family. A black man could never be certain whether a child borne by his "wife" was his own, so he broke connections with all black children. Moreover, he could not provide an inheritance to his offspring. A family was usually held together by a man who assumed responsibility for feeding and sheltering his children and providing them with an inheritance. In return, the man could expect respect and could control his family members' actions. Black men who could not even protect their women and children from rape or daily beatings found their usefulness reduced to the level of a beast of burden.

As a natural consequence of this, the black man developed a casual attitude toward coupling with black females, ensuring that no enduring affection or sense of mutual responsibility developed between them. The South abounded with stories of male slaves who elected to migrate with kind masters even if it meant separation from their black women. "If you got a good master, foller him," was the saying in Virginia, according to a former slave. An equally common story was that blacks were not greatly disturbed by forced separation and soon found new partners.[23]

The Protestant slavery code's affects on black families and children was devastating. Children's dependence on their parents was removed, so black parents could not command obedience from and control their children. Black children had a high mortality rate, and only a quarter of the black babies born survived. The connection between mother and child was broken, as the mother was required to return to work immediately after the baby was born. Children were brought up in a communal nursery under the care of an older woman or man too feeble for more strenuous work. Black children had to learn how to minimize pain and get used to the lash. Educating them was forbidden on pain of punishment. By their eighth year, children were expected to help with light chores. Heavier chores like carrying wood and water, helping in the kitchens, and cleaning cabins were expected at age twelve. It was up to the master to decide when children were fit to work in the fields. Children also got used to growing up without a father. A typical example was that of a Tennessee slave woman who bore six children, each from a different father. Three of her men had been sold, one had died, and two had failed to develop any lasting attachment. Her daughter recalled, "We all raise up without any regular pappy but we got along just fine."[24]

Slave women were first full-time workers for their owners. They also had to help nurse white children and cook in the communal kitchen, and were in no position to nurse their own children or the children's father if any of them fell ill. As parents had little to do with raising their own children, children soon learned that their parents had little authority. It was usual for a mistress to give a black mother twenty lashes for some infraction in front of her children. Lacking autonomy, slave families could not offer their children shelter or security from the frightening forces around them.

The matriarchal system was forced on black slaves because children's only links were with their mothers. The black man at most was the woman's assistant, her companion, and sex partner. He was often thought of as her possession, as in the case of Mary's Tom in *Uncle Tom's Cabin,* since they lived in Mary's cabin. A mother and her children were commonly considered a family without reference to the father.

Given the prohibition against black slave marriages, the slaveholders' success in preventing black family formation was assured. This was reinforced by the fact that black parents had no social or economic significance. Even the biological family group's ability to live close to one another in the same set of slave quarters was prevented by forced separations through sales. A slave family could be widely dispersed as a result of one or more of these factors. An advertisement for a North Carolina fugitive, for example, said he was presumed to be "Lurking in the neighborhood of E. D. Walker's, at Moore's Creek, who owns most of his relations, or Nathan Bonham's who owns his mother; or perhaps near Fletcher Bell's, at Long Creek, who owns his father."

When a black man asked permission to marry another of his owner's slaves, their Virginia master read them a statement warning that he might be forced to separate them "so Joushua must not say I have taken his wife from him." In this way every black family was destroyed even before it started, because no master could promise that his debts would not force sales, or guarantee that his death would not cause divisions.

Yet another consequence of black family disruption was that black males and females learned to deny the very existence of black children. An angry Virginian attributed a slave infant's death to the unnatural neglect of his infamous mother. Fanny Kemble observed the reaction of slave parents to children's deaths. "I've lost a many; they all goes so," was the only comment of one mother. When another child died, the father went out to his enforced labor without word or comment.[25]

The status of black men, women, and children was clearly summarized by the North Carolina Supreme Court: "The relationship between slaves is essentially different from that of man and wife joined in lawful wedlock. With slaves it may be dissolved at the pleasure of either party, or by the sale of one or both, depending on the caprice or necessity of the owners." The law did not recognize fornication or adultery between slaves, nor bastardy, for as a Kentucky judge noted, the father of a slave was "unknown" to the law. The black family's fate resembled that of Humpty Dumpty falling off the wall. Once the family was destroyed, all the nation's forces could not put it back together again.[26]

No Immunity for White Families

White men believed they were immune from any results of their actions in destroying black families and raping black females. In the long run every action had a reaction, and there was no way of protecting themselves from the consequences. One obvious consequence was for the mulattos born, who inherited slave status from their black mothers. This led to several dilemmas and problems for white men because these children, their own flesh and blood, were treated like slaves and their existence denied by white society.

Whenever two races meet, it is impossible to prevent intermingling, especially when there is wide disparity between the numbers of males and females in the population. After the initial stages it becomes an accepted practice. Southern white male behavior was not unexpected, because in the initial stages there was a shortage of white females in the colonial population.

A Kentucky judge told Olmsted: "It [the rape of black women] was a practice, but too common, as we all know, that pervaded the entire society." A Virginian wrote, "How many have fallen before this temptation? So many that it has almost ceased to be a temptation to fall." Many white parents traced the moral ruin of their sons "to temptations found in female slaves in their own or neighbor's households." With this in mind, one slaveholder advised families to use "elderly servants only" and to put all young slaves to work in the fields. Permitting them to grow up in the house, he warned, was "fraught with evil." This interracial sex resulted in a sizable mulatto population. According to the census of 1860, over half a million colored people in the slave states were mulattos.[27]

Many white men found comfort only in black women whom they could not legally marry. The white man's parents often made too many demands. On the other hand, the black nurse who raised him always loved him and asked no questions. Many white men thus found a necessary retreat in black women. Others were ashamed and tried to hide their actions by selling the women and children far from those who could recognize the father's features in their issue.

Mulattos were in the most unenviable position, as they could not identify with either whites or blacks. Some whites preferred mulattos as domestics, while others paid premium prices for mulatto women as prostitutes and concubines. Most masters, however, saw the inconvenience in owning mulattos who were nearly white, because they could easily escape. One former mulatto slave with blue eyes recalled his master's repeated attempts to sell him, all of which failed. A Kentucky mulatto who was almost white was adjudged worth only half as much as black slaves because he could not be sent into the fields for work, since he could easily escape.[28]

Frederick Douglass relates in his autobiography that:

> The opinion was whispered that my master was my father. The fact remains, that slaveholders have ordained, and by law established, that the children of slave women shall in all cases follow the condition of their mothers; and this is done too obviously to administer to their own lusts, and make a gratification of their wicked desires profitable as well as pleasurable. I know of such slaves invariably suffer greater hardships, and have more to contend with,

than others. They are, in the first place, a constant threat to their mistress. She is ever disposed to find fault with them, they can seldom do anything to please her; she is never better pleased than when she sees them under the lash, especially when she suspects her husband of showing to his mulatto children favors which he withholds from his black slaves. The master is frequently compelled to sell this class of his slaves, out of deference to the feelings of his white wife, and cruel as the deed may strike any one to be, for a man to sell his own children to human flesh-mongers, it is often the dictate of humanity for him to do so.[29]

Although associations between slaveholders and slave women were regarded as an assault on the white family, masters' white children sometimes manifested affection for their mulatto half brothers and half sisters. The mulatto Clarke tells us that at least one of his mother's white half sisters respected the blood tie when the estate was sold:

> When I was about six years of age, the estate of Samuel Campbell, my grandfather, was sold at auction. When everything else had been disposed of, the question arose among the heirs, "What shall be done with Letty (my mother) and her children." Judith, the wife of Joseph Logan, told her brothers John and William Campbell "Letty is our own half sister, and you know it; father never intended they should be sold." Her protest was disregarded and my mother, and her infant son Cyrus, about one year old, were put up together and sold for $500! Sisters and brothers selling their own sister and her children.[30]

Southern white women believed they suffered from white men's attitude toward black women. One of them wrote bitterly:

> Under slavery we live surrounded by prostitutes. Like the patriarchs of old, our men live all in one house with their wives and their concubines and the mulattos one sees in

every family partly resemble the white children. Any lady
is ready to tell you who is the father of all the mulatto
children in everybody's household but their own. These
she thinks, drop from the clouds. My disgust sometimes
is boiling over.

A Virginia woman grieved for the "White mothers and daughters of the South who had seen their dearest affections trampled upon, their hopes of domestic happiness destroyed by husbands, sons and brothers who gratified their passions with female slaves."[31]

Southern white men argued that raping black females was a boon for white women because it protected their chastity. In the South, white men justified using black women for recreational sex and experimentation on the grounds that doing so protected white women. Many poor whites did not bother with moral codes. The number of cases regarding bastardy in Southern court records appears to confirm the conclusion that women of the poor white class "carried about the same reputation for easy virtue as their sable sisters."

Since colonial times, when males outnumbered females, poor white female indentured servants worked side by side with black slaves and could have their pick of black or white men. Contacts between poor white women and blacks were discouraged by law but could not be prevented. A Maryland statute of 1663 noted that, "divers freeborn English women, forgetful of their free condition, and to the disgrace of our nation, do intermarry with Negro slaves." The penalties provided in this and other statutes did not put an end to this practice. A Southerner told Olmsted, "there must be always women of the lower class whites, so poor that their favors can be purchased by the slaves."

These women were not all paupers or prostitutes. Some women of the lower classes had sex with black men to teach a lesson to white husbands who had sex with black women. For the poor white woman, there were hardly any consequences to worry about. If she gave birth to a mulatto or an unwanted child, she could always abandon it on a refuse heap or let it grow up like the rest of the black and mulatto children on the farm where the black father worked.[32]

Rich white women also found ways to get even with white husbands who caused them suffering and neglected them. Such women often wondered about the charms black women possessed that seduced white males, wondered what they themselves lacked. As white men would not always satisfy white women, the women turned their attention to black males out of curiosity.

In New Orleans a "seemingly respectable" white woman was arrested on a charge of having been in an "indecent companionship" with a slave. In one such case the woman not only admitted her intimacy with a slave but confessed that he made her love him, "better than anybody in the world, and she thought he must have given her something." With equal candor, a Virginian white woman told her husband "that she had not been the first nor would she be the last guilty of such conduct, and that she saw no more harm in a white woman having a black child than a white man's having one, although the latter was more frequent."

Occasionally a white female who loved a black man lived with him as a common-law wife. There was always a danger that the white woman might be discovered or get pregnant. If this happened, a respectable white female could be in trouble and lose face. To save herself, she often accused her black lover of raping or attempting to rape her, even if there was no convincing evidence. The black man was promptly lynched or executed. The white woman could then get rid of the unwanted child. She could, however, go through this routine only once. Black slaves were also aware of these methods, and routinely warned black boys to avoid contact with white mistresses.[33]

Some white women tried to protect their mulatto children by marrying white men. Several cases came to the Supreme Court of North Carolina in which white men sought divorces because their wives had borne mulatto children. In arguing for a divorce, one petitioner asserted that he knew his wife had a child at the time of their marriage, but he thought it was his. After their marriage, he discovered that the child was a mulatto. At the same time, another husband sought a divorce on the grounds that his wife had become the mother of a mulatto child. In that case the plaintiff was denied a divorce because, in marrying her because of pregnancy, he could not have presumed her to be chaste. Justice Ruffin pointed out that the petitioner was "criminally accessory to his own honor in marrying a woman whom he knew to be lewd."[34]

The Protestant slavery code's rules were strict and unbending because of fear of a free Negro population. No matter how large the proportion of white blood in his veins and no matter whether the part-Negro mother was slave or free, the offspring resulting from miscegenation was always Negro. This meant that every person was indelibly branded as either white or Negro and amalgamation had to be prevented at all costs. The wall thus erected was not to be breached.

As a young lawyer, Thomas Jefferson vainly defended Samuel Howell, an octoroon (of one-eighth black ancestry), who was bound to slavery until the age of thirty-one, as his grandmother and mother had been before him, under a Virginia law which punished sexual intercourse between whites and Negroes by enslaving their progeny. Jefferson noted slavery's effects on white families as follows:

> The whole commerce between master and slave is a perpetual exercise of the most boisterous passion, the most unremitting despotism on the one part, and degrading submissions on the other. Our children see this, and learn to imitate it; for man is an imitative animal …. The parent storms, the child looks on, catches the lineaments of wrath, puts on the same airs in the circle of smaller slaves, gives loose to his worst of passions, and thus nursed, educated, and daily exercised in tyranny, cannot but be stamped by it with odious peculiarities. The man must be a prodigy who can retain his manners and morals undepraved by such circumstances.[35]

From the slave's point of view, the system's ambiguities provided constant evidence of white hypocrisy. An ex-slave commented on the anti-miscegenation laws and their fate at white man's hands:

"He made that law himself and he is the first to violation." A slave's petition for freedom in 1774 summarized the situation as follows:

> We are deprived of everything that hath a tendency to make life even tolerable, the endearing ties of husband and wife we are strangers to for we are no longer man and wife than our masters or mistresses thinkes proper marred or onmarred. Our children are also taken from us by force and sent maney miles from us wear we seldom or ever see them again there to be made slaves of for Life which sumtimes is vere short by Reson of Being dragged from their mothers Breest Thus our Lives are imbittered to us on these accounts. By our deplorable situation we are rendered incapable of shewing our obedience to Almighty God how can a slave perform the duties of a husband to a wife or parent to his child. How can a husband leave master to work and cleave to his wife. How can the wife submit themselves to there husbands in all things. How can the child obey thear parents in all things ... [36]

Slaveholders came up with sundry arguments and rationales to justify their actions. They claimed that most miscegenation in the South occurred in towns and cities, not on plantations or even farms. Sexual ratios in towns and cities propelled interracial concubinage, for white males usually outnumbered white females; and breaking black families was justified by the explanation that slavery and family life were inherently incompatible. Slaveholders also argued that Negro domestic ties were at best weak and that family separations were no more frequent than those suffered by free laborers in the North, where families were often forced apart by economic necessity. If a finger must be pointed, Yankees were to blame, because they brought the slaves from Africa and sold them to the South individually, without regard to family ties.

To top it all, there was a photograph showing five generations of one black family on Smith's plantation in Beaufort, South Carolina, which supposedly proved that slaveholders' actions to break black families were unsuccessful. The argument that accompanied this photograph was that the enslaved and their children possessed such strong adaptive capacities to recreate their families that family breakups were inconsequential, and therefore did not matter in the first place.[37]

In this debate, white non-slaveholders were a silent majority who would pay dearly for their indifference. Their silence and cooperation was secured by slaveholders through emotional appeals to white supremacy and the need for unity. They did not reveal that almost all miscegenation and mulattos resulted from white males' lawbreaking in raping black females. Black males were harmless and culturally impotent because they could not protect black females or black children. Instead, word was spread that black males lusted after white females and free blacks would take revenge by raping the wives, mothers, and sisters of non-slaveholders and destroy their Southern way of living.

Non-slaveholders did not realize that by breaking black families indiscriminately, violating all religious and moral precepts, slaveholders were spreading slavery to new states and territories. This precluded non-slaveholders from the same territories because they refused to compete with slaves if given a choice. If the slaveholders had been permitted to acknowledge their mulatto offspring and free them or provide them with education and property, over a two-hundred-year period whites and blacks might have learned to live with each other. Mulattos could have served as a bridge between the two races. That was not to be; and broken homes, along with the absence of this escape clause in the Protestant slavery code, combined to contribute to the factors that led to the Civil War.

CHAPTER 5

HUMAN RIGHTS

*Treating people as animals often makes
something rather like animals of them.*

> —Southern Planter before the Civil War

*They'll church you if you sip a dram,
And damn you if you steal a lamb;
Yet rob old Tony, Doll, and Sam,
Of human rights, and bread and ham;
Kidnapper's heavenly union.*

> —Frederick Douglass, "The Parody," 1854

George Washington was not only a planter. He also had one of the largest estates in the Commonwealth of Virginia and owned slaves all his life. An inventory at the time of his death would show that he possessed 124 Negroes in his own right, another 153 dower Negroes belonging to Martha Custis Washington, and he had leased an additional forty from a Mrs. French. After all, Washington lived in a Virginia where slaves were bred to sell to other colonies. Thus in 1772, Washington ordered "musty" flour from wheat raised on his estates to be sold in Jamaica and the proceeds spent on Negroes, provided the "choice ones" could be had for forty pounds sterling or less. The requirements were straightforward enough:

> Let there be two-thirds of them males, the other third fe-
> males. The former not exceeding (at any rate) 20 years of

age, the latter 16. All of them to be straight-limbed and in every respect strong and likely, with good teeth and good countenances, to be sufficiently provided with clothes.

Like other Virginia slaveholders, Washington made no provision to educate his Negroes, but as a matter of course encouraged their promiscuity. He however urged his manager to be "particularly attentive to my negroes in their sickness" and complained that overseers, as a general rule, "view the poor creatures in scarcely any other light than they do a draught horse or ox, neglecting them as much when they are unable to work instead of comforting and nursing them when they lie on a sick bed."[1]

Such cruelty was very much in keeping with the spirit of the times, fostered by the Protestant code. The Kentucky high court pronounced in 1828: "However deeply it may be regretted, and whether it be politic or impolitic, a slave by our code is not treated as a person, but (negotium) a thing." A South Carolina court held in 1809 that "the young of slaves … stand on the same footing as other animals." A mother-child relationship was recognized not because of human or social significance but because it affected property interests.[2]

The human rights of blacks were continuously violated by denying their humanity and treating them as animals and things. One Southern planter boasted that a Negro was what the white man made him. As Harriet Beecher Stowe stated, "Treat 'em like dogs, and you'll have dogs' work and dogs' actions. Treat 'em like men, and you'll have mens' work. That is to say, the Lord made 'em men, and it's a hard squeeze getting 'em down into beasts."[3]

Blacks' Humanity Denied

What is the difference between a human being and an animal? They are both living creatures who reproduce and can learn. Self-awareness is certainly one characteristic that is far more evolved in man than in animals, making humans more responsive to the various different stimuli in their environment; controlling their reactions depending upon their goals. It endows them with greater ability to learn from self-experience and those experiences of their parents, family, the community, and past generations.

To create animal-like behavior in a slave, it was necessary for slaveholders to minimize contacts between the individual and his parents and family; the community around him, and to deny the slave any opportunity for education that affected his ability to learn from previous generations. Food and shelter were provided to guarantee dependence, while all opportunities were denied that might enable the slave to exercise responsibility or freedom of choice, two activities that exercise the mind. This treatment was designed to numb a slave's mind into accepting the fact that he must follow orders or suffer pain while destroying all self-motivation or hope for change.

Slaveholders designed their program to transform blacks into animal-like creatures in the most efficient manner and the shortest time possible, taking on the family first. The family is the most important component in man's socialization process, with the parents serving as the child's primary role models. A child also has expectations of his parents in terms of food, shelter, and protection from a hostile environment. In return he gives his parents respect and obedience. One way a father could attempt to motivate the child and enforce his authority was by providing him with an inheritance. This provided children with hope and a stake in maintaining a long-term relationship with parents. Slaveowners denied black children opportunities to be with their parents and their parents any prospect of providing an inheritance. A master could make a black child an orphan the day he was born.

The community then emerged as a more important bonding factor and as a learning resource. No black could separate himself from the black community, no matter how educated or wealthy or different he was. Community power and sanctions were essential in a minority group based on color which could not be hidden or camouflaged, because in the majority white culture every slave's actions was attributed to every other. If one black man committed a crime, white society saw all blacks as criminals. If one black woman was a prostitute, whites regarded all black women as such. A black man was guilty unless proven innocent; the benefit of any doubt always went to the slaveholder. A black man was a slave unless he could produce a court judgment testifying that he was free. If a black man did not carry a written traveling pass, he could be challenged by any white man and whipped on the spot. Any black female could be raped at any time and place by anyone, simply because she was black.

Yet the blacks were not entitled to operate as a normal community, to assemble and hold such meetings as they chose, which is a basic human right. Allowing blacks to meet in groups was asking for trouble. Even religious meetings were denied them as the danger from conspiracy against whites far outweighed the advantages of putting the fear of God into slaves. There were laws specifying the number of blacks who could attend funerals, which had to be completed before sundown.

Literacy, the third source of learning, had to be denied, too, because a literate black might find access to newspapers, learn what was going on not only in the immediate neighborhood but in the country as a whole, and absorb a wide range of ideas and study the concepts of liberty and equality that the slaveholders had used to obtain freedom from the British. Any black who acquired a writing ability could pen traveling passes for himself and other blacks, creating havoc in the slave policing and enforcement system. Slaveholders took no chances and passed laws in every state of the South making it a crime to teach a black person to read or write. There were even laws forbidding the *Bible* being read to blacks. The only religious instruction allowed slaves was verbal.

Having ensured an uneducated mind, the slaveholders wanted to destroy black willpower and command unquestioned, automatic obedience. This could only be achieved by the pain minimization principle and by eliminating any prospect of slaves planning for the future or using their brains to make decisions or solve problems. For blacks, there was no such thing as planning for tomorrow.

An Arkansas master in 1850 explained his slave management technique:

It is necessary to implant in the bondsmen themselves a consciousness of personal inferiority. They had to know and keep their places, to feel the differences between master and slaves, to understand that bondage was their natural status. They had to feel that African ancestry tainted them, that their color was a badge of degradation. In the country they were to show respect for their master's non-slaveholding neighbors, in the towns they were to give way on streets to the most wretched white man. The line between the races must never be crossed, for familiarity caused slaves to forget their lowly station and to become impudent.[4]

Next the slaves were conscientiously dazzled by their masters' enormous power. Slavery could only be maintained through fear. The final step was to impress Negroes with their helplessness and create in them "a habit of perfect dependence" upon their masters. A Virginian was alarmed to find that his slaves, while working at an iron furnace, "… got a habit of roaming about and taking care of themselves." Independent spirits were less likely to develop among slaves kept on the land, where they became accustomed to having their basic needs met by masters and were taught that they were unfit to look after themselves.

Here then was the recipe for the production of the perfect slave: accustom him to rigid discipline, demand unconditional submission from him, impress him with his innate inferiority, develop in him a paralyzing fear of white men, train him to adopt the master's code of good behavior, and instill a sense of complete dependence in him. Slaveholders, Olmsted noted, were able to gratify, with little restraint, man's "natural lust for authority." They did not have to endure employees who made demands, who could legally refuse to obey, or who cherished their own self-respect and personal dignity.[5]

According to Frederick Douglass, slavery's continuation depended on keeping blacks ignorant:

To make a contented slave, you must make a thoughtless one. It is necessary to darken his moral and mental vision, and, as far as possible to annihilate his power of reason. He must be able to detect no inconsistencies in slavery. The man that takes his earnings, must be able to convince him that he has a perfect right to do so. It must not depend on mere force; the slave must know no Higher Law than his master's will. The whole relationship must not only demonstrate, to his mind, its necessity, but its absolute rightfulness.[6]

Blacks as Animals and Things

The slaveholders treated black slaves on a par with animals so that non-slaveholders too would feel superior to them and treat them the same way. A farmer who had no mule would lash a slave to the plow. Whites gave black men names like Toby, Mando, Mingo, Hector, and Hagar, and made them sleep outside while the owner's best dogs rested in bed with him. Dogs were used to track down runaway slaves. Groups of slaveholders sometimes rode through swamps with their dogs and made fugitive catching a game comparable to fox hunting. Others preferred to hire professional slave catchers who provided their own "Negro dogs." A Mississippi master described a slave catcher's mode of operation: "He follows a Negro with his dogs 36 hours after he has passed and never fails to overtake him. It is his profession and he makes some $5,600 per annum by it." Southern newspapers carried advertisements of professional slave catchers who solicited slaveholders' patronage and of those who trained "Negro dogs" for sale.[7]

To match their lack of status, black slaves did not have surnames and had to answer to "Boy" or "Girl" all their lives. Most slave inventories carry no last name. In Missouri, Mark Twain explained: "If Mr. Harbison owned a slave named Bull, Tom would have spoken to him as 'Harbison's Bull,' but a son or dog of that name was 'Bull Harbison.'" In the Carolina rice country, "Scarcely ever did a Negro choose the name of his owner but often took that of some other slaveholding family of which he knew, so that they had surnames amongst themselves." The Catholic slavery code's influence made Louisiana an exception. The inventory of Isaac Franklin's West Feliciana Parish plantations shows more slaves with surnames than without. Frederick Douglass noted: "It was seldom that a slave, however venerable, was honored with a surname in Maryland and so completely has the South shaped the manners of the North in this respect that their right to such honor is tardily admitted even now."[8]

Matters were equally sorry when it came to slave hygiene. In Africa, blacks usually bathed at least once a day, often using soap made of palm oil and wood ash. America's Southern black field hands were as dirty as their clothes, of which they had too few to spare any for washing. Even humane masters allowed only a weekly "half hour by Sun" for slaves to wash their clothes. Therefore all hands wore the same clothes for a week at a time, if not longer, hence their reputation for "Negro funk," an especially acrid odor deemed to be innate. Thomas Jefferson observed that Negroes sweated more, "which gives them a very strong and disagreeable odor." Charles Mackay, a traveler, noted in 1859: "The whites in the North object to a negro not alone for moral and political, but for physical reasons. They state that he smells, and that it is almost as offensive to come near him as it would be to fondle a skunk." In a church that held seven to eight hundred blacks, he discussed the absence of odor with a Virginian gentlemen who accompanied him, and got the response: "The month is March. In June or July the odor would be perfectly intolerable, and I, for me, should not have ventured to have done myself the honor of accompanying you."[9]

Slaveholders used flogging freely and severely to instill in blacks a fear of them. Frederick Douglass describes the technique of Mr. Hopkins:

> His chief boast was his ability to manage slaves. The peculiar feature of his government was that of whipping slaves in advance of deserving it. He did this to alarm their fears, and strike terror into those who escaped. His plan was to whip for the smallest offenses, to prevent the commission of larger ones.

Bennet H. Barrow, a planter who refused to employ overseers because of their bad reputations, broke his sword cane on the head of one offending slave, and "beat" another "very bad." Advertisements for fugitive slaves and sheriffs' committal notices show the results of frequent flogging. A Mississippi slave had "large raised scars of whelks in the small of his back and on his abdomen nearly as large as a persons finger;" Nancy, a Georgia slave, was "considerably marked by the whip."[10]

If simple flogging did not cause a slave to obey, it was continued until it resulted in crippling, maiming, or death. "Salting," or washing cuts received from the whip with brine, was performed on the most obstinate slaves. If these actions failed, an obstinate slave could be sent to a professional "slave breaker." Frederick Douglass remembered a ruthless man in Maryland who had a reputation for being "a first rate hand at breaking young Negroes." Some slaveholders sent their new hands to him for training.[11]

Slaves were branded for easy identification. Punishment by mutilation was widespread. A Louisiana jailer gave notice in 1831 that he had a runaway in his custody: "He has been lately gelded, and is not yet well." Another Louisianian recorded his disgust for a neighbor who had castrated three of his men. Others hunted them with shotguns. A North Carolinian advertised for an escaped slave who had, "… some marks of shot about his hips, thighs, neck and face." A Mississippian, wishing to give his slaves a stern warning, promised to compensate whoever captured his fugitive "dead or alive."[12]

Dogs were allowed to maul fugitive slaves severely if the owner was in the mood. After a Mississippi master caught an escaped slave, he allowed his dogs to "… bite him very severely." On another occasion his dogs tore a slave naked; he then "… took him home before the other Negroes, and made the dogs give him another overhauling."[13]

To reinforce the idea that blacks were on a par with animals, slaveholders treated black children as pets. Many masters gave their children each a younger black child as a pet to play with and keep him company. Thus in 1779, Richard Taliaferro of Virginia left each of his grandchildren, "a negro Boy and Girl apiece, as near their own age as conveniently may be out of my own stock of Slaves." At other times black children were given out to whoever would take them, like kittens. Historian W.E.B. DuBois bluntly asserts that planters viewed Negro women as brood mares and black children as puppies. Of course, professional breeders were in business for profit.

The profitability of using female slaves for breeding was not lost on slaveholders. With the magnitude of the interstate trade in slaves, the opportunity to supply speculators with merchandise was alluring. In Virginia, Olmsted, who was traveling through the South, remarked, "The cash value of a slave for sale, above the cost of raising it from infancy to the age at which it commands the highest price, is generally considered among the surest elements of a planter's wealth—that a slave woman is commonly esteemed least for her laboring qualities, most for those qualities which give value to a brood mare."

Slaveholders were often remarkably candid about their desire to exploit the procreative talents of their slaves. A Virginia planter, writing in an agricultural periodical, stated that, "Young Negroes will breed much faster when well clothed, fed and housed, which fact offers an inducement to those slaveowners whose hearts do not overflow with feelings of humanity." A Georgian observed that the capital invested in black slave females yielded a substantial return from the women's offspring alone. He claimed that many Southern slaveholders had accumulated wealth merely by increasing their slaves through breeding.[14]

Church congregations in Kentucky and Virginia commonly invested in slaves for hire to pay the minister's salary. In one such case in Virginia, the original investment was in two Negro women bought in 1767, whose successive generations of descendants, fathered nobody cared how, were retained until liquidation in 1835, when the total was some seventy head of human livestock.[15]

Some owners used black females for prostitution. A trader in Lexington, Kentucky, who paid $1600 and $1700 for two young slave women, obviously had the market for "fancy girls" in mind, because these prices were considerably above the current market prices for female field hands, domestics, or even promising "breeding women." Luis C. Robards, a well-known trader from Lexington in the 1850s, had special quarters on the second floor of his "Negro Jail" for his "choice stock" of quadroon and octoroon girls. A visitor reported: "In several rooms I found very handsome mulatto women of fine persons and easy genteel manners sitting at their needlework, awaiting a purchaser. The proprietor made them get up and turn around to show to advantage their finely developed and graceful forms and slaves as they were, this I confess rather shocked my gallantry."[16]

The black slave's utility was enhanced by his market value; the profit he could generate from being sold and therefore treated as a thing. A black slave was inspected, mortgaged, and treated like a horse, cow, or pig. Annual taxes and import duties were imposed on slaves as on any other property.

An inspection determined a slave's price. Prospective purchasers usually examined the merchandise minutely to make sure slaves bore no physical defects or extensive whip marks, which might indicate bad character. Buyers were not expected to invest in an expensive piece of property without this precaution, and anyone who had, or pretended to have, a mind to purchase was free to satisfy his curiosity. Though they offered little entertainment, an inspection and the accompanying sale never failed to attract a crowd of spectators. A visitor in Louisville attended a public auction where a pregnant slave woman was offered to the highest bidder: "... the auctioneer standing by her side, indulged himself in brutal jests upon her thriving condition, and sold her for four hundred dollars."[17]

Masters discussed black slaves in impersonal terms; slave prices were discussed with as much interest as cotton or tobacco prices. Commenting on extraordinarily good prices in 1853, a South Carolina editor reported, "Boys weighing about fifty pounds, can be sold for about five hundred dollars." A North Carolina editor remarked, "It really seems that there is to be no stop to the rise ... .

This species of property is at least 30 per cent higher now, than it was last January ... what Negroes will bring next January, it is impossible for mortal man to say."[18]

Obviously then the death of a slave was no more than the loss of property. A Mississippi editor reported a tragedy on the Mississippi River involving the drowning of six "likely" male slaves "owned by a couple of young men who had bought and paid for them by the sweat of their brows." A young North Carolina planter, who seemed doomed to misfortune, "lost through an accident a slave he had inherited from his grandmother" and was thus "minus the whole legacy." One morning, James H. Hammond discovered that his slave Anny had brought forth a dead child. "She has not earned her salt for four months past," he grumbled. "Bad luck my usual luck in this way."[19]

Consequentially, blacks were victims of disputes over titles and actions between owners and renters. A Kentucky slave "died in consequence of injuries inflicted on him by Thomas Kennedy and others." The owner sued and recovered a judgment for one hundred and ninety-five dollars and costs. A Tennessee slave was hired by a man who then permitted him to die of neglect. An indignant judge affirmed that "the hirer of a slave should be taught ... that more is required of him than to extract from the slave the greatest amount of service, with the least degree of attention to his comfort, health or even life," and ordered five hundred dollars as the sole penalty for the master. An Alabama slave was scarred by severe whippings inflicted by his hirer. The owner brought suit on the ground that the slave's "market value was permanently injured."[20]

Blacks' Psychological Syndromes

As the slaveholders intended, blacks got used to idling away their spare time and living in a void. Their only emotional release was in dance and music on Saturday nights, with the master's permission. U. B. Phillips, a historian, claimed:

> the traits which prevailed with the black slaves were an
> eagerness for society, music and merriment, a fondness

for display whether of person, dress, vocabulary or emotion, a not flagrant sensuality, a receptiveness towards any religion whose exercises were exhilarating, a proneness to superstition, a courteous acceptance of subordination, an avidity for praise, readiness for loyalty of a feudal sort, and last but not least a healthy human repugnance toward overwork.[21]

Historian Nathan Huggins states:

The breakup of the black slave from all affectionate connections, of a lack of sense of father or mother, being traded from place to place, suffering continually as the victim of one-sided violence pushed the black man to care only about himself, finding as much pleasure in the pain of others as in avoidance of pain for oneself. Such a spirit volatile, unsettling, disruptive would move within the slave quarters, stealthily, slyly, sometimes with a disarming charm and wit but always as a corrupting force. While shrinking from the master's power the black slave might urge others into foolhardy acts while currying favor with whites through tales of plots and misdeeds. A personality type common enough among all victims of tyranny, would also undermine the slave community.[22]

Blacks were forced to protect themselves from victimization and the duplicity practiced by slaveholders. Fear, deception, and hatred endangered slaves' personalities, because each placed his entire being at the oppressor's disposal. Black reality narrowed to what white masters did or willed.

The predominant and overpowering emotion whites aroused in black slaves was fear. "We were always uneasy," an ex-slave recalled. When "… a white man spoke to me, I would feel frightened," another confessed. In Alabama, a visitor who lost his pocketbook noted that the slave who found it "… was afraid of being whipped for theft and had given it to the first white man he saw, and at first was afraid to pick it up." The white masters themselves provided vivid evidence of the frightening image whites had assumed in slave minds. Advertisements for fugitives revealed the slaves' emotional nightmare with such descriptive phrases as these: "… stutters very much when spoken to"; "speaks softly and has a downcast look"; "a very down look, and easily confused when spoken to"; "stammers very much as to be scarcely understood." A black woman who had escaped to Canada affirmed, "I feel lighter—the dread is gone. It is a great heaviness on a person's mind to be a slave."[23]

Another defense mechanism developed by blacks was to flatter whites, show complete subservience, and behave like buffoons. When Olmsted was introduced to a slave preacher, he took the Negro's hand and greeted him respectfully; but the black man seemed to take this for a joke and laughed heartily. The master explained in a "slightly humorous" tone that the preacher was also the driver, that he drove the field hands at the cotton all week and preached the gospel on Sunday. At this remark the preacher "… began to laugh again, and reeled off like a drunken man entirely overcome with merriment." Olmsted remarked that the preacher, having concluded that the purpose of the interview was to make fun of him, "generously assumed a merry humor."[24]

Some blacks became very suspicious, harboring habitual distrust for the white race, which resulted in unending conflict with whites. Blacks felt they were entitled to use every tactic of deception or chicanery they could devise. Many ex-slaves recalled with particular pleasure some time when they had outwitted or beguiled their masters, "… cause us had to lie." To defend their self-images, some blacks openly expressed contempt for poor white trash. Some masters tolerated and were amused by this, not realizing that blacks used this mechanism to express their opinion of the entire white race.[25]

Another black defense against whites was religion and the practice of voodooism. Slaves needed a spiritual life in which they could participate vigorously and which transported them from slavery's dull routine and promised that a better time was within reach. A visitor to the South explained: "The doctrine of the savior comes to the Negro slaves as their most inward need, and as the accomplishment of the wishes of their souls. They themselves enunciate it with the purest joy .... Their prayers burst forth into flame as they ascend to heaven." A former slave recalled the ecstasy he felt when he learned there was a salvation "for every man" and that God loved black men as much as white: "I seemed to see a glorious being, in cloud of splendor, smiling down from on high, ready to welcome me to the skies." Some blacks practiced voodooism because they had to try every method available to protect themselves from whites. Frederick Douglass learned from an old African medicine man who was said to have magical powers that if a slave wore the root of a certain herb on his right side, no white man could ever whip him.[26]

How successful slaveholders were in applying their behavior therapy to black slaves can be seen by the class system slaves developed among themselves based on their masters' example. This system, developed among blacks themselves, enabled one black to feel superior to another based on skin shade or work assignment and would treat the other accordingly. Slave society's stratification was based on a pathetic quest by black individuals for personal prestige. Slaves yearned for their worth as individuals to be recognized, if only by those in their own limited surroundings. Each slave cherished whatever shreds of self-respect he could preserve.

Many domestic slaves adopted the white behavior code for blacks: they were proud of their honesty and loyalty to their white families and frowned on disobedient or rebellious behavior. Some slaves feared or disapproved of a troublemaker lest he cause them all to suffer the master's wrath. Most domestics were proud of their responsible positions, fine manners, and correct speech, their handsome clothing and other badges of distinction. Indeed, domestics, artisans, and foremen constituted slave society's aristocracy. An ex-slave who had been his master's body servant confessed: "I considered my station a very high one." Many visitors to the South commented on how the domestics flaunted their superiority over "... the less favored helots of the plough ... their assumption of hauteur when they had occasion to hold intercourse with any of the 'field hands.'" Former slaves described the envy and hatred felt by the "helots" for the "funglemen" who "put on airs" in imitation of whites. Blacks reached the upper stratum of their society through intimate contact with the master, by learning to mimic his manners, and by rendering him personal service, as well as by heaping abuse on brother and sister slaves who had to work in the fields.[27]

Because of their desperate need to find some group to feel superior to, black slaves learned to make social distinctions among themselves, based on wealth and poverty and the kind of work they did,. Field hands, who suffered contempt from domestics, lavished their own contempt on "coal pit niggers" hired to work in the mines. Everywhere in the South, slaves of all ranks ridiculed non-slaveholders, especially poor whites—the dregs of stratified white society—whom they scornfully called "po' buckra" and "white trash." Blacks who belonged to a master with great wealth and social prestige looked disdainfully upon slaves who belonged to humbler ones. Frederick Douglass wrote: "… the slaves seemed to think that the greatness of their masters was transferable to them." A former slave criticized the foolish pride which made them love "… to boast of their master's wealth and influence. I have heard of slaves object to being sent in very small companies to labor in the field, lest that some passer-by should think that they belonged to a poor man who was unable to keep a large gang."

A Northern visitor described the house servant of a wealthy planter as "… full of his master's wealth and importance, which he feels to be reflected upon himself." A domestic on a Louisiana sugar plantation was once asked to attend to a sick overseer. "What do you think he says?" reported the irritated mistress. "He ain't used to waiting on low rank people."[28]

Slaves, seeing their masters exhibit wealth as evidence of social rank, developed their own measure of worth and exhibited their price tags. Many black slaves boasted about the prices their masters had paid for them, or the handsome offers their masters had rejected from would-be purchasers. A thousand-dollar slave felt superior to an eight-hundred-dollar one. An amused traveler wrote, "When we recollect that the dollars are not their own we can hardly refrain from smiling at the childlike simplicity with which they express their satisfaction at the high price set on them."[29]

Evidence that the masters' message of white superiority had been effective could be seen in the slave community, where mulattos sought status by boasting about white ancestors or took pride in a light complexion. Fanny Kemble told of a slave women who came to her and begged to be relieved from field labor "... on account of her color." This slave made it evident that "... being a mulatto, she considered field labor a degradation. This was a reflection of the white man's thinking who preferred mulattos as house servants."[30]

Sharp wits and strong muscles were black men's chief survival weapons. Young men prided themselves on their athletic skill and physical prowess and often matched strength in violent encounters. Since they had to submit to their masters' superior power, slaves learned to be aggressive toward one another. "They were," insisted a Georgian, "by nature tyrannical in their dispositions; and if allowed, the stronger will abuse the weaker, the men will abuse the women and mothers their children." Slave foremen were severe taskmasters and were rewarded by white masters for using the whip more cruelly than white overseers. Fanny Kemble discerned the brutalizing effects of slavery in the "... unbounded insolence and tyranny" that slaves exhibited toward one another. Frederick Douglass wrote that: "Everybody, in the South, wants the privilege of whipping somebody else."[31]

Blacks had no way of breaking the monotonous grind of their existence. A visitor to South Carolina observed: "The life of a slave was removed from civilization, it was mere animal existence, passed in physical exertion or enjoyment." Fanny Kemble saw grown slaves "... rolling, tumbling, kicking, and wallowing in the dust, regardless alike of decency, and incapable of any more rational amusement; or lolling, with half-closed eyes, like so many cats and dogs, against a wall, or upon a bank in the sun, dozing away their short leisure hour."[32]

The boredom of their daily lives made black slaves look forward to every holiday with great fervor. Feasting was one of the slave's chief pleasures, one of his "… principal sources of comfort." Slaves looked forward to feasts not only at Christmas, but also when crops had been harvested or when there was a wedding. A former slave recalled, "… only the slave who has lived all the year on his scanty allowance of meal and bacon, can appreciate such suppers." Occasions such as Christmas or a corn-shucking were not only times for feasting but also for visiting slaves on nearby establishments—with the master's permission. A visitor to Virginia observed that many slaves spent Sundays "… strolling about the fields and streets finding joy in their relative freedom of movement. They dressed in bright colored holiday clothes, which contrasted pleasantly with their drab everyday apparel."[33]

Saturday night dances and songfests were the only regular forms of physical and emotional release most blacks had. Most masters permitted a dance at least occasionally. A Louisianian wrote: "This is Saturday night and I hear the fiddle going in the Quarter. We have two parties here among the Negroes. One is a dancing party and the other a praying party. The dancers have it tonight, and the other party will hold forth tomorrow." Slaves danced to the music of fiddle or banjo, or beat out their rhythm with sticks on tin pans or by clapping hands or tapping feet. The kinds of jigs and double shuffles slaves performed were once described to "… agitate every part of the body at the same time." Such dances were physical and emotional orgies to help slaves forget their lot, at least for an evening.[34]

One lesson blacks learned from masters, in spite of efforts to discourage slaves from the practice, was how to make leisure hours more agreeable with the aid of alcohol in its crudest but cheapest and most concentrated forms. In preparing for Christmas, slaves somehow managed to smuggle "fresh bottles of rum or whiskey into their cabins," for many thought of each holiday as an occasion for an orgy. A former slave recalled that sobriety during the holidays was considered disgraceful in the black community, and any member who could not afford to drink whiskey during Christmas was esteemed lazy and improvident. No law and no threat from masters could keep liquor out of slaves' hands or stop the illicit alcohol trade between them and "unscrupulous" whites. Some masters themselves furnished whiskey for holiday occasions or winked at violations of state laws and their own rules.[35]

Slaveholders' Rationalizations

Having accomplished the dehumanization of the slaves, the masters still had to deal with their own consciences. Slaveholders therefore looked for any excuse to justify their treatment of blacks. Each and every argument, starting with the climate and proceeding through religion, science, history, and economics, was advanced to rationalize the consequences of slavery. These arguments held only one point in common: slaveholders did not want to accept responsibility for treating blacks as animals and things.

Some slaveholders blamed the weather for slavery's growth and the South's treatment of blacks. Though admitting great climatic variations within the South, they emphasized the humid heat of their subtropical summers. Because of these conditions, proponents argued, slaves were necessary because only those who were forced to work would do so. Since Southerners were unable to control the weather, they had to come to terms with it. They therefore argued that the climate determined the nature of their institutions and the structure of their society. One historian wrote: "Let us begin by discussing the weather which is the chief agency in making the south distinctive."[36]

If climate alone could not explain slavery, perhaps (the argument ran) certain additional factors, such as soil, topography, and watercourses, contributed to broader geographical determinism. Combine the long growing seasons with the rich Southern soils and many navigable rivers, which facilitated the movement of bulky staples from considerable distances and all the requirements for commercial agriculture existed. Commercial agriculture induced a trend toward large landholdings, which in turn created a demand for labor. Thus, some have argued, Southerners, in permitting slavery's growth, merely submitted to compelling natural forces.[37]

Another rationale for slaveholders' actions was that blacks had to be brought to the South to perform labor that Europeans were unable to undertake themselves. According to a Southerner: "The white man will never raise … can never raise a cotton or a sugar crop in the United States. In our swamps and under our sun the Negro thrives, but the white man dies. Without the productive power of the African whom an all wise creator had perfectly adapted to the labor needs of the South, its land would have remained a howling wilderness."[38]

For those who were scientifically inclined, doctors and scientists found physiological basis for the alleged temperamental and intellectual differences between blacks and whites that ideally suited blacks for slavery. Dr Samuel W. Cartwright of Louisiana argued that the visible difference in black skin pigmentation also extended to "the membranes, the muscles, the tendons, and … to all the fluids and secretions. Even the Negro's brain and nerves, the chyle and all the humors are tinctured with a shade of the pervading darkness." Dr Josiah C. Mobile was the leader of a group that supported one of the more extreme opinions: the denial that Negroes and whites belonged to the same species.[39]

Some slaveholders claimed they did what was best for blacks. These slave owners argued that primitive Negroes brought to America could only learn civilized ways over the course of many generations of gradual cultural growth. These slaveholders maintained it was their duty to guide, protect, and instruct blacks until the slaves learned to cope with America's more advanced culture; in return, blacks owed their masters labor for this generous assistance. One historian described the Southern plantation as "a school constantly training and controlling pupils who were in a backward state of civilization … on the whole the plantations were the best schools yet invented for the mass training of that sort of inert and backward people which the bulk of the American blacks represented."[40]

Slaveholders found considerable solace in the fact that they had not invented slavery. They traced slavery's history back to the dawn of civilization and showed that it had always existed in some form, from ancient times right down to their own day. Ancient Egyptians obtained slave laborers from their Semitic and Ethiopian neighbors. The Athenians attained unprecedented heights of artistic achievement in a society built on a foundation of slavery. The Romans made chattel slaves of captives taken in Europe, West Asia, and North Africa. Slavery flourished in various forms in the Middle Ages. The lands of European nobles were cultivated by serfs whose status was above that of chattel slaves, but who were nevertheless bound to the soil in hereditary servitude. Christian and Muslim zealots made each faith regard the other as infidels, entitling them to enslave members of the other faith taken as captives. Spaniards and Portuguese brought to Europe cargoes of black servants from Africa's west coast. In short, Southerners were only following a historical tradition in civilization's progress.[41]

Another favorite explanation was that blacks were unfit for freedom. Slavery existed because of the "race problem"; free Negroes would pose an immense social danger and threaten Southern civilization. According to this theory, slavery was a method of regulating race relations, an instrument of social control. Masters kept possession of their slaves because it was their duty to society and the white race. Destroying the system would be a tragedy for both races.[42]

"The truth is," affirmed George Fitzhugh of Virginia, "that some men are born with saddles on their backs and others booted and spurred to ride them, and the riding does them good." Fitzhugh, along with other Southern conservatives, concluded that the best way of protecting property and preventing proletarian revolution was to reduce the laboring population to slavery. He states:

> Where slavery does not exist, there is a conflict—a constant, unremitting struggle for mastery between capital and labor, which not infrequently leads to strikes, mobs, bloodshed, and revolution. But is there no remedy for this state of things? ... We answer yes, in a system of labor such as the South is blessed with—a system which proclaims peace, perpetual peace, between the warring elements. Harmonizing the interest betwixt capital and labor, southern slavery has solved the problem over which statesman have toiled and philanthropists mourned from the first existence of organized society.[43]

Some Southerners were concerned only with slavery's benefits and did not need any theory or philosophy to justify their actions. Their rationale was, "Never inquire into the propriety of the master, but just do as others do." Their ancestors owned slaves and the present generation owned them. They invested their money in this property, just as they invested in cattle or real estate, leaving others to discuss the right and justice of the institution. Only maudlin weaklings held "morbid sensibilities" about owning slaves or thought of freeing them in wills. Newspapers encouraged such thinking by publishing arguments such as this one:

> Let our women and old men, the persons of weak and infirm minds, be disabused of the false notion that slavery is sinful, and that they will peril their souls if they do not disinherit their offspring by emancipating their slaves. It was high time masters put aside all care or thought what northern people say about them. Let us be independent in this at least.[44]

To convince themselves they were blameless, and in reply to their own consciences, some masters recited the arguments justifying slavery to one another over and over, as if to still inward doubts. A slaveholder wrote to a fellow slaveholder in 1849:

> My views respecting the responsibility under which the master of Negroes rests correspond precisely with yours. That description of property is in our hands, and, I believe, by the will of providence; and the fact of possessing them, is justified by the example and the language of Patriarchs, Prophets and Apostles, from the day of Abraham to the period of St John's revelation. The slaves were in a far happier condition than if they were liberated and so my conscience is clear.[45]

President Jefferson in his annual message of December 2, 1806, presented a Bill in Congress to ban slave importation, during which he made the following remarks about the treatment of blacks:

> I congratulate you, fellow citizens on the approach of the
> period at which you may interpose your authority con-
> stitutionally to withdraw the citizens of the United States
> from all further participation in those violations of hu-
> man rights which have been so long continued on the
> unoffending inhabitants of Africa …

Slaveholders' thinking was explained by Daniel Webster in 1850
as follows:

> Such is the influence of a habit of thinking among
> men, and such is the influence of what has been long
> established, that even minds, religious and tenderly con-
> scientious, such as would be shocked by any single act of
> oppression, in any single exercise of violence and unjust
> power, are not moved by the reflection that slavery is a
> continual and permanent violation of human rights.[46]

Though the demands of political correctness made the
Constitutional Convention keep the word "slave" out of the
Constitution, slaveholders successfully included the concept of
slavery in it in the form of the fugitive slave and the federal ratio
clauses. Not only were the non-slaveholders passive accomplices of
the slaveholders in the violation of human rights of the blacks, but
they were also to be the major victims of the Civil War and pay for
their participation in such violations with their lives.

CHAPTER 6

CIVIL RIGHTS

Glittering Generalities

—Herbert Friedenwald (Historian)

We wonder how such saints can sing,
Or praise the Lord upon the wing,
Who roar, and scold, and whip, and sting,
And to their slaves and Mammon cling,
In guilty conscience Union.

—Frederick Douglass, "The Parody," 1845

We hold these truths to be self evident, that all men are
created equal.

—The Declaration of Independence

An English visitor observed: "The Federal Constitution is silent about race or color, but in interpreting it American lawgivers arrive at the conclusion that the United States are the property of whites, that persons with a tinge of dark color in their countenance, though born free, are not citizens." Representative Charles Pinckney of South Carolina, a delegate to the Constitutional Convention in 1787, claimed that he had been responsible for the section on the rights and duties of citizens. He explained to Congress in 1821 what he had in mind regarding civil rights for blacks: "I perfectly knew that there did not then exist such a thing in the Union as a black or colored citizen, nor could I then have conceived it possible such a thing could ever have existed in it; nor notwithstanding all that is said on the subject, do I now believe one does exist in it." He further charged that the Northern states were seeking to rid themselves of the black population by treating them on every occasion with the most marked contempt and denying them their civil rights. Roger Taney, Andrew Jackson's attorney general, gave his opinion regarding Negroes' constitutional rights in 1831:

> The framers of the Constitution had not regarded Negroes as citizens, and the present condition of that race warranted no change in their legal status. The African race in the United States even when free are everywhere a degraded class, and exercise no political influence. The privileges they are allowed to enjoy, are accorded to them as a matter of kindness and benevolence rather than of right …. And where they are nominally admitted by law to the privileges of citizenship, they have no effectual power to defend them and are permitted to be citizens by the sufferance of the white population and hold whatever rights they enjoy at their mercy. Negroes were thus a separate and degraded people and each state could grant or withhold such privileges as it deemed proper and expedient.[1]

Most blacks in Southern states being slaves, civil rights for blacks were considered unnecessary because, slaveholders claimed, slavery and civil rights were incompatible. On the other hand, the Northern states abolished black slavery because it was incompatible with white wage slavery. Northern citizens preferred not to have blacks amongst them and passed laws to prevent black immigration and drive out those blacks who were there. Blacks who remained had to live as "untouchables." A framework to deny Northern blacks civil rights evolved before 1860. The violation of black civil rights in the North, South, and at the federal level held consequences for blacks, non-slaveholders, and slaveholders alike.

Blacks' Role in the Revolution

In 1776, America's founding fathers realized they had to accept black slavery if they were going to fight the British effectively. Most Southern slaveholders regarded their investment in slaves as more important than the fight for independence. Northern merchants, importing and selling slaves to the South, profited from the trade that played such an important role in the colonial economy. In order to unite all Northern and Southern colonies—including slaveholders, non-slaveholders and merchants—against the British, the Declaration of Independence was formulated to read as follows: "We hold these truths to be self-evident, that all men are created equal, that they are endowed by their Creator with certain inalienable rights, that among these are life, liberty and the pursuit of happiness."[2]

The original draft of the Declaration of Independence submitted to the Continental Congress by Thomas Jefferson contained specific charges against the king for violating black rights to life and liberty. It stated: "He has waged cruel war against human nature itself, violating its most sacred rights of life and liberty, in the persons of a distant people who never offended him, captivating and carrying them into slavery in another hemisphere or to incur miserable death in their transportation thither."

Southern slaveholders and Northern slave merchants were concerned about this language because it was too descriptive of their own activities. Southerners had no intention of giving up slavery after the war ended and did not want to give blacks any ideas about demanding freedom; northern slave traders wanted to continue with their profitable pursuit. Both sides therefore agreed to forego accusing the king of engaging in the slave trade and forcing slavery upon them against their wishes. It was more prudent to adhere to "glittering generalities" vaguely connecting the status of the black with the philosophy of freedom for all men. If anyone tried in the future to apply the declaration of rights to blacks, the founding fathers could always point out that this paragraph had been eliminated. The precedent having been set, everything that followed was a natural consequence of this line of thinking.[3]

From the beginning of hostilities in 1775, the Patriots had to grapple with the status of blacks, both free and otherwise, in the war with the British. Some blacks fought at Lexington and Concord in April 1775. In May 1775, the Committee on Safety, commonly known as the Hancock and Warren Committee, took up the matter of blacks in the armed forces and concluded that only free men should be enlisted, since using slaves would be "inconsistent with the principles that are to be supported." Some blacks were allowed to take part in the Battle of Bunker Hill and had to be manumitted (released from slavery) so that they could join the army.

An overall policy for military service, formulated shortly after General Washington took command, averred that services of the black were not needed. An order to recruiting officers stated that they were not to enlist "any deserter from the ministerial Army, nor any stroller, Negro or vagabond or person suspected of being an enemy to the liberty of America nor any under eighteen years of age." This was indicative of the blacks' status in slaveholders' minds at that time. Edward Rutledge of South Carolina confirmed this by introducing a motion in the Continental Congress calling for all blacks to be discharged from the army. After due deliberations in war councils and civilian groups, it was agreed that blacks should not be recruited. In November, General Washington issued a formal order instructing recruiters not to enlist Negroes, boys unable to bear arms, or old men unable to endure the fatigues of campaign. Thus blacks, both free and slave, were rejected from the new army under George Washington.[4]

At the time George Washington issued his order, Lord Dunsmore, the Governor of Virginia, issued a proclamation that caused immediate concern among slaveholders. In part, he said, "I do hereby ... declare all indentured servants, Negroes, or others free, that are able and willing to bear arms, they joining his Majesty's troops, as soon as may be, for the more speedily reducing this colony to a proper dignity." Washington was alarmed when he learned of Dunsmore's designs, as wholesale enlistment of blacks in the British army would have been dangerous for the Patriots. In a letter to Richard Henry Lee, Washington asserted that if Dunsmore was not crushed before spring, he would become their cause's most formidable enemy, because his strength would increase "as a snowball, by rolling, and faster, if some expedient cannot be hit upon to convince the slave and servants of the impotency of his designs."[5]

Washington quickly reported to the president of the Congress that he was permitting free blacks to enlist in the army. He said that blacks discarded from the American army would join the British army if not allowed to serve with the patriots. Congress approved Washington's action for free blacks but made it clear that slaves were not to be admitted. In consequence, many slaves, seeking freedom, ran away to join the British lines. Edmund Pendleton wrote to Richard Henry Lee that slaves were flocking to Dunsmore. Dunsmore himself reported to the British secretary of state that Negro enlistments were proceeding very well. Wherever it went, the British armies attracted many blacks. As late as 1781, Richard Henry Lee wrote to his brother that two neighbors had lost "every slave they had in the world." This was true for almost all slaveowners with holdings near any location approached by the enemy.[6]

The British bid to wrest away blacks led the colonists to liberalize policies toward Negroes, especially in the North. A New York law permitted the army to accept black substitutes for whites who had been drafted. Virginia started permitting mulattos and blacks with certificates of freedom secured from a justice of the peace to enlist. Rhode Island and Massachusetts changed their laws to permit black slaves to enlist. North Carolina decided that penalties against fugitive slaves would not be applied to blacks who enlisted in the Patriot army. As black enlistments increased, Massachusetts and Rhode Island formed their own black regiments. New Hampshire offered black soldiers the same enlistment incentives it gave to whites and masters were also paid bounties for freeing their slaves to fight. Before the end of the war, most states, as well as the Continental Congress, were enlisting slaves with the promise that they would receive their freedom at the end of their service.

Most blacks in the Patriot army were from the North while the majority of blacks in America were slaves in the South, where matters were very different. Although black slaves made up a third of the Southern population, the planters there had no intention of involving blacks in the Revolutionary War. Allowing the blacks to participate would lend a powerful argument to those who might later contend that Negroes should share liberty's blessings in a land they had helped to defend. Most Southern slaveholders preferred abandoning the Revolution to engaging slaves in the war. They maintained that if they had to give up their slaves to the army, it would be unjust; this would require planters to bear a disproportionate share of the burden of defense, sacrificing their property for the safety of the whole. In their view, British rule could not be worse than relying on Negroes to defend the country. That was not independence, but a new kind of dependence.[7]

In consequence, Southern states sharpened their vigilance to prevent black slaves from running to British lines. Several states authorized augmented patrols to pick up fugitives and return them to their masters. Georgia directed one-third of the troops raised in each county to stay in their home counties to guard against slave uprisings and mass flights. Slaveowners in Virginia and North Carolina locked up their small boats to prevent slaves from stealing off down the river at night. Others removed their slaves from coastal areas and sent them to work in lead mines and elsewhere in the back country, far from British lines. Showcase executions were staged to frighten slaves who might be tempted to flee. In South Carolina, one free Negro was hanged and then burnt in August 1775, despite the Governor's protest, because the executed man had allegedly been arming slaves and urging them to flee to the British.[8]

Thus, during the war of independence, Northern and middle-state slaveholders made tall promises to discourage blacks from joining the British. However, after the war, there was hardly any change in the condition of blacks who continued to live as slaves and untouchables. Some masters sought to repossess former slaves who had fought in the war, leading George Washington to appoint several courts of inquiry to establish the validity of such claims. Finally, Virginia passed a law granting freedom to blacks who could prove they had served in the war on the Patriot side. A clear distinction had to be made so that blacks who merely ran away from their masters or escaped to British lines were not rewarded for this conduct. Even George Washington expressed alarm at the news that blacks were embarking with the defeated British fleet at various American ports and asked a friend in New York to help him retrieve some of his own runaways whom he suspected of being in that vicinity.

The Slaveholders' Constitution

After winning the war of independence, slaveholders used their power to structure the Constitution so that blacks were the responsibility of individual states and out of the reach of the federal government. The founding fathers agreed that although slavery was recognized, it should not be sanctioned by the Constitution. The words "slave" or "slavery" should not mar the Constitution; so great an inconsistency must not be proclaimed to the world. In the end they did, however, write slavery into the Constitution after a long debate and only non-slaveholders were deceived. This inclusion took the form of three clauses: counting blacks for Congressional representation, the ban on importing slaves, and the fugitive slave clause providing that slaves who fled from one state to another would be returned to their masters if apprehended.

At the Constitutional Convention, the delegates from Georgia and South Carolina wanted to count slaves in determining Congressional representation due to the large slave population in their states. Northern delegates wanted black slaves to be treated as property and, therefore, not counted for representation. This was a consistent demand of the Northerners, since there were few blacks in the North and most Northern whites wanted to rid themselves of even those few. Governor Morris declared that the people of Pennsylvania would revolt if placed on an equal footing with slaves. The Constitutional Convention therefore compromised by splitting the difference and counting a black slave as equivalent to three-fifths of a white man for the purpose of Congressional representation. The compromise was stated as follows:

Representatives and direct taxes shall be apportioned among the several States which may be included within this Union, according to their respective numbers, which shall be determined by adding to the whole number of free persons including those bound to service for a term of years, and excluding Indians not taxed, three-fifths of all other persons.[9]

It was significant that blacks were not referred to directly as slaves, but in a roundabout way. The convention circumvented the basic problem of blacks and left the solution to future generations. As blacks were not citizens and could not vote, providing federal representation to them was an absurd proposition. Under the federal ratio clause, a slaveholder who owned five slaves was allowed three Congressional representation units, while his fellow countryman who owned five horses or five ships would have only one unit. This representation system gave constitutional sanction to the fact that the United States comprised some persons who were "free" and others who were not. It established a new principle for American democracy: a slaveholder had more votes than a non-slaveholder. With one stroke, despite the disclaimers of James Madison, this representational formula acknowledged slavery and rewarded slaveholders. Madison observed:

Slaves are considered by the law in some respects, as persons, and in other respects as property. In being compelled to labor for a master; in being vendible by one master to another master, and in being restrained in his liberty and chastised in his body, by the capricious will of another—the slave may appear to be degraded from the human rank, and classed with irrational animals which fall under the legal denomination of property. In being protected, on the other hand, in his life and in his limbs ... and in being punishable himself for all violence committed against others—the slave is no less evidently regarded by the law as ... [a] person, not as a mere article of property.[10]

In the end the federal ratio clause in the Constitution would prove a major disaster for the nation. The federal government collected no revenue from this clause as the states were never assessed to finance the federal government. As noted by Judge William Paterson of New Jersey and others at the convention, it encouraged the slave trade as the Southern states would seek to increase their strength in Congress by importing and smuggling slaves. For the Northern states, the federal ratio clause was a constant reminder of slavery's injustice—because they did not have any black slaves to increase their own representation. If the federal ratio clause had been kept out of the Constitution, the Northern states would not have cared what the Southern states did to their slaves and would gladly have allowed the South to kidnap all free Northern blacks as fugitives. The Thirteenth Amendment to the Constitution became necessary after the Civil War to neutralize the federal ratio clause.[11]

The debate over the role of blacks in the Revolutionary War once again emphasized the need to restrict the proportion of blacks in the population in both the North and the South. The Northern delegates wanted to ban the import of blacks because they would only increase the South's leverage in Congress under the federal ratio clause. Virginia and Maryland went along with the North and banned the importation of blacks because, being overstocked with slaves, they knew the danger a surplus held for the value of their investment. However, South Carolina and Georgia, aware of the profit potential in growing short staple cotton in the back country, refused to confederate on "such unequal terms." The fear of rupture at this critical moment led the Northern and upper Southern states to compromise with the lower Southern states to permit the slave trade to continue for twenty years, as follows: "The migration or Importation of such Persons as any of the States now existing shall think proper to admit, shall not be prohibited by the congress prior to the Year one thousand eight hundred and eight, but a Tax or duty may be imposed on such Importation, not exceeding ten dollars for each Person."[12]

Here again was an implicit acceptance of black slavery by the Constitutional convention. However, during the next twenty years, fear of blacks was reinforced in the colonies by the French Revolution and the subsequent takeover on the island of Santo Domingo, leading to formation of the Republic of Haiti. In consequence, Congress was able to pass a law in 1808 prohibiting further slave importation. At this time, a crucial challenge against federal authority to enforce this law was mounted by congressmen from the Deep South. If the government could regulate coastwise slave trade among the states, could it not regulate all interstate domestic slave trading? Southern slaveholders were convinced that slavery could endure without a legal foreign slave trade, but transporting slaves across state lines was crucial for slavery's survival. If the federal government could regulate slave importation, it might be led to regulate domestic slave trading. It had the power of life and death over the entire slavery system. Therefore, Southern congressmen and senators fought to make practical enforcement of the law impossible. Although Jefferson signed the Act into law, it was a law, as noted by historian Ulrich B. Phillips, "which might be evaded with relative ease wherever public sanction was weak."[13]

The law banning slave importation provided that smuggled blacks were to be taken from their captors and delivered to officers of the state into which they had been imported, for disposal under that state's laws. In practice, this provision, when enforced at all, appears to have turned into an arrangement whereby slaves seized by a customs collector were delivered on demand to agents of the governor, then committed under bond to a planter, whereby the nominal bond was simply forfeited. In one recorded case, smuggled slaves seized by a United States marshal in Alabama were taken from his jurisdiction by a federal judge; the judge then appointed a group of his cronies as the slaves' "guardians." These guardians rented out the slaves, making a nice profit for themselves and depriving the marshal of his own fair "pittance."[14]

When the South won clear recognition at the Constitutional Convention for states to continue slavery, they demanded that Northern states give up fugitive slaves to their owners. At this stage there was no opposition to this, and the provision was included in the Constitution as follows:

> No person held to service or labor in one State, under the
> laws thereof, escaping into another, shall, in consequence
> of any law or regulation therein, be discharged from such
> service or labor, but shall be delivered up on claim of the
> party to whom such service or labor may be due.[15]

The casual way in which this clause—so pregnant with peril to blacks, both slave and free—was adopted tells volumes about the plight of blacks in a nation governed by whites. The United States was a miserable place for blacks because the government was in no way answerable to them. While Southern slaveowners wanted to enforce their property rights over blacks in all the states, the Northerners did not want blacks among them and were willing to oblige. As General Charles Pinckney noted in a 1788 speech urging ratification of the Constitution: "We have obtained a right to recover our slaves in whatever part of America they may take refuge, which is a right we had not before."[16]

As enforcement of the Constitution's fugitive slave clause was not clear, Congress passed legislation in 1793 empowering the master of an interstate fugitive to seize him wherever found, carry him before any federal or state magistrate in the vicinity, and procure a certificate warranting his removal to the state from which he had fled. A $500 fine was imposed on anyone obstructing the recovery of runaways. Although the law was severe in its treatment of people who might help slaves to escape, it prescribed no penalties for those who sought to kidnap and re-enslave freed Negroes. It failed to protect either blacks' civil rights or liberty.[17]

The Act of 1793 was not good enough for Southern slaveholders, and jockeying for power in Congress continued until the passage of the Fugitive Slave Act of 1850, which ensured a speedier return of runaway slaves. Any claimant who could establish proof of ownership by affidavit before a special commissioner could take possession of a black. The captive had no recourse to common legal safeguards such as a jury trial or judicial hearing. Indeed, the new law awarded the commissioner $10 if he directed a captive's return but only $5 if he ordered a runaway's release. The relative cost of paperwork involved in the two transactions allegedly justified this difference. Critics, however, termed it an open bribe.

The Act further empowered federal officers to call upon all citizens to help enforce its provisions and imposed fines, imprisonment, and civil damages for concealing or rescuing a fugitive. It was obviously a threat to free Northern blacks, who could "mistakenly" be identified as fugitives and taken South. Encouraged by the new legislation, slaveholders appeared in Northern communities or employed agents to reclaim their lost slaves. Paid informers who would testify to anything could be used to purchase Negroes from the North by paying the commissioner $10 apiece. The law's operation confirmed the impression that it was rigged in favor of the claimants. In the first fifteen months after its passage, eighty-four "fugitives" were returned to slavery and only five released. Rather than risk the prospect of being kidnapped by slaveholders and their agents from the South for a new lifetime of slavery, Northern blacks fled to Canada or England, ridding the Northern states of blacks.[18]

As far as blacks were concerned, whether slave or free, the Constitution was rigged by slaveholders so that the benefit of the doubt lay with the states. According to General Charles Pinckney of South Carolina, in a 1788 speech urging ratification of the Constitution, "We have a security that the general government can never emancipate them [slaves], for no such authority is granted; and it is admitted, on all hands, that the general government has no powers but what are expressly granted by the Constitution, and that all rights not expressed were reserved by the several states." Various "internal regulations" left to the states by the Constitution included "instruction of slaves in morality and religion, rules governing their care and maintenance, marriage laws and family life, and provision for cases of 'sickness, age and infirmity.'" Significantly, included in this catalogue of responsibilities of the states was the "seizure, transportation, or sale of free Negroes." The fugitive slave clause required the federal government to protect white citizens against the flight of slaves. By this interpretation, however, no agency of government was authorized to prevent the re-enslavement of free blacks.[19]

Blacks' Federal Status

Reflecting the popular conception of the United States as a white man's country, early Congressional legislation excluded blacks from certain federal rights and privileges and sanctioned a number of territorial and state restrictions. In 1790, the Congress limited naturalization to white aliens. In 1792, a militia was organized and membership restricted to able-bodied white male citizens. In 1810, blacks were excluded from working in the U.S. Mail Service. In 1820, Congress authorized the citizens of Washington, D.C., to elect "white city officials and to adopt a code governing free blacks and slaves." Moreover, the nation repeatedly approved the admission of new states whose constitutions severely restricted free blacks' legal rights.

It appears that from the outset the Congress had no intention of treating blacks, slave or free, as citizens of the United States. The Naturalization Act of 1790 extended citizenship to all free white persons who had resided in the United States and shown good behavior for one year, who expressed the intention of remaining, and took an oath of allegiance. During discussion the pros and cons of including Roman Catholics and Jews as citizens was debated, but there was not even a suggestion of including blacks. In 1857, the Supreme Court of the United States dispelled all doubts regarding the status of the country's black residents. By then the Chief Justice, Roger B. Taney, could find appropriate precedents in Congressional Acts and the executive department's conduct. According to Taney, no black could qualify as a citizen of the United States. So far as the Constitution was concerned, he added, blacks had no rights that whites were bound to respect.[20]

To support his claim that Negroes were not citizens of the United States, Chief Justice Taney cited the refusal of secretaries of state to grant passports to Negroes. Secretary of State James Buchanan explained in 1847 that regular passports certified that the bearer was a citizen of the United States. Consequently, it was customary to grant free Negroes in the merchant marine special certificates "suited to the nature of the case" rather than passports. Two years later, Secretary of State John M. Clayton insisted that no passports had been granted to Negroes and that protection abroad had been granted to them only when they were in the service of the United States' diplomatic agents.

The question of Negro citizenship, Assistant Secretary of State J. A. Thomas noted in 1856, had arisen repeatedly in both federal and state governments. In Attorneys General William Wirt and Caleb Cushings' opinions, and certain state judicial decisions, Negroes could not be regarded as citizens, either at home or beyond the federal government's jurisdiction. Nevertheless, the State Department was willing to grant qualified Negroes special forms certifying that they were free and born in the United States. If any of them should be wronged by a foreign government "while within its jurisdiction for a legal and proper purpose," American diplomatic officials would seek to protect their rights.[21]

So far as mail delivery by blacks was concerned, the Post Office Department simply enforced an earlier Congressional Act that it helped to conceive. In a confidential letter to the chairman of a senate committee, Postmaster General Gideon Granger explained in 1802 that major objections had been raised against Negro mail carriers:

> ... of a nature too delicate to engrave into a report which may become public, yet too important to be omitted or passed over without full consideration. Such Negroes constituted a peril to the nation's security, for employment in the postal service afforded them an opportunity to coordinate insurrectionary activities, mix with other people, and acquire subversive information and ideas.

The Postmaster General's warning aroused sufficient alarm to spur legislative action. In 1810, Congress ruled that "no other than a free white person shall be employed in conveying the mail," and provided fines for any offending mail contractors. Not until after the Civil War began did Congress consider changes.[22]

Negro rights to the public domain were always restricted. On several occasions, exclusionary sentiment prompted Congress to pass amendments restricting blacks' rights through land and homestead bills. In organizing the Oregon and New Mexico territories, for example, Congress agreed to limit public land grants to white settlers. An Ohio representative exclaimed:

> I have no sympathy for Negroes in a common residence with the white race. God had ordained, and no human law can contravene the ordinance, that the races shall be separate and distinct ... I will vote against any measure that has a tendency to prolong their common residence in this confederacy, or any portion of it.

Prior to 1857 the federal government had no consistent policy governing Negros' rights to public land. The United States Supreme Court's Dred Scott decision dealt black rights a crushing blow. Shortly afterwards, the Commissioner of the General Land Office announced that since Negroes were not citizens, they could not qualify for preemption benefits. Consequently, any black who desired to settle newly opened western lands now faced not only various territory and state anti-immigration laws, but also the federal government's open hostility.[23]

Efforts by a few Southern states to control American and British black seamen's movements required the attorney general's opinion to define the Constitutional position on free blacks. Obsessed with fear that Northern or foreign blacks had instigated a recent slave uprising, in 1822 the South Carolina legislature directed that black seamen be imprisoned while vessels employing them remained in port. Unless the vessel's owner paid the costs of such confinement, Negro seamen were to be sold to recover the damages. Several other Southern states adopted virtually identical measures. Attorney General John Berrien confirmed their action and found the legislation to be a lawful exercise of state police powers. "The general right of a State to regulate persons of color within its own limits," Berrien ruled, "is one clearly recognized by the tenth amendment to the Constitution to be drawn into controversy." In this case, according to Berrien's decision, the state had simply moved to protect its white and colored citizens from the "moral contagion" of insurrection.[24]

In 1842, Senator John Calhoun succeeded in excluding blacks from the navy except as cooks, stewards, and servants, defeating a proposal that they be recruited for service in "unhealthy climates." Calhoun asserted that it was wrong "to bring those who have to sustain the honor and glory of the country down to a footing of the negro race—to be degraded by being mingled and mixed up with that inferior race." Northern sentiment regarding civil rights for blacks was explained by Representative Henry C. Murphy of New York as follows: "As long as that degraded race remained in the South, it might be happy and contented. Once Negroes entered the free States, however, they would certainly, be the objects of contumely and scorn." Under these circumstances he appealed to the South to retain its Negro population. Indeed, he stated, he would favor the adoption of severe laws "against any who shall bring the wretched beings to our free States, there to taint the blood of whites, or to destroy their own race by vicious courses." Thus for different reasons, the North and South jointly denied citizenship and civil rights to blacks at the federal level.[25]

Code Noir Civil Rights

In any event, civil rights for slaves were inconceivable under the South's Protestant slavery code. The general attitude was that if blacks were going to be slaves forever, why bother with civil rights? Every slave had to have a master to watch over him; therefore the question of civil rights and relations with non-slaveholders did not arise. However, the Catholic slavery code's operation in Louisiana, before it became a territory and then a state, made it apparent that a slave could have civil rights. The Catholic slavery code encouraged manumitting slaves who had opportunities to purchase their own freedom or whose freedom was purchased by relatives. Blacks were allowed to join the militia and give evidence in court when necessary. Slaves also had some protection: the church protected them as Christians, while the king extended them some rights and protection as citizens and subjects.

The *Code Noir* assumed the existence of a free Negro population when Louisiana was a French colony and blacks were granted "the same rights, privileges, and immunities which free persons enjoy." Any master twenty-five years of age or older could manumit his slaves, but only with the permission of the colony's Superior Council. This latter provision was intended to prevent masters from freeing slaves who were old, sick, or otherwise apt to become charges on the colony. The Superior Council was instructed to grant permission for good reason. Therefore, the slave was permitted freedom if the master was father of the mulatto child; if the slave had attained a level of education and skills sufficient to purchase his own freedom; or if a free black wanted to purchase a slave spouse or child. The benefit of the doubt was always on the side of freedom; a slave could be freed by the master in his will, or if the slave accompanied the master on a trip to France (Louisiana being a colony of France with laws based on the *Code Noir* of 1724), or if the slave became a priest in the Catholic Church.[26]

There were a number of cases in Louisiana history of slaves being purchased in order to be emancipated. The St. Charles Parish Police Jury authorized the emancipation of a mulatto named Charles in 1842 because Charles' late master had bought him in order to set him free. Free Negroes often bought relatives in order to manumit them. Two free men of color who wished to emancipate their recently purchased sister were authorized to do so in 1832. Authorities were usually sympathetic to such cases during the early part of the century when the Catholic slavery code's influence still prevailed.[27]

Some slaves were sufficiently fortunate to be able to buy their freedom in Louisiana by hiring out their own time. Under these circumstances the slave usually turned over some amount agreed on in advance to his master and kept any surplus earnings for himself. In 1849, Amades Landry was authorized to emancipate Eulalie, a slave who had purchased her freedom.[28]

Slaves could hire themselves out to those in need of labor who contracted with the slaves themselves for Sunday work. The usual wage for this labor appears to have been fifty to seventy-five cents a day. Thus on Sunday, September 26, 1841, a storekeeper hired six Negroes to cut hay for six *escalin chacun*. (The word *escalin*, which originally referred to a small Dutch coin, was used in southern Louisiana to mean "bit.") An account left by a Frenchman named Dumont during the colonial period gives this explanation:

> Most of the slaves clear lands which they cultivate to their own profit, they grow cotton, tobacco, and other products which they sell. There are settlers who give their Negroes Saturday and Sunday for their own; and during this time the master is relieved of care for their nourishment; they work then for other Frenchmen who do not have slaves, and who pay them. Those who live in the capital or its environs take advantage, ordinarily, of the two hours rest given them at noon to go cut wood that they afterwards sell in the city, others sell ashes, or the fruits of the country when one is in season. Some of the Negroes do so well that they have earned the wherewithal to buy their liberty, and have built their habitations in this province in imitation of the French.[29]

Travel was another route to freedom. During the early part of the nineteenth century, it was not uncommon for wealthy Louisianians of French ancestry to travel to France. If such travelers took slaves with them, the slaves became free under French law, and Louisiana courts recognized them as such. This escape hatch in the Catholic slavery code was closed by the Louisiana legislature in 1846, when the legislature ruled that going into any free territory, with or without his owner's consent, did not affect a slave's status.[30]

Three-fourths of all Negroes emancipated in Louisiana were mulattos, and only concubinage would explain why so many young women with young children were emancipated. The Louisiana Supreme Court noted in 1845: "The testimony establishes that the deceased was living in open and notorious concubinage with a mulatress named Fanchon, who ... was later emancipated." One

Sinnot provided that his natural son Thomas, a mulatto, should be set free and should inherit all his property. Sinnot's wife was, however, to have possession for the rest of her life.[31]

Using armed slaves for defense was not unheard of during the colonial period in Louisiana. During the Natchez Massacre of 1729, armed slaves fought against the Indians so bravely that it was proposed that those who had given the best account of themselves should be freed. Consideration was also given to a plan to form a regular company of black soldiers. In January 1804, a free Negro militia marched in force at the ceremony transferring Louisiana to the United States. Federal officials disliked the idea of armed, free Negro militiamen and suggested the governor use his discretion to incorporate free Negro units into the white American forces. The governor initially persuaded the free Negro militia to accept white officers, but by October 1804 lawmakers deactivated the company by simply omitting it from the Act establishing a territorial militia. After destroying the free black militia, in 1806 the territorial legislature barred free Negroes from carrying guns without proof of their status from a justice of the peace.[32]

Matters began to change after Louisiana became a United States territory; and by the time of the Civil War, the Protestant slavery code was firmly entrenched. Since the Protestant slavery code could not tolerate free blacks, slave emancipation had to be prevented at all costs, and steps were taken to get rid of free blacks by every possible means. Under the Act of 1807, no slave could be freed unless he was at least thirty years old and had not been guilty of bad conduct for the preceding four years. Estate executors who were under instructions to emancipate slaves belonging to the estate had to follow the same procedure. An Act of 1830 placed barriers against emancipation with a provision that any person who freed a slave must post a bond of one thousand dollars to guarantee that the freed slave would leave the state within thirty days. An Act of 1842 provided that a Negro who returned to Louisiana after being freed and expelled was subject to five years' imprisonment; and it specifically stated that a master might not take a slave to free territory and then bring him back without making him subject to the same punishment.[33]

As the law did not completely prevent the emancipation of slaves, the legislature ruled in 1852 that no slave could be emancipated under any condition unless he was to be sent out of the United States within twelve months. The master who set a slave free was required to post $150, which was to be used to pay for transportation to Africa. When the 1852 Act resulted in a flood of petitions to the legislature for special authorizations to emancipate, a new Act passed in 1855 required a person who desired to emancipate a slave to bring a suit against the State of Louisiana in a district court. This law was declared unconstitutional by the Louisiana Supreme Court, so in 1857 the legislature ruled that "from and after the passage of this Act, no slave shall be emancipated in this state."

The Protestant slavery code triumphed fully in 1859 when the legislature allowed free Negroes to choose masters and re-enslave themselves. Furthermore, if a mother with children under ten years of age so enslaved herself, the children automatically became slaves.[34]

Southern Civil Rights

Since free blacks were not supposed to exist in the Protestant slavery code, all possibilities for manumission or emancipation had to be discouraged. Every slaveholding state restricted manumission of Negro slaves. Several states prohibited domestic manumission— that is, manumission to take effect within the state. In Mississippi, Alabama, and Maryland, manumission by will was void. In South Carolina, Georgia, Alabama, and Mississippi. manumission was valid only with the consent of the state legislature. In 1801, a Georgia master was fined two hundred dollars for attempting to manumit a slave without the legislature's consent and the slave continued in bondage as before. In 1818, it imposed a fine of one thousand dollars on anyone giving effect to a last will and testament that freed a slave or permitted him to work for himself beyond a master's control.[35]

Denying the slave his civil rights was the easy part. A greater challenge for the Protestant slavery code was controlling free blacks, the trouble-makers, who were not supposed to exist. The first step was to prohibit them from immigrating into the state. Virginia took the lead in 1793. At about the same time, Georgia required that all free black immigrants give proof of their industry and honesty within six months of their arrival or face deportation. Two years later, North Carolina limited free Negro immigrants by requiring Negroes entering the state to post a bond of two hundred pounds or be arrested, jailed, and sold at public auction. In 1800, South Carolina banned free Negro entry. In 1807, when Maryland whites complained that "Many beggarly blacks have been vomited upon us," the state legislature enacted a similar ban. Three years later, Delaware enacted a total prohibition and Georgia slapped a twenty-dollar tax on all Negro freemen entering the state.[36]

After 1822, free Negroes in South Carolina were subject to a series of heavy taxes and compelled to have white guardians. Thus the requirement of a two-hundred dollar bond in North Carolina was not severe in comparison with the treatment blacks were receiving in neighboring states. In 1827, the North Carolina General Assembly passed a law banning free Negroes from migrating into the state and subjected them to a five-hundred dollar fine for breaking the law. Any black who was unable to pay the fine was liable to be sold into slavery for a term not exceeding ten years. Anyone guilty of transporting free Negroes into the state was also subject to the five-hundred dollar fine.[37]

Another way of disposing of free blacks was for the state to do nothing if they were stolen or kidnapped and sold into slavery. An Act of 1779 declared it illegal to steal, carry off, and sell free Negroes, but provided no penalties for such activity. Therefore, in 1801 a new Act provided penalties to correct this glaring omission. However, enforcement was left at the discretion of the authorities. The *Raleigh Register* reported the following incident in 1801:

> On the 29th Instant, about midnight, four men came to the House of Valentine Lowst, an aged free Negro, who resides on Leek Creek, in Wake County ... instantly knocked down the old man and his wife and beat them

to such a degree as scarcely to leave life, and whilst they were in that situation the robbers carried off two of their children.

In 1772, a free Negro mother became alarmed at the disappearance of her children and placed an advertisement with their description in the *Raleigh Register* requesting information in which she noted: "It is supposed that some dishonest Person has taken them off, for the purpose of selling them as Slaves."[38]

Prohibitions on interstate migration still left state lawmakers with the problem of controlling free Negroes within their borders. To distinguish slaves from free blacks, Southern states established a system of registering free blacks. A 1785 North Carolina law required all urban free Negroes to register with the town commissioners and to wear a shoulder patch inscribed with the word "Free." In 1793, the Virginia General Assembly, complaining of the "great inconvenience" of slaves passing as free in cities, required urban free Negroes to register with the town clerk. The clerk would record their name, sex, color, age, stature, identifying marks, and how they were freed. The "Register of Free Negroes" was to be kept in the town hall and a copy, which had to be renewed annually for a fee of twenty-five cents, issued to every free Negro.[39]

Another method of controlling free blacks was to pass laws against vagrancy. In 1795, Maryland required that all indigent free Negroes be jailed and either give security for their good behavior or be expelled from the state. Free Negro vagrants who remained in the state were to be sold into slavery for six months, and at the end of their service the process was to be re-initiated. An 1801 Virginia law with a similar goal declared that all registered free Negroes who "intruded" into another county could be arrested and, if judged vagrants, fined and sold in default of the fine and court costs. Other states attempted to extort free Negro labor directly. In 1808, Georgia legislators, complaining about the "dangerous tendency" of permitting "free negroes and persons of color to rove about the country in idleness and dissipation," empowered the justice of the peace and any three freeholders to bind out all such free Negro men between eight and twenty-one years of age. In 1810, Georgia took the final step of inviting free Negroes to take white guardians to supervise their affairs.[40]

Another way of solving the free Negro problem was to make life miserable for them by denying them their civil rights so that they would beg for protection as slaves under a new master. Thus Lucinda, who had been manumitted under a will requiring her removal to another state, petitioned the Virginia legislature in 1815 to become a slave of her slave husband's master. William Bass petitioned the South Carolina general assembly, stating:

> that as a free Negro he is preyed upon by every sharper with whom he comes in contact, and that he is very poor though an able-bodied man and is charged with and punished for every offense, guilty or not, committed, in his neighborhood, that he is without house or home, and lives a thousand times harder and in more destitution than the slaves of many planters in the district.

He, accordingly, asked permission by special Act to become a slave of Philip W. Pledger, who had consented to receive him if he could lawfully do so.[41]

To provide for the systematic conversion of free blacks into slaves, the legislators of several states from Maryland to Texas enacted laws in the mid- and late-1850s authorizing free persons of color, at their own instance and with the approval of magistrates, to enslave themselves to such masters as they might select. The Virginia law, enacted at the beginning of 1856, safeguarded creditors' claims against a Negro by requiring a month's notice during which protests might be entered and also required the prospective master to pay the state half the Negro's appraised value.[42]

Many Southerners called for complete expulsion of free blacks or the re-enslavement of those who would not leave. Petitions poured into state legislatures demanding laws that would implement one or the other of these policies. In 1849, a petition from Augusta County, Virginia, asked the legislature to make an appropriation for a program to gradually expel blacks. All free blacks who refused to go to Liberia should be expelled from the state within five years, it stated. In 1859, the Arkansas legislature required sheriffs to order the state's handful of free Negroes to leave. Those who remained were to be hired out as slaves. In their final sessions before the Civil War, Missouri and Florida lawmakers ordered free Negroes from their states under threat of enslavement. Maryland lawmakers provided for a referendum in which whites might vote blacks into slavery in 1860.[43]

Just before the Civil War, most Southern states were prepared to enslave all free blacks who remained within their boundaries. The border states were trying to wrestle with the free black problem by controlling their movements between counties, restricting their interactions with slaves, preventing access to education, limiting access to firearms and liquor, and declining their offers to join the militia. This resulted in a "Free Negro Code," which further curtailed the civil rights of that unfortunate group. If the border states were to maintain the status quo, freedom of thought had to be restricted, since the system's critics were becoming more active. The Assembly of North Carolina therefore passed an act to prevent circulation of seditious publications. It made it unlawful to circulate any books and papers that tended to "excite insurrection, conspiracy or resistance in the slaves or free Negroes and persons of color within the State."[44]

The Legislature of North Carolina in 1830 restricted free Negroes' movements with an Act against peddling wares out of one's home county unless a license was granted by the county court. To grant the license seven or more justices had to review the applicant's good character and the clerk was entitled to eighty cents. Free Negroes violating this Act were subject to a fifty-dollar fine for each offense or imprisonment not exceeding six months at the discretion of the court.[45]

Then came the firearms restrictions. After 1840, North Carolina restricted firearm possession and consumption of spirituous liquor by free Negroes. The law did not forbid possession and carrying of firearms but restricted it to those free Negroes who could get a license. When the Act was challenged before the state supreme court, the judge ruled:

> From the earliest period of our history free people of color have been among us as a separate and distinct class requiring from necessity in many cases, separate and distinct legislation. The Act of 1840 is one of police regulation. It does not deprive the free man of color of the right to carry arms ... but subjects it to the control of the county court, giving them power to say ... who of this class of persons shall have a right to a license, or whether any shall.

In 1856, a group of Robeson County citizens asked the Assembly to pass an Act providing that no free Negro be permitted to have a gun and also regulate the possession of dogs by them. Finally, in 1861, a law was passed that made the possession of arms by Negroes a misdemeanor punishable by a fine of not less than fifty dollars.[46]

By disenfranchising the free Negro vote in 1835, North Carolina was merely catching up with the other Southern states. At no time during the national period could free Negroes vote in Virginia or South Carolina. After 1789, Negroes in Georgia were excluded from suffrage on the basis of an understanding, and in 1799 Kentucky introduced "free white men" into its franchise clause. In the nineteenth century, other Southern states fell into line, including Maryland in 1809, and Florida, Alabama, and Mississippi when they entered the union. In 1834, Tennessee restricted suffrage to white men.[47]

The experience of Charleston free Negroes indicates how vehemently whites opposed any improvement in blacks' status. In 1791, Peter Mathews, a free Negro butcher, along with several other free Negro artisans and tradesmen, petitioned the state legislature to expand their rights as free men. The law which barred them from testifying in court against whites "for which cause many Culprits have escaped punishment," made it impossible for them to collect their debts, and subjected them to numerous frauds. At the same time, they were tried without jury in courts in which slaves could testify. For many years, Mathews went on, free Negroes had supported the government, paid their taxes and upheld the peace. "Your Memorialist," he tactfully concluded, "do not presume to hope that they shall be put on an equal footing with free White Citizens of the State in general but humbly solicit such dictate in their favor by repealing the clauses of the Act above mentioned ... " Although the petition did not threaten the whites, it received no hearing from the legislature. However, as an answer, three years later white vigilantes broke into his house looking for arms, fearing insurrection.[48]

In almost all the Southern states before the Civil War the slaves' most important civil right, manumission, was severely restricted if not practically eliminated. Even in Louisiana the Catholic slavery code was replaced by the Protestant slavery code after it joined the union, and the civil rights of slave and free blacks became indistinguishable from the lack of rights in other Southern states.

Northern Civil Rights

Northern whites attacked the civil rights problem in a way more suited to their economic situation. The Northern states, with the exception of New York and New Jersey, had only a small number of blacks, and their economies were not dependent on black labor. They further lessened their dependence on blacks by encouraging white immigration from Ireland and Europe. The North, too, did not want any confusion regarding free blacks and black slaves. Black slaves provided unwanted competition for white immigrants who provided a major part of the labor needed in the textile mills, iron and coal mines, and railroad and canal projects. All the Northern states therefore decided to abolish slavery. By 1830, whether through legislative, judicial, or constitutional action, black slavery had been virtually abolished in the North.

Northern slaveholders did not have to suffer any economic losses, because they could sell their slaves to the South, where there was a great demand for them on cotton plantations. As it was, all the slave trade and supply of slaves to the South was controlled and financed by Northern Yankees. The North continued to grow, its population doubling from 1830 to 1860 from white immigrants who reduced the North's free blacks to an insignificant minority.

The principal for abolition of slavery was the competition slaves offered to non-slaveholders and poor whites, and therefore all poor whites on juries wanted to free black slaves at every opportunity. John Adams, who represented several slaves in such cases, recalled that he "never knew a jury, by a verdict, to determine a Negro to be a slave. They always found them free." This, however, had nothing to do with rights of man and freedom and equality for all men.[49]

The status of the northern blacks depended on their numerical strength, the state's geographic position, political and economic factors, and public opinion. Nearly every Northern state considered and adopted measures to restrict further black immigration. The objective was to settle the race relations problem by expelling blacks, or at least by preventing any sizable increase in their numbers. The white man's argument was based on the dangers that were inherent in integrating blacks into the political and social community, for "the natural tendency has been proved by experience, not to be the elevation of the degraded, but the deterioration, the lowering of the better class, towards the standard of the lower class."[50]

Immediate and practical considerations also prompted demands to exclude blacks or restrict their movements. In the absence of adequate legislation, whites feared that the northern states would be inundated with emancipated blacks who would be nothing but a burden on the community. This fear was particularly strong in those free states bordering slave states, and it prompted most of them to adopt restrictive measures. In defending the Illinois Statute, Senator Stephen A. Douglas asserted that his state would not become "an asylum for all the old and decrepit and broken down Negroes that may emigrate or be sent to it." Indiana also indicated its unwillingness to become "The Liberia of the South." The adoption of restrictions against blacks in western states and territories impelled several older states to pass their own laws.[51]

In several newly formed states, whites threatened drastic action if legislative protections against black immigration were not forthcoming. The people of Southern Illinois, a native warned, "would take the matter into their own hands and commence a war of extermination." An Indianian told a state constitutional convention that "It would be better to kill them off at once, if there is no other way to get rid of them." After all, he added, "We know what the puritans did with the Indians, who were infinitely more magnanimous and less impudent than the colored race." In Southern Ohio, aroused groups stopped an attempt to settle 518 emancipated slaves who formerly belonged to John Randolph in Virginia. Defending their action, an Ohio Congressman warned that, "If the test must come and they must resort to force to effect their object, the banks of the Ohio would be lined with men with muskets on their shoulders to keep off the emancipated slaves." Three states—Illinois, Indiana, and Oregon—incorporated anti-immigration provisions into their Constitutions. In separate votes their electorates overwhelmingly approved the changes.[52]

In 1856, an Indiana court convicted a black man of violating the law by bringing a black woman into the State in order to marry her. The state's Supreme Court upheld the conviction. It declared: "The policy of the State is clear. It is to exclude any further ingress of Negroes and to remove those among us as speedily as possible. The law specifically voided all contracts made with blacks entering the State and this applied to marriage agreements."[53]

Anti-immigration laws provided whites with a convenient excuse for mob violence and frequent harassment of the black population, which was indeed the legislation's intention. An Ohio legislative committee reported in 1838 that:

> It was never believed that the law would ever be complied
> with, nor was it intended by the makers that it ever should
> be. Its evident design was to drive this portion of our pop
> ulation into other States. It was an unrighteous attempt
> to accomplish, indirectly and covertly, what they would
> shrink from doing openly and frankly.[54]

Ohio provided a classic example of how anti-immigration legislation could be invoked to harass black residents. The state's restrictive statutes, enacted in 1804 and 1807 as part of the black laws, compelled blacks entering the state to post a five-hundred dollar bond and produce a court certificate as evidence of their freedom. No effort was made to enforce the bond requirement until 1829, when rapid increases in the black population alarmed Cincinnati. City authorities announced that the black laws would be enforced and ordered blacks to comply or leave within thirty days. Impatient for results, white mobs roamed thorough Cincinnati's Negro quarters, spreading terror and destruction. Subsequently, about 1,500 blacks had to flee to Canada.[55]

By 1840, about ninety-three percent of the Northern blacks lived in states that excluded them from the vote. From the admission of Maine into the Union in 1819 until the end of the Civil War, every new state restricted voting rights to whites in its Constitution. In New Jersey and Connecticut, where no racial distinctions had figured in the original Constitutions, the legislatures limited the right to vote to whites and subsequent Constitutions incorporated the restrictions. A Philadelphian told Alexis de Tocqueville in 1831 that blacks could not appear at the polls without being maltreated. The French traveller asked, "And what becomes of the reign of law in this case?" The Philadelphian replied, "The law with us is nothing if it is not supported by public opinion." In 1837, an English visitor asked why blacks did not vote, since the law did not specifically bar them. He was told: "Just let them try." In July 1837, the Pennsylvania Supreme Court ruled that blacks could not legally exercise the right to vote. The Chief Justice cited a 1795 court decision excluding blacks from voting, and although no record of this case existed, he declared that the memory of a good friend and Philadelphia lawyer was "perfect and entitled to full confidence." Besides, as he proceeded to demonstrate, the decision had been based on "true principles of the Constitution."[56]

Northern whites did not consider it necessary to protect black life or liberty. In the South, a black could not be a witness against a white, he could not sit on a jury, and the idea of a black judge could not even arise. In the North restrictions on black rights extended from the polls to the courtroom. Five states—Illinois, Ohio, Indiana, Iowa, and California—prohibited black testimony in cases where a white man was a party, and Oregon forbade blacks from holding real estate, making contracts, or maintaining lawsuits. Under these circumstances an Oregonian protested that the black man "is cast upon the world with no defense, his life, liberty, his property, his all, are dependent on the caprice, the passion and the inveterate prejudices of not only the community at large but of every felon who may happen to cover an inhuman heart with a white face." This accurately reflected the black man's judicial plight in the Northern free states.[57]

Where courts refused to admit black testimony, there could be no legal protection for blacks. A white man could assault, rob, or even murder a black person in the midst of a number of black witnesses and escape prosecution unless another white man had been present and had agreed to testify. After dismissing a case because black testimony had been admitted, an Ohio judge protested from the bench that in all his judicial experience, he could not recall a single instance where this law had served the purpose of justice. "The white man may now plunder the black, he may abuse his person, he may take his life: He may do this in open daylight and he must go acquitted unless there be some white man present." In 1849, Ohio finally removed the ban on black testimony, but observers admitted that the repealed law was still in force.[58]

Between 1832 and 1849, Philadelphia mobs set off five major anti-black riots. In 1834, a white mob stormed through the black section, clubbed and stoned its victims, destroyed homes, churches, and meeting halls, forced hundreds to flee the city, and left many others homeless. In assessing the riot's cause, a citizens' committee cited frequent hiring of blacks during periods of depression and rising white unemployment as a major factor. At the same time, the blacks' tendency to protect and rescue their brethren when the latter were arrested as fugitive slaves caused problems.[59]

In August, 1843, a Columbia mob invaded the city's black section, destroyed homes, and forced many of its victims to hide in nearby woods until order was restored. Subsequently, white leaders met with black property holders to discuss the disposition of their property at "a fair valuation" and to advise them not to receive any black residents from other areas. Most of the property holders were ready to "sell as fast as funds could be raised." A meeting of local "capitalists" was called to give serious consideration to the "very profitable investment of their funds." Meanwhile, mob violence continued and finally prompted a black coal and lumber dealer to offer his entire stock at fire sale prices in order to close his business.[60]

In the North, blacks were educated in separate schools, punished in separate prisons, nursed in separate hospitals, and buried in separate cemeteries. The black quest for educational opportunities prompted strong and violent protests in the North. The possibility of black children mixing with white in the same classroom aroused even greater fears and passions than those that directed blacks to a secondary place in church, theater, or railroad car. Blacks were expected to be grateful for the privilege of even using these facilities.

Blacks in the North were restricted to menial or unskilled jobs. White men refused to accept black apprentices, thus preventing blacks from attaining many skills. Because of the black man's "untouchable" social status, whites even refused to work under the same roof as blacks. As late as 1855, some eighty-seven percent of employed blacks in New York City worked in menial or unskilled jobs; this reflected their economic condition in other Northern cities too. In New York, Philadelphia, and Boston, black men worked as laborers, mariners, servants, waiters, barbers, coachmen, porters, and second-hand clothing dealers, while women worked as washerwomen, dressmakers, seamstresses, and cooks.

The "untouchable" role served by blacks was alluded to by the Senate Foreign Relations Committee in 1828 when it objected to the plan for colonizing American Negroes in Africa. Since blacks performed "various necessary menial duties," the committee concluded that colonization would create a vacuum in seaboard cities. Just as slavery allegedly freed Southern whites for the leisurely pursuit of culture, so did blacks enable Northern whites to engage in more vital activities. If blacks had been sent to African colonies, a New England journal warned, "White men must hew our wood, draw our water, and perform our menial offices. They supply the place of so many whites, who may be spared for higher purposes." Finally, blacks performed a psychological service, in that their work allowed whites to assume aristocratic airs. In New York, for example, an English traveler observed that whites preferred black hackney coachmen because they could order them about in the tones of masters, and also because a black coachman driving a hired cab gave the impression that the whites were riding in their own carriages.[61]

To keep blacks in their place, white businessmen refused to advance credit. When Frederick Douglass, a skilled caulker, escaped to the North and sought work in the New Bedford shipyards, he was told that employing him would drive every white man away. White laborers did not want to lose their social status by associating with blacks, either at work or at mealtime. One English traveler concluded that white men "would rather starve than accept a menial office under a black. Where the two races worked together in the service occupations, whites insisted on different titles in order to preserve the sanctity of their color." One traveling Englishman commented,

> As is well known, a domestic white American born servant who condescends to help the mistress or master of a household in making the beds, milking the cows, cooking the dinner, grooming the horse or driving the carriage is not a servant but a "help." "Help wanted" is a common heading of advertisements in the North where servants are required. Let blacks be servants and if not blacks let Irishman fill their place, but for an American, an Englishman or a Scotsman, that is a Protestant to be a servant or a waiter is derogatory.[62]

By the 1830s, the rapid increase in white immigration into the North threatened even the black hold on lowly jobs. Blacks were excluded from turnpikes, canals, coal mines, brick-making, street-paving, and street-cleaning jobs. The panic of 1837 and the ensuing depression weakened the blacks' economic position further. The poverty-stricken Irish in the cities sought employment regardless of wages or conditions. One black man wrote,

> These impoverished and destitute people transported from the transatlantic shores are crowding themselves into every place of business and of labor and driving the poor American born black out. Along the wharves, where the colored man once done the whole business of shipping and unshipping—in stores where his services were once rendered, and in families where the chief places were filled by him, in all these situations there are substituted foreigners or white Americans.[63]

In California, black laborers had to compete with Chinese immigrants, though both groups faced legislative and judicial restrictions on their rights. California whites applied legal disabilities against both groups, as public opinion sanctioned and enforced social proscription. The vigorous exclusion of blacks from white residential neighborhoods in all the Northern states made blacks virtual prisoners of the ghettos. Property values fell in areas inhabited by blacks. In this way Northerners made blacks untouchables in the economic class system by eliminating all opportunities for work and restricting them to menial jobs.[64]

Even northern churches placed restrictions on blacks, and the message for black members was that they would know their place or get out. After 1830, blacks began to leave white churches and start black ones. Segregation in the North followed blacks to the grave. Symbolic of the black position in the North was the public cemetery, or Potter's Field, of Cincinnati, where whites were buried east to west and blacks north to south. The touch of black skin was to be avoided even among the dead.[65]

Because both the North and the South refused to recognize black civil rights at the state and federal levels, blacks were without a place to stand in America. A civil war became necessary to define their role, but more importantly to establish a new order between powerful white slaveholders and the more numerous white non-slaveholders.

Chapter 7
Educational Opportunity

Separate and unequal

> —Northern state laws prior to the Civil War

They'll read and sing a sacred song,
And make a prayer both loud and long,
And teach the right and do the wrong,
Hailing the brother, sister throng,
With words of heavenly union.

> —Frederick Douglass, "The Parody," 1854

Benjamin Franklin was interested in Negro education as early as the 1750s. He supported a school for black children run by the Reverend William Sturgeon, which taught catechism and where students learned to read. Franklin visited this school in 1763 and observed:

> I was on the whole much pleas'd, and from what I then saw, have conceiv'd a higher Opinion of the natural Capacities of the black Race, than I had even before entertained. Their apprehension seems as quick, their Memory as strong, and their Docility in every Respect equal to that of white Children. You will wonder perhaps that I should ever doubt it, and I will not undertake to justify all my Prejudices, nor to account for them.

Franklin's mistaken notion about Negro intelligence was entirely in keeping with the belief of the times that it could never be innately equal to that of whites. Franklin was probably the first to oppose the prevailing viewpoint. On March 20, 1774, he wrote to the French mathematician and philosopher Marquis de Condorcet, that Negroes were "not deficient in natural Understanding, but have not the Advantage of Education."[1]

The importance of education for the nation as a whole was well known. The founding fathers believed that an ignorant electorate could not be trusted to preserve democracy. As early as 1647, a Massachusetts law required every town to support a public school, leading to a modest network of educational establishments. In cities, master craftsmen set up evening schools for their apprentices. By the time of the Revolution, over half the colonial white men could read and write, a rate substantially higher than in Europe. The objective was to create a nationwide system of public schools in which all male citizens would receive a free education.

For the blacks, however, matters were different. Both the government authorities and slaveholders believed that black education was important only to enable them to understand the Bible and be converted to Christianity. This gave them some hope of reward and justice, if not in this world, then in the next, and helped them accept their condition submissively. Educational opportunity for blacks was systematically denied in both the North and South.

In the South

There were several reasons offered by Southerners for denying black education. Most Southern slaveholders believed that educating blacks produced a craving for liberty, and that the more cruelly slaves were treated, the more pliant they became. The following explanation was advanced by Mr. Auld, Frederick Douglass' master before he became a freeman. Mr. Auld forbade Mrs. Auld to teach the child the letters of the alphabet because he said it was unlawful, as well as unsafe, to teach a slave to read:

If you give a nigger an inch, he will take an ell. A nigger should know nothing but to obey his master—to do as he is told to do. Learning would spoil the best nigger in the world. Now if you teach that nigger [referring to Frederick Douglass] how to read, there would be no keeping him. It would forever unfit him to be a slave. He would at once become unmanageable, and of no value to his master. As to himself, it would do him no good, but a great deal of harm. It would make him discontented and unhappy.[2]

Between 1800 and 1825, Southern slaveholders found two more reasons to prohibit black education. The first was the worldwide industrial movement, which included processes that revolutionized spinning and weaving, increasing demand for cotton fiber. This provided a golden opportunity for Southern planters to move west into the virgin territories of Alabama and Mississippi and grow cotton using plantation slavery. The planters concluded that educating blacks was a waste of time because of their utility as beasts of burden. It was more profitable to work a black slave to death in seven years and buy a new one than to educate and humanize him with a view to increasing his efficiency.

The second reason for prohibiting black education was that black refugees from Haiti, who settled in Baltimore, Norfolk, Charleston, and New Orleans, gave American blacks a firsthand account of how blacks in the West Indies had righted their wrongs by adopting the bloody methods used in the French revolution. Following revolts and insurrections planned and executed by blacks with some education, Southern states passed laws of increasing severity to restrict educational opportunities for them.

Their initial concern sprang from the accomplishments of the Spanish and French Catholic missionaries who were teaching blacks and baptizing them into the church. The missionaries educated the numerous mulatto offspring and provided free blacks access to education at par with whites, raising the specter of manumission. To secure the black's status as a slave, slaveholders obtained a formal declaration from the Bishop of London that changed the law prohibiting holding Christians as slaves.

From the earliest times Southern colonists had to confront the Quakers, who preached in slaveholding communities as part of their duty to help all men. Quakers were then denounced as undesirable for bringing unnecessary doctrines into America that were subversive of the aristocratic planters' institutions. Virginian slaveholders demanded legislation to prevent this religious group from gaining ascendancy over the minds of black slaves, and a law was enacted in 1672 prohibiting Quakers from taking blacks to their meetings. In 1678, the colony excluded Quakers from the teaching profession by providing that no person should be allowed to run a school in Virginia unless he had taken the oath of allegiance and supremacy. Taking this oath was inconsistent with the Quakers' creed, so they had to close the schools and leave the colony.[3]

North Carolina's settlers followed the same procedure as Virginia to check the Quakers' influence. The slaveholders' apprehension was so strong that Governor Tryon was instructed to prohibit any person who did not have a license from the Bishop of London from teaching in the colony. As missionaries of the established church were not available in all parts of the colony, this action was directed at the Quakers of North Carolina who had formed local schools and taught black slaves.[4]

As slavery became established in the eighteenth century, the slaveholders were concerned that educated blacks could write passes, which would play havoc with the policing system for the slaves. Because of several rebellions from 1730 to 1739 led by blacks who had received some instruction from missionaries, South Carolina enacted a law in 1740 prohibiting any person from teaching and causing to be taught, or from employing or using a slave as a scribe in any manner of writing.[5]

A missionary, Bishop Secker, came up with a more prudent plan in 1741 whereby he would employ young Negroes to teach their countrymen. The Society for the Propagation of the Gospel in Foreign Parts purchased two Negroes named Harry and Andrew and qualified them through instruction in the principles of Christianity and the fundamentals of education, to serve as schoolmasters to their people. Under the direction of Reverend Garden, a building was erected in Charleston, South Carolina, and a school opened in 1744 where Harry and Andrew served as teachers. The directors of the institution planned to send out annually between thirty and forty youths, "well instructed in religion and capable of reading their Bibles to carry home and diffuse the same knowledge to their fellow slaves." In 1764 the Charleston school had to be closed because one of the teachers died and no instructors could be found to continue the work.[6]

At the time of the American Revolution the Quakers and the American Convention of Abolition Societies continued attempts to establish a school for colored people. Robert Pleasants, a Quaker of Virginia, circulated a pamphlet in 1782 entitled, "Proposals for establishing a Free School for the Instruction of Children of Blacks and People of Color." Pleasants proposed to establish a school on a 350-acre tract of his own land near Four-Mile Creek, Henrico County. Although the outcome is not known for certain, the abolitionists reported the cause had been hindered by the "rapacious disposition which emboldened many tyrants to trample upon the rights of colored people even in violation of the laws of the State."[7]

Meanwhile, there were continuous reports on insurrections. Gabriel's insurrection in 1800 prompted a statute prohibiting church wardens from teaching black pauper children apprenticed by them. Some masters in North Carolina, who were sending their slaves to a Sunday school opened by Levi Coffin and his son Vestal, were so alarmed that such instruction would make them discontented when they learned to spell a few words, that they threatened the teachers with the law and induced other slaveholders to prohibit their blacks' attendance. The school had to be closed.[8]

After the Gabriel insurrection, slaveholders concluded that education was the chief culprit behind black revolts. Discussing the plot of the Gabriel revolution in 1800, Judge St. George Tucker said:

> Our sole security consists in their ignorance of this power [doing us mischief] and their means of using it—a security which we have lately found is not to be relied on, and which, small as it is, everyday diminishes. Every year

adds to the number of those who can read and write: and the increase in knowledge is the principal agent in evolving the spirit we have to fear.[9]

Insurrection disturbed Camden in 1816 and Charleston in 1822. The Charleston insurrection had a formidable plot that officials believed was due to the "sinister" influence of enlightened blacks. The moving spirit of the organization behind the plot was Denmark Vesey, who had purchased his freedom in 1800. He had learned to read and write and had accumulated an estate worth $8000. Jack Purcell, an accomplice of Vesey, weakened in the crisis and confessed. He said that Vesey was in the habit of reading to him all the passages in newspapers that related to Santo Domingo and, apparently, every accessible pamphlet that had any connection with slavery. This confirmed whites' worst fears about educated blacks. A statement made by South Carolina's governor also showed the influence attributed to educated blacks. This official felt that Monday, a slave belonging to a Mr. Gill, was the most daring conspirator. According to the governor, Monday, being able to read and write, had "attained an extraordinary and dangerous influence over his fellows."[10]

States enacted stringent laws to control black education. Missouri passed an Act in 1817 designed to prevent insurrections by regulating slave travel and assembly. In 1819, the General Assembly of Virginia passed a law stating that slaves, free blacks, and mulattos could not assemble for purposes of teaching, reading, or writing. Mississippi, even when it was a territory, declared it unlawful in 1823 for more than five Negroes to meet for educational purposes.[11]

Yielding to slaveholders' demands, Georgia passed a law in 1831 providing that any black who taught another to read or write should be punished by a fine and whipping. If a white person committed this offense, he should be punished with a fine not exceeding five hundred dollars and with imprisonment in the common jail at the committing magistrate's discretion. Virginia, where the prohibition did not apply to free blacks, enacted a new law in 1831 providing that any educational meeting of free blacks or mulattos was to be considered an unlawful assembly. For this purpose, the judge or justice of the peace could issue a warrant to apprehend such persons and inflict corporal punishment not exceeding twenty lashes. White persons convicted of teaching blacks were to be fined fifty dollars and could be imprisoned for two months. For imparting rebellious information to slaves, the offender was subject to a fine of not less than ten dollars nor more than one hundred dollars.[12]

The Southern slave states were disturbed by insurrection again in Southampton County, Virginia, in 1831. This was a striking example of an insurrection led by an intelligent black man. Nat Turner, who had started reading so easily that he did not remember when he had first learned to do so. Given unusual social and intellectual advantages, he developed into a man of considerable "mental ability and wide information." His education was chiefly acquired in Sunday schools in which "the textbooks for the small children were the ordinary speller and reader, and for the older blacks the Bible." Turner also received instruction from his parents and his indulgent young master.[13]

Subsequent reactionary legislation aimed at completing the task of preventing dissemination of information among blacks. This was achieved by prohibiting slaves from communicating with one another, preventing contact between better-informed free blacks and white liberals, and closing all schools that had been open to blacks. States passed laws providing for a more stringent pass regulation, defining unlawful assemblies, and fixing penalties for these. Other statutes either prohibited religious worship or brought it under the direct supervision of the slaveowner concerned and forbade teaching blacks privately in any manner whatsoever.

Mississippi, which already had a law to prevent black education, enacted another law in 1831 to expel free blacks from the state, asking them to leave within ninety days. The same law stated that no black should preach in the state unless to slaves on the plantation where he lived, and with his owner's permission. Delaware went even further in 1831, providing that no congregation or meeting consisting of more than twelve free blacks or mulattos should be held later than midnight, except under the direction of three respectable white persons who were to attend the meeting. The law further provided that no free black should attempt to call a meeting for religious worship, to exhort or preach, unless he was authorized to do so by a judge or justice of the peace, upon the recommendation of five "respectable and judicious citizens." In 1832, Delaware passed a measure to prevent black assemblages for instruction and all other meetings apart from religious worship and burials. Following Delaware's example, in 1832 Florida passed a similar law prohibiting all meetings of blacks, and made these regulations more stringent in 1846.[14]

Alabama had some difficulty in passing a law that satisfied whites. In 1832, it had enacted a law that imposed a fine of $250 to $500 on persons who attempted to educate any black. It appeared that the state had gone too far in that it had infringed on the rights and privileges of certain Creoles who, as residents of the Louisiana territory when it was purchased in 1803, had been guaranteed the rights of United States citizens. Accordingly, in 1833 Mobile's mayor and alderman were authorized to grant licenses to instructors in Mobile and Baldwin Counties, where the free colored children were descended from colored Creoles who had resided in the district since 1803.[15]

Certain states had to overcome another difficulty. Though Georgia had incorporated into the state law adequate provisions to prevent blacks' mental development, employed as they had been in various positions, blacks could pick up the rudiments of education without access to schools. The state then passed a law imposing penalties of up to $100 for employing any slave or free blacks "in setting up type or other labor about a printing office requiring a knowledge of reading or writing." In 1834, South Carolina realized the same danger. In addition to enacting a more stringent law to prevent whites or educated blacks from teaching blacks and to destroy black schools, the new law provided that "persons of African blood" should not be employed as clerks or salesmen in or about any shop or store or house used for trading. This ensured that blacks could not even come into contact with written materials.[16]

North Carolina was among the last states to take drastic measures to prevent black education. Until 1835, some free blacks attended schools open to both races. Then a new law passed that year prohibited public instruction of blacks, making it impossible for black children to get any education beyond that they were able to acquire within their family circles. The public schools system established thereafter specifically provided that its benefits should not extend to anyone descended from black ancestors, down through the fourth generation. Unable to bear their loss of social status after they had toiled up from poverty, free blacks left the state.[17]

The western states did not have to deal as severely with their slaves as the southern states did. In 1847, Missouri passed a law directing that no one should keep or teach any school for the education of blacks. In states such as Tennessee and Kentucky, no laws prohibited instructing slaves though public sentiment made it impossible. This was also true of Maryland.[18]

To justify all the new restrictive legislation, Southern whites came up with two arguments explaining their actions. They said that because of blacks' "defective comprehension of the Bible and the laborious nature of this employment to them," such reading was an inefficient method of religious instruction. Another reason whites gave was that Christianizing and educating black slaves had a tendency to elevate them above their masters and to destroy "legitimate distinctions" in the community.[19]

After the new round of Southern legislation, slavery extended its reach from slavery of the body to slavery of the mind. Education was thereafter regarded as positively inconsistent with the institution of slavery. Berry summed it up in the Virginia House of Delegates in 1832 when he said this:

> We have as far as possible, closed every avenue by which light may enter the slave's mind. If we could extinguish the capacity to see the light, our work would be completed. They would then be on a level with the beasts in the field and we would be safe. I am not certain that we would not do it, if we could find out the process, and that on the pleas of necessity.

With free blacks leaving the South, in some large Southern districts it was surprising to find even one black who could read the Bible or sign his name.[20]

Even these stringent laws could not make all Christian sects stop offering slaves religious training. The richest slaveholders were Episcopalians who did not break the laws, which served their own interests. The Methodist and Baptist churches were indifferent to slavery and just wanted to do their best without breaking laws. The Presbyterians, however, were against slavery and did not want to give up teaching slaves.

To save black souls, Southern ministers hit on the scheme of teaching Christian principles verbally to illiterate blacks. This new form of religious instruction involved memorization from the most simplified books. Some slaveholders became sufficiently alarmed to object to verbal instruction on the ground that it would eventually lead to education. It was feared that it would increase slaves' desire to learn, and the slaves would neglect their duties and engage in religious worship as a cover for originating and executing plans for insubordination and revolt.

After 1835, even the use of verbal religious instruction was prohibited. Some slaveholders asserted that blacks were such stubborn creatures that there could be no such close dealings with them, and that when converted to Christianity, they became more saucy than pious. Others maintained that blacks were so ignorant and indocile, so far gone in wickedness, so confirmed in their evil ways, that it was vain to undertake teaching them. Yet others used the excuse that instructing blacks required more time and labor than masters could well spare from their business, while some frankly confessed that being ignorant and unlearned people themselves, they could not teach others. Some slaveholders were smart enough to work out a logic for neglecting black education altogether. They argued that African racial inferiority was so well exhibited by blacks' lack of wisdom and goodness that the race's continued heathenism was justifiable.[21]

A few blacks who had learned the importance of early Christian training organized local study groups among themselves. They often appointed an old woman on the plantation to teach children too young for fieldwork to say prayers, repeat a little catechism, and memorize a few hymns. This, however, too closely resembled systematic instruction and was prohibited by masters who were, they claimed, only obeying the law. The slaveholders' actions were summed up by Rev. John G. Fee, an abolitionist minister: "Sealing up the mind of the slave lest he should see his wrongs, was tantamount to cutting off the hand or foot in order to prevent his escape and unwilling servitude." That Southern slaveholders were successful in achieving their objectives is evident from the statement of William Jay, son of the first chief justice of the United States, who said in 1835 that only one in ten slaves had any knowledge of Christ.[22]

Louisiana, however, continued to be different. Here mulattos and blacks were assured the privilege of an education. In 1724, the *Code Noir* made it incumbent upon masters to enlighten their slaves so that they might grasp the Christian religion's principles. After 1726, when Law's Company was importing many slaves to meet Louisiana's demand for laborers, there are more accounts of French Catholics instructing Negroes. Writing about this task in 1730, Le Petit, a Jesuit priest, spoke of being "settled to the instruction of the boarders, the girls who live without, and the Negro women." In 1738, he wrote, "I instruct in Christian morals the slaves of our residence, who are Negroes, and as many others as I can get from their masters." Years later, Francois Philibert Watrum, seeing that some Jesuits had 130 slaves on their estates, inquired why instructing the Indian and Negro serfs of the French did not give these missionaries enough to do.[23]

Matters changed after Louisiana became a United States territory and educating blacks became more difficult. Contrary to the stipulation in the purchase treaty that the territory's inhabitants should be admitted to all the rights and immunities of United

States citizens, state legislation denied the right of education to a large class of blacks and mulattos. Many of them had, thanks to the Catholic slavery code, been freed and had educated themselves, accumulated wealth, and compared favorably with whites of refinement and culture.[24]

Louisiana's initial step was to keep out intelligent blacks who might inform slaves about insurrections and revolts in other places, thus creating trouble for their masters. Accordingly, in 1814, the state passed a law prohibiting free blacks from immigrating into the state. This precaution was not deemed sufficient after the black insurrection in North Carolina. In 1830, Louisiana enacted another measure providing that whoever should write, print, publish, or distribute anything that had the tendency to produce discontent among slaves should, on conviction thereof, be imprisoned with hard labor for life or suffer death, at the court's discretion. Whoever became instrumental in bringing into the state any paper, book, or pamphlet inducing such discontent should suffer virtually the same penalty. All persons who taught, or permitted to be taught, any slave to read or write, should be imprisoned for not less than one month nor more than twelve. Thus, long before the Civil War, Louisiana joined the other Southern states and denied blacks all educational opportunities under threat of criminal penalties.[25]

In the North

The North, which did not want blacks, enacted laws prohibiting black immigration and made life miserable for those already there. Preventing the establishment of black schools, harassing teachers, and, if necessary, burning black school buildings were the standard fare. Later, when the black taxpayers demanded public education for blacks, such tactics became more sophisticated. First, the whites decided that blacks should have separate schools so as not to pollute white children by dragging them down to black children's level of base ignorance. This agenda was not difficult to push through as blacks had no political or fundamental rights and were not even citizens of the United States. The second step was to make it impossible for blacks to open their own schools.

In the North, there was trouble of yet another kind brewing. Many whites feared that they would be overrun by old, sick, and other undesirable blacks driven out of the South. This resulted in anti-abolition riots in the North. In 1818, a black school opened in Washington, D.C., under an association of free blacks called the Resolute Beneficial Society to improve black youths' intellects and morals. It sought patronage from benevolent ladies and gentlemen. The Society declared that "to avoid disagreeable occurrences no writing was to be done by the teacher for a slave, neither directly nor indirectly to serve the purpose of the slave on any account whatsoever." The District of Columbia's black schools sought to recover lost ground. A school was started by Alexander Hays, a former slave emancipated by the Fowler family of Maryland, supported by three teachers from England, Thomas H. Mason and Mr. and Mrs. Fletcher. Strong feelings against white people instructing blacks led to these philanthropists' school houses being burned and to their being expelled from white churches and eventually driven from the city.[26]

Attempts to start schools for blacks in New Haven and Canterbury, Connecticut, saw townspeople vigorously protest against them lest they attract blacks from other states or threaten the town's property values and peace. In 1831, Prudence Crandall, a young schoolmistress, established a successful and popular boarding school for girls in Canterbury. Her welcome proved short-lived, for a year later she agreed to admit a black girl. This aroused the town, brought protests from white parents, and resulted in most students withdrawing. The schoolmistress thereupon decided to admit only black girls in 1833. A Canterbury town meeting a week later appointed a committee to persuade Miss Crandall to abandon her project in view of "… the injurious effects and incalculable evils that would follow." At the same time, certain "responsible" town citizens offered to purchase her newly acquired house on condition that the school be discontinued. However, Miss Crandall refused to back down, and the school opened in April. The town adopted a new form of opposition: harassment. Stores denied the school necessary provisions; townspeople insulted students in the street and filled the school's well with manure, forcing Miss Crandall to arrange for water to be transported from her father's farm two miles away. The village physician refused to treat the pupils, and civil authorities threatened to invoke an old vagrancy law against them. [27]

Andrew T. Judson, a local official, denounced the plan to establish a school for blacks in Canterbury, Connecticut, or in any other part of the state. He believed that blacks, who could never rise from their menial condition in the United Sates, should not be encouraged to expect to elevate themselves in Connecticut. He considered them inferior servants who should be sent back to Africa to improve themselves and Christianize the natives. When attempts to close the "nigger school" failed, local officials appealed to the legislature, which was only too willing to help. They adopted a law that prohibited establishment of "any school, academy or literary institution, for the instruction or education of colored persons who are not inhabitants of this State." The law's preamble declared that the evil to be obviated was any increase in the Commonwealth's black population. This law's enactment in 1833 was greeted with town bells and cannon and made Canterbury go wild with joy. In Boston, the *Liberator* cried "Georgia outdone."[28]

Miss Crandall did not wilt under this overwhelming legal and extra-legal pressure, and was thereupon arrested on charges of violating the new law. The controversy had thus been transferred to the courts. The chief justice regretted "that I should add to the degradation of this race of men; but I am bound, by my duty, to say, they are not citizens." The jury found Miss Crandall guilty but an appellate court reversed the conviction on a technical defect in the information. Meanwhile, villagers subjected the school to continual harassment; it was frequently stoned and an attempt was made to burn it down. Finally, in September 1834, the siege ended. Miss Crandall abandoned the school and departed for Illinois.[29]

Some whites wanted to provide free blacks with facilities for higher education in the hope that their enlightenment would make blacks so discontented with the United States that they would emigrate to Liberia. This plan was acceptable only if those blacks who were "permanently attached" to this country could be kept in ignorance. Realizing that they could not count on educated free blacks to leave the country, whites did not want to increase any blacks' intelligence, which might have jeopardized slavery. Whites decided it would be better to educate the blacks after they emigrated and settled in Liberia.[30]

Between 1830 and 1840, blacks were barred from white colleges. Before 1840, not even fifteen blacks were admitted to colleges in the United States. Only after much debate did Union College agree to accept a black student—on condition that he swear that he had no Negro blood in his veins.

Restricting educational opportunity also occurred among artisans. In opposing black encroachment into their fields of labor, Northerners took their cue from Southern white mechanics. As the Northern population doubled with an influx of white European immigrants between 1830 and 1860, there were riots against blacks in Cincinnati, Philadelphia, New York, and Washington, D.C., primarily due to ill feelings between white and black skilled laborers. White artisans prevailed on the Pennsylvania and Maryland legislatures to enact measures hostile to blacks.[31]

The North was in the throes of industrial unionization. White labor unions, seeking to protect their interests, refused to accept black youths as apprentices or even work for employers who persisted in hiring blacks. After being refused employment by the master mechanics of Cincinnati, a black cabinetmaker finally found an Englishman who was willing to hire him; but the shop's other employees objected, refusing to allow the newcomer even to work in a room by himself. A black man, preaching in a northern black church, could not get a contract to build new edifices for his congregation. A black man could not get his son into a blacksmith's shop to blow the bellows and wield the sledgehammer.[32]

Free blacks decided to set up a vocational school in New Haven, Connecticut. Before their well-laid plans could mature, unexpected opposition developed. Local citizens said that a black college so near Yale might cause friction between the two student bodies and that the vocational school might attract an unusually large number of undesirable blacks. New Haven citizens called a meeting at which they passed a resolution stating that founding colleges for educating colored people was an unwarrantable and dangerous undertaking to the internal concerns of other states and ought to be discouraged. New Haven's mayor, alderman, common council, and freemen would resist the movement by every lawful means. No such protests were made by New Haven's citizens, however, when colonizationists planned a mission school to prepare blacks for emigration to Liberia.[33]

When a plan was made to subsidize the Noyes Academy of Canaan, New Hampshire, as a model academy for black education "on the manual labor system," these modern Canaanites destroyed the academy, dragging the building to a swamp with a hundred yoke of oxen. Mrs. Harriet Beecher Stowe, the author of *Uncle Tom's Cabin,* wanted to raise funds on her tour of England to start a vocational school for blacks but saw the futility of her plans after her return to the U.S.[34]

Free public schools were first regarded as a system to educate the poor, but blacks stayed away from them lest they be accused of becoming public charges. In the course of time, the charity stigma was removed as a wider network of free schools was developed at public expense. Blacks concluded it was not dishonorable to share the benefits of institutions they were taxed to support. Although Baltimore's blacks were paying $500 in annual taxes to support public schools just prior to the Civil War, their children were not allowed to attend them. The blacks insisted that money be appropriated for black children's education. Complying with these petitions, the Boards of Education provided for black schools that were to be partly or wholly supported at public expense. The only catch was that the amount appropriated to support black schools was inadequate to supply the necessary equipment or competent teachers. This procedure was repeated in most Northern states.

In 1802, 1804, and 1809, Pennsylvania passed Acts in the interest of the poor which authorized their education at public expense. These Acts were interpreted to exclude blacks from the benefits provided. In 1834, the Pennsylvania legislature established a public school system, but black claims to public education were neither granted nor denied. Consequently, black children were conveniently ignored. Finally, the School Law of 1854 provided that the state's school districts could establish separate schools for black and mulatto children whenever they could be so located as to accommodate twenty or more pupils. Another provision stated that wherever such schools should "be established and kept open four months in the year," the directors and comptrollers should not be compelled to admit black students to any other schools in that district. As a result, the children of Robert B. Purvis were turned away from Philadelphia's public schools on the grounds that special educational facilities for blacks had already been provided. Pennsylvania and other Northern states established public school systems with a built-in caste system to separate the "untouchables."[35]

In 1823, the State of New York, following its Superintendent of Schools' recommendation, adopted a policy under which schools were organized exclusively for blacks. In Rhode Island, where the black population was proportionately larger than in some other New England states, special schools for blacks, separate from white public schools, were considered necessary. Since few blacks lived in Connecticut, there were no schools for black children there. With whites preventing blacks from attending the public schools, in 1830 Hartford blacks presented a petition to the School Society of the City, asking for a separate school for blacks with part of the public school funds apportioned to them, according to their number. The state legislature authorized several separate schools for blacks to be established, but the arrangement proved unworkable due to the small number of blacks in Connecticut towns. Their pro-rata share was inadequate for the maintenance of separate schools.[36]

In Boston, which had a larger black population than all other Massachusetts towns combined, there were separate schools for blacks and whites. No black from a public school there had ever qualified for a secondary institution. It was evident that in cities with separate schools for black and white students, blacks derived practically no benefit from the school tax they paid. Solicitor Chandler presented the opinion of the majority of the School Board, which refused the request for common schools for whites and blacks. They based their action on the natural distinction of the races, stating that "no legislature, no social custom can efface and which" renders a promiscuous intermingling in the public schools disadvantageous to both races. The controversy continued for ten years until 1855, when the Massachusetts legislature enacted a law prohibiting school admissions based on race, color, or religious opinion. It was further provided that a child excluded from school for any of these reasons might bring a suit for damages against the offending town. This set a precedent for the future, in that legislatures placed all sorts of laws on the books for display without the smallest practical prospect of those laws being enforced. As Solicitor Chandler warned, no legislature could force the people to act against their wishes.[37]

The question of educating the increasing number of blacks at public expense was also perplexing people's minds in the West, especially Ohio. An Ohio law of 1825 provided that a tax of half a million dollars be appropriated for the support of common schools in the respective counties and that these schools should be "open to the Youth of every class and grade without distinction." Some interpreted this law to include blacks and objected to the school officials ignoring black children's education. The state passed another law in 1829 to clarify the situation, excluding blacks from the new system and returning to them the amount accruing from the school tax on their property. Not until 1849 did the legislature pass a law authorizing schools for black children to be established at public expense. Unfortunately again, the per capita division of the fund was insufficient to support black schools. Even if the funds had been adequate to pay teachers, the blacks had no school houses, and lawyers contended that the Act of 1849 said nothing about constructing buildings for schools.[38]

In 1824, Indiana was very "solicitous" for an educational system that would guard against caste distinction. However, in 1837, it decided that only white inhabitants of each Congressional township could be included in the local school corporation. In 1841, a petition sent to the legislature requested a reasonable share of school funds be allocated for black education. With the exception of prohibiting black immigration into the state, no action was taken until 1853.

Then the legislature amended the law authorizing public schools in townships, but specifically excluded black children from them and excluded all property belonging to blacks and mulattos from taxation for school purposes. The amendment stated that black children should not derive any benefit from the state's common schools. This provision had actually been incorporated into the former law but had been omitted by oversight on the part of the engrossing clerk.[39]

An Indiana House resolution instructing the educational committee to report on a Bill establishing schools for the state's blacks was overwhelmingly defeated in 1853. Explaining their position, opponents said that it was held "to be better for the weaker party that no privilege be extended to them," as the tendency to such "might be to induce the vain belief that the prejudice of the dominant race could ever be so mollified as to break down the rugged barriers that must forever exist between their social relations."[40]

The situation in Illinois was better than in Indiana but far from encouraging. The Constitution of 1847 restricted the school law's benefits to white children, stipulating the word white throughout the act to make the legislators' intention abundantly clear. It provided that school taxes collected from blacks should be returned. Exactly what should be done with such money, however, was not stated in the Act. The provision was little help to blacks, since the clause providing for the return of school taxes was seldom put into effect. In the few cases in which it was carried out, the funds thus raised were not adequate to support a special school for black children because they were widely dispersed. Some unsuccessful attempts were made to remove the word "white" from the law.[41]

In other northwestern states, where few blacks were to be found, the solution to the problem was easier. In 1848, blacks were allowed to vote in school meetings in Michigan. Wisconsin and Iowa allowed blacks similar privileges in 1857. It became convenient to provide all the theoretical rights for black access to education, so long as these rights could not be enforced.[42]

In California, the general feeling was that if equal educational privileges were provided for blacks, other blacks would flock there. On the pretext that educational privileges for blacks would antagonize Southern whites, a California mayor vetoed appropriations for black schools as "… particularly obnoxious to those of our citizens who have immigrated from southern states."[43]

Knowledge Base: A Northern Advantage

Amidst all this denial of educational access to blacks, the non-slaveholding whites suffered, especially in the South. As yeoman farmers and Northern white wage slaves were not competing with black slaves as in the South, they were provided educational opportunities. Just before the Civil War, the North led the world in educational facilities and literacy. Over ninety-five percent of its adults could read and write; three-fourths of children aged five to nineteen were enrolled in schools, which they attended for an average of six months a year. This educational system was offered by British observers as an explanation for the North's economic efficiency and the reputation for Yankee ingenuity. Of 143 important inventions patented in the United States from 1790 to 1860, ninety-three percent came out of the North. Education in the North was shaped by its utility. Consequently, Northern yeoman farmers enhanced productivity to produce enough food to feed the South. Most manufactured goods were also produced by Northern factories while Northern merchants and traders controlled the commerce of the United States.[44]

Slaveholders, who controlled the South's government and infrastructure, provided only themselves and their white children with educational opportunities. They did not provide education for utility, as in the North, but for development of character and grace. Thus, provisions for common schools or public education were neglected, while Southern colleges were in general decently supported, decently staffed, and well attended. In 1860, out of 6,000 private academies nationwide, the South had 2,640 but only about 30 public high schools out of the 321 listed nationwide. The South was for the most part a land without free public schools—a land where the poor man's son was likely to go untaught, and the working man or small yeoman farmer apt to be ignorant, if not illiterate.[45]

Statistics from 1857, quoted by Hinton Rowan Helper, show the gulf separating the North and South. In the South the proportion of free white children between the ages of five and twenty found at any school or college was not even one-fifth of the whole. The proportion was over three-fifths in the Northern states. The South had less than one-third as many public schools as the North and less than one-twentieth as many public libraries.[46]

Besides fostering ignorance among the masses, Southern slaveholders controlled the press and eliminated free speech, which was considered treason against slavery. Only the pro-slavery argument could be expressed. Any questioning of the morality or policy of slavery in the South resulted in the terrors of lynch law. Southern states' legislation suppressing freedom of speech and the press was absolute and total in its reach.[47]

This was achieved by ensuring the mass ignorance of Southern white non-slaveholders, taking advantage of the competitive economic relationship between the two groups. The lack of educational opportunities for white non-slaveholders ensured that all industry and manufacturing stayed out of the South. Since the support of the non-slaveholders was critical for the slaveholders to preserve slavery and eventually secede from the Union, mass ignorance among non-slaveholders was a necessary condition for the Civil War. Failure to provide blacks with educational opportunities in turn eliminated the option of freeing the blacks in the face of a fall in the value of slave property.

Chapter 8

The Reckoning

Rich man's war and a poor man's fight

—AWOL Mississippi Farmer (Civil War)

A roaring, ranting, sleekman—thief,
who lived on mutton, veal and beef,
Yet never would afford relief
To needy, sable sons of grief,
Was big with heavenly union

—Frederick Douglass, "The Parody," 1854

In her book *Gone with the Wind*, Margaret Mitchell made the following observation about the Civil War:

> All wars are sacred to those who have to fight them. If the people who started wars didn't make them sacred, who would be foolish enough to fight? But, no matter what rallying cries the orators give to the idiots who fight, no matter what noble purposes they assign to wars, there is never but one reason for a war. And that is money. All wars are in reality money squabbles. But so few people ever realize it. Their ears are too full of bugles and drums and fine words from stay-at-home orators. Sometimes the rallying cry is "Save the Tomb of Christ from the Heathen!" Sometimes it's "Down with Popery!" and sometimes "Liberty" and sometimes "Cotton, Slavery and States Rights!"

Even with American Civil War, notwithstanding other contributory factors, the major issue was economic. The non-slaveholders, who actually fought the war, were, however, rallied around a false slogan.[1]

As Jefferson Davis, the president of the Confederacy, later claimed, slavery was not the real issue in the Civil War, but a red herring; and for over a century, historians have disagreed about the causes of the Civil War. In 1858, Senator William H. Seward of New York took note of the two competing explanations of the sectional tensions that were then inflaming the nation. On one side were those who believed the sectional hostility to be "accidental, unnecessary, the work of interested or fanatical agitators." Opposing them were those who believed there to be "an irrepressible conflict between opposing and enduring forces." The Civil War could not have been accidental and unnecessary and yet an inevitable conflict between opposing forces.[2]

Competing Theories

What is undisputed is that the Civil War lasted over four years, cost over half a million white lives, and was the bloodiest war in American history. It was unlikely that it was accidental and unnecessary. The issues involved in the war had been discussed and debated for almost a century by experienced politicians on both sides because the blacks had been brought to America in 1619 and the North and South had over two hundred years of experience with black slavery. Even the question of black participation in battle on the Patriot side had arisen during the 1776 revolution. Slavery was extensively debated at the Constitutional Convention in 1787 before provisions protecting slaveholders' interests were written into the Constitution and subsequently ratified by the states. In 1807, Congress banned the import of slaves. In 1820, the question of slavery in the territories was temporarily resolved by the Missouri Compromise, and again temporarily by the Compromise of 1850. For the entire decade that followed, it claimed the attention of Congress and was a prominent subject in election debates. It was unlikely then that the Civil War was accidental.

The "irrepressible conflict" that caused it could only have been an amalgam of ideological, cultural, political, and economic differences. The competing ideologies theory places the South on one side with its racist supremacy position and the North on the other on a moralist plank. To put matters in perspective, Abraham Lincoln said: "If slavery is not wrong then nothing is wrong," but he also pledged himself to enforce the fugitive slave clause of the Constitution and deferred the goal of emancipation into the remote future. A valid explanation is that Lincoln termed slavery immoral as an excuse to keep slaves out of the territories and reserve them for whites only; immoral not because of what it did to the blacks but for what it did to whites. It would appear that what happened to the blacks was secondary as Lincoln was willing to amend the Constitution to guarantee protection to slavery in states that chose to retain it.[3]

This mindset of slavery in itself posing no ethical problem was shared by the majority of the Northern population where it was legal during the colonial period. Even after its abolition, many Northern Constitutions banned the immigration of blacks because they were not wanted. The Northern public was conspicuously hostile to the tiny proportion of abolitionists amidst them, and there was no agreement in the North or South over what constituted morality and what its consequences were.[4]

However, the rallying cry of white supremacy was useful for the Southern slaveholders, who controlled the state governments and spread the word through the press that most of the Northerners were abolitionists. They also engaged in effective propaganda on the horrors of slave freedom. If anything, these arguments clouded the issue of the acute impoverishment of white non-slaveholding farmers. Had white supremacy been the true goal, it would not have made sense to bring poor whites down to the level of slaves. As things stood, the economic condition of Southern non-slaveholding whites was virtually on par with that of the blacks and was by no means comparable to that of better-off Northern white wage earners.[5]

Ideological programs are always the best motivators for the general public, who fight the wars or vote in elections. They rarely reveal the actual issues for which wars are started. The pro-slavery argument of the South was an ideological program to propagate slaveholders' interests in Congress and to unite the South. Similarly, the position of the Republican Party in the North, that slavery was immoral, was an ideological position to win votes by guaranteeing new territories for whites only.

The cultural difference theory—focusing on culturally divergent civilizations of the South and the North with different values and lifestyles—was yet another myth. The North was a dynamic, expanding urban population, concentrating on industry, while the South was static, rural, and agricultural. The real difference was that over a third of the Southern population was black, living with whites, while the North had a very small population of blacks who were treated as "untouchables." The Southerners argued that as only they lived with blacks, only they were competent to judge the conditions under which Southern blacks and whites should coexist. The slaveholders chose the Protestant slavery code and the Northerners did not realize that the South could not free the slaves even if they wished to because they had no infrastructure for free blacks. Even the U.S. Constitution lacked a place for free blacks.[6]

This did not however create any great cultural divide. The North held that it did not want the South to abolish slavery; no major political party, including the Republicans, ever called for its abolition. The North was in fact party to letting the South kidnap blacks into slavery by the terms of the Fugitive Slave Act of 1850. Abraham Lincoln sympathized with the South saying that he would not know what to do if he were in their shoes. Culturally, the inhabitants of the North and the South had the same roots, language, common history, and Constitution; and problematic issues surrounding black slavery affected both Northerners and Southerners because they both benefited from it and would have to find a mutually acceptable solution to it.[7]

A more serious explanation features the loss of slaveholders' political clout in the Federal government, referred to as the slave-power conspiracy or even as the States' Rights doctrine. The Southern slaveholders who had protected slavery in the Constitution in 1787, contradicting the claims of the Declaration of Independence and winning an unfair advantage over the North, used the unfair federal ratio clause (counting a slave as three-fifths of a person in the census count that determined each state's representation in Congress) and the fugitive slave clause, delaying the ban on slave imports until 1807.[8]

Using this power, the slaveholders perpetuated their control of the country for sixty years, and not until the Northern population grew to twice the size of the South in that period, could the South be dispossessed of federal control. The slaveholders tried to further their objectives by using the presidency of James Buchanan, the Supreme Court Chief Justice Roger Taney, and the theory of States' Rights, but could not continue after the election of Abraham Lincoln. Was this sufficient reason for the South to secede? It is important to appreciate that the loss of political power was an effect and not a cause of the Southern dilemma.[9]

Another explanation was the divergence in the economic power of the North and South. The fundamental problem lay in the Southern population and economy remaining static, while the North's grew hugely, leading to certain inherent antagonisms between the Northern industrialists and the Southern planters. The North wanted high tariffs on imports, public appropriations for improving means of transport such as the railroad to the Pacific, a central bank, and homestead laws. The South opposed all of them. The North sold the South all its food and manufactured goods in exchange for the South's cotton, which was exported to Europe. The high tariff forced the South to buy its goods from the North rather than from Europe while it received only competitive European prices for its cotton. Appropriations for transport would only help the Northern population to migrate west and grab new territories for whites only. The homestead laws would also encourage the movement of Northern and Southern white non-slaveholders to new territories, thus keeping slaveholders and black slaves out.[10, 11]

Historian Eugene Genovese underscores the disproportion of income distribution in this statement:

> The structure of income distribution needs to be more closely analyzed, but we already know that slaveholders in general, and planters in particular, got a disproportionately high share. Planters siphoned off much of the yeoman's cotton profits by charges for ginning and other services and through a cotton market that operated to give big producers higher prices than small producers. Average cotton prices disguised a big spread in the returns of social groups.

The distribution of income and wealth between slaveholders, non-slaveholders, and slaves was an important component of the American economic divide; it was its class system that did not officially exist. There was a small wealthy class and a small poor class, with the majority constituted by the wage-earning middle-class. The socio-economic dynamics between them were important contributory factors to the Civil War.[12]

To examine the causes of the Civil War, historian Kenneth M. Stampp has suggested investigations along three separate but interdependent lines: (1) The differences over slavery that only arose when it came to supporting slavery in the new territories; (2) the causes prompting the states of the deep South to secede after Lincoln's election in 1860; (3) the reason that the great majority of Northerners preferred to use force rather than recognize Southern independence.[13]

It would be worthwhile to again acknowledge that the Northern abolitionists were a tiny group, certainly not representative of the views of the Northern majority; the Southern slaveholders were a small minority but controlled the government and power; black slaves made up over a third of the Southern population but had no political power and were inconsequential in a country where both the South and the North were admittedly racists.

Southern Dilemmas

Lincoln was aware of the South's dilemma and the difficulty of finding practical and satisfactory solutions:

> When southern people tell us they are no more responsible for the origin of slavery than we, I acknowledge the fact. When it is said that the institution exists, and that it is very difficult to get rid of it in any satisfactory way, I can understand and appreciate the saying. I surely will not blame them for not doing what I should not know how to do myself. If all earthly power were given me, I should not know what to do, as to the existing institution.

The South faced three fundamental dilemmas. (1) The static population of the South in effect meant a decline when compared to the growing population in the North and a qualitative decline in a majority of this population, with the Southern white non-slave-holders virtually at par with the slaves in terms of economic well-being. The incomes of all white non-slaveholders—the unskilled workers, skilled workers, and yeoman farmers—were being hurt by the institution of slavery. (2) White workers had little bargaining power so long as the employers could hire slaves and keep them at subsistence levels. (3) The declining utility of black slaves who could not be set free because the Protestant slavery code did not provide for free blacks. Significantly, none of these concerns related to the well-being of the slaves.[14]

The import of blacks was stopped to ensure that America remained a white man's country and because of the possible threat of a large black population, the experience of Santo Domingo being fresh in everyone's mind. From a white security and white supremacy point of view, the limits on the black population had essentially been reached. The number of blacks exceeded a third of the population in the South. In South Carolina and Mississippi, blacks actually outnumbered whites. In four other states—Florida, Georgia, Alabama, and Louisiana—the numbers of blacks and whites were about equal, indicative of violation of the 1808 law prohibiting the importation of blacks.[15]

Much of the South's white population had been brought to America as indentured servants before the Revolution and had stayed on after their term had been completed. Most Europeans who came to America in the nineteenth century were not, however, indentured servants. They had a choice of either going North, where there was no competition from black slaves, or South, where they were in direct competition with black slaves. Many wage-earning white immigrants saw scant opportunity in the South because slaves were given preference by their masters when steady occupations were to be filled and odd jobs were often the only recourse for outsiders. Still more important was the repugnance that the newcomers felt at working and living alongside blacks, which was not so much a consequence of the Negroes being slaves as of the slaves being Negroes. Slavery thus stood as a barrier to white immigration into the South, making its population static in a situation in which blacks too could not be allowed to grow.[16]

The second issue around the non-slaveholding whites, who constituted three-quarters of the white population, was their abysmal poverty and the fact that they actually had to compete with the slaves. In 1860, the average annual wage for textile workers in New England was $205, while in the South it was $145. Even in industries that employed no slaves, there was the threat to employ them. For example, a strike in Richmond's Tradegar Iron Company was broken when the white workers were replaced by black slaves. Therefore, a standard of living at the subsistence level for the Negro also meant the same living standard for white laborers.[17]

A petition to the Atlanta city council complained: "Negro mechanics can afford to underbid the regular resident mechanics of your city, to their great injury," but the slaveholders generally successfully opposed the white mechanics' efforts. Laws for the protection of white mechanics, a slaveholder protested, were "a monstrous invasion of the right of private property." A supply of slave mechanics "is our bulwark against extortion and our safeguard against the turbulence of white mechanics, as seen in the great strikes, both in England and in the North, and is the only protection we have in any possible struggle between capital and white labor." Therefore, even white skilled craftsmen were not unaffected by the institution of slavery in the South.[18]

Nor could the Southern yeoman farmer escape slavery's economic competition. Prices for cotton and other commodities were dependent on the production cost of the planter with his superior efficiency and cheap labor. The white yeoman farmer's reward for his toil was, therefore, directly affected by the meager rewards slaves received. Southern poverty was contagious. Moreover, slaveholders owned most of the fertile land. Those yeoman farmers who had land suitable for commercial agriculture either prospered and became slaveholders, or they sold their land to neighboring slaveholders. [19]

With the white non-slaveholding majority actually a victim of Southern slavery, the slaveholders' dilemma was around obtaining their cooperation in terms of inducing them to stay on instead of seeking greener pastures in free territories and motivating them to support the status quo and even fight the Yankees if necessary. The depreciating value of slave property, following the falling productivity of soil, and the inability to free redundant slaves, was a pressing problem for slaveholders, who had a profitable labor system with a $2 billion capital investment at stake. Even Abraham Lincoln was aware of the surplus of slaves in some border states and could remember attempts by Virginia, Kentucky, and Missouri to enact plans for gradual emancipation that were frustrated because they were impractical.[20]

Slavery had forced the South into continued dependence on exploitative agricultural methods, which even prevented reclamation of the greater part of the degraded land. Land, being abundant, was cheap in comparison to labor, and there was no incentive to practice crop rotation or fertilize the land with livestock. It was more profitable to breed slaves for sale and sell otherwise surplus slaves to the cotton states. If the Southern frontier stopped expanding, the surplus slaves could not be sold, which decreased their value, especially since they could not be disposed of.[21]

Therefore, instead of freeing slaves, most of the South took pride in legislation to eliminate free blacks by offering them the opportunity to leave the state or select a master and re-enslave themselves. As the North did not want blacks, the South was stuck with its blacks and had to find its own solution to the dilemma. The South could increase, decrease, or maintain the size of its black population, or free it and distribute it throughout the country.[22]

A federal ban prevented an increase in the numbers of blacks. The Louisiana legislature several times considered an "African Apprentice Bill" that would have authorized importation of Negro laborers under fifteen-year indentures. A group of Mississippians unsuccessfully considered forming an African Labor Immigration Company to import indentured Negro apprentices. Similar attempts in Florida and Arkansas failed because the slaveholders of the Upper South feared competition from African traders in the slave-importing states. Also, slaveholders who owned an adequate supply of slaves opposed a measure that would inevitably depress the value of slaves already on hand.[23]

The advantages of this course of action lay in lowering the prices of slaves and making them affordable to non-slaveholders. More importantly, every five slaves imported gave the South representation at the federal level equivalent to three Northern whites. Ultimately, the falling property value of slaves did not warrant the benefits promised by this speculative scheme of importing indentured Negro apprentices and so this option was rejected.[24]

Getting rid of all four million blacks in the South—the Colonization solution—proposed by Thomas Jefferson, involved emancipating the slaves, followed by immediate colonization in Africa or Central America. This solution had occurred to Abraham Lincoln, who also noted its impracticality:

> My first impulse would be to free all the slaves, and send them to Liberia—to their own native land. But a moment's reflection would convince me, that whatever of high hope (as I think there is) there may be in this, in the long run, its sudden execution is impossible. If they were landed there in a day, they would all perish in the next ten days; and there are not surplus shipping and surplus

money enough in the world to carry them there in many times ten days.[25]

Colonization would involve a financial loss for the slaveholders, who would expect compensation. Even so, some Southern states supported the American Colonization movement and prominent men lent their names to the cause. Only 11,909 immigrants went to Africa and only 6,000 of them were freed for this purpose. Not many slaveholders were willing to free their slaves without compensation even if the blacks were to leave the country.[26]

Nor could the South spread the slaves throughout the country, as Thomas Jefferson suggested in 1820:

> But as it is, we have the wolf by the ears, and we can neither hold him, nor safely let him go. Justice is in one scale, and self preservation in the other. Of one thing I am certain, that as the passage of slaves from one State to another, would not make a slave of a single human being who would not be so without it, so their diffusion over a greater surface would make them individually happier, and proportionally facilitate the accomplishment of their emancipation by dividing the burthen on a greater number of coadjutors ....

Lincoln also analyzed this option in his debates with Douglas:

> Free them all, and keep them among us as underlings? Is it quite certain that this betters their condition? I think I would not hold one in slavery, at any rate; yet the point is not clear enough for me to denounce people upon. What next? Free them, and make them politically and socially our equals? My own feelings will not admit to this; and if mine would, we well know that those of the great mass of white people will not.[27]

The fundamental flaw in the dispersion plan was in its prospective effects on the productivity of the black. They would be freed only if slaveholders were compensated. Certainly the North would not provide the compensation funds to free the slaves who might then go to the North where they were not wanted. The reality then was that the South could neither import nor export blacks, nor could they share their burden of blacks with the North by freeing them. Blacks and whites had to live together in the South, so the slaveholders had to do their best to prevent the value of their slave property from falling.

More serious than the black dilemma was the problem of controlling the South's white non-slaveholding population. Attracting new white wage earners was not easy because, under the prevailing conditions, the life of a Negro slave was more valuable than a white wage earner to the slaveholder because of the investment the slaveholder had made to acquire the slave. Under these conditions, the only way of attracting white wage earners to the South was by freeing the slaves so that white wage earners would get preference over their black counterparts. Of course, freeing the slaves to attract whites was out of the question for the slaveholders. A slaveholder explained the situation as follows: "Fill the South with immigrant laborers and you will have voters enough among these newcomers to abolish slavery in every State where it exists." Therefore, trying to attract new whites to the South was not a viable proposition for the slaveholders.[28]

Yet, the possibility of white non-slaveholders leaving the South terrified the slaveholders, whose security in larger white numbers depended on the non-slaveholders' presence. Already blacks were the majority in some Southern states. Before the proportion of Southern blacks increased any further, the non-slaveholders would be forced to massacre them. That this possibility was not far-fetched is expressed in a letter from President John Quincy Adams to Louisa Adams:

> I shudder when I think of the calamities which slavery is likely to produce in this country. You would think me mad if I were to describe my anticipations. If the gangrene is not stopped, I can see nothing but insurrection of the blacks against the whites … till at last the whites will be exasperated to madness—shall be wicked enough to exterminate the Negroes as the English did the Rohillas.

[The Rohillas, a tribe of Afghan descent that occupied territories in Uttar Pradesh, India, were subjugated and broken by the British in alliance with the Nawab of Oudh in 1774].[29]

Under no circumstances then were white non-slaveholders to flee the South. In a war they would do the actual fighting to protect the slaveholders' interests and, therefore, had to be kept within the boundaries of the South, if necessary by imprisoning them. One way of doing this was to diffuse slave ownership more generally among them to reinforce the foundation of the slave institution. Pro-slavery leaders claimed that every white family should own at least a household servant: in fact, "we do not wish to see the white man of the South act as a bootblack, a cook, a waiter, or one of a gang of laborers in the sugar and cotton fields." Also, small farmers should have slaves so that they were not compelled to toil in their fields and to put their young sons to work "when they should either be at school or at play." What was not said was that there were more non-slaveholders than there were slaves. The wide distribution of the slaves would be the end of the plantation system that depended on the economics of scale and overseers for the slaveholders' profits. The slaveholders were unlikely to distribute their slaves if no new ones could be imported from abroad.[30]

Slaveholders' Survival Plan

The slaveholder then had to launch a three-pronged attack: (1) Fight tooth and nail for new territories where slavery was legal. Not only would this provide fresh land to keep the slaves working, but would prevent Southern non-slaveholders from emigrating to the new states. (2) Start a program to keep white non-slaveholders in the dark about slaveholders' real ambitions. This would be done by controlling the press and the mail, and prohibiting free speech in the South, contrary to the Constitution in a bid to control the non-slaveholders' discontent. (3) Play the race card to arouse the non-slaveholders' emotions in order to motivate them to support and even die for the goals of the slaveholders. This they would do with pro-slavery arguments: appeals for the preservation of white supremacy, and calls for unity to protect their lives and families from Black Republicans and Northern abolitionists like John Brown.

Protecting slavery in the South and obtaining an equal share of the nation's territories for slavery would entail the control of the federal government, which was a difficult proposition given Lincoln' ascendancy. An embittered South Carolina planter wrote in 1856 that:

> The northern abolitionists are threatening and planning to take away or destroy the value of our Slave property, and the demon democracy by its leveling principles, universal suffrage and numerous popular elections, homestead laws, and bribery are sapping the foundations of the rights of property in everything.[31]

By controlling the Senate, the presidency, and through them the Supreme Court, slaveholders had total control over the legislative, executive, and judicial branches of government. As the Supreme Court was the interpreter of the Constitution, the slaveholders also hoped to change the rules as they went along if necessary. Thus slaveholders were all set to protect slavery and win new territories for the South.

They had a first close call in the presidential election of 1800 when Jefferson and Burr tied for first place and the winner had to be decided by the House of Representatives. Party division was so close that during thirty-five ballots the House was deadlocked amidst talk of preventing an election and Civil War as the Virginia militia prepared to march on Washington, D.C. Thomas Jefferson won the election only because of the extra slave state votes provided by the federal ratio clause in the Constitution. He later obliged the Southerners with the controversial Louisiana Purchase that brought a vast territory into the Union, the most accessible parts of which appeared fit for cultivation only by slavery. Now the Southerners were in the driver's seat of the federal government and would maintain control until Abraham Lincoln's election in 1860.[32]

The Southerners made a first slip while preparing the Constitution of the United States when the Northwest Ordinance of 1787 was passed, specifically excluding slavery from western lands not yet organized and admitted as states. This implied that the federal government had jurisdiction over western lands and territories. This was unacceptable to the South, which created confusion in interpreting the Northwest Ordinance by making Kentucky enter the Union as a slave state without ever being a federal territory. Later, the Alabama and Mississippi territories were ceded as states in the Union by North Carolina and Georgia with stipulations that Congress must not disturb the existing status of slavery in those areas.

The North and South came to an unwritten understanding that the number of senators from slave and free states was to remain equal; slave and free states were to be admitted to the Union in pairs. In consequence, the slave states, starting with the admission of Tennessee in 1796, held an equal number of seats or occasionally, for short periods, just two seats short of equality in the Senate. This position continued until 1819, when there were twelve free states and twelve slave states.[33]

In 1819, Missouri applied for admittance to the Union as a slave state. By this time it was clear to the North that slavery was too entrenched to disappear soon. Admitting Missouri as a slave state would give the South an extra two votes in the Senate. Therefore, the North decided to oppose Missouri's application on the basis of the 1787 Northwest Territory ordinance, which had not been directly invoked until then. After violent political convulsions, a new compromise was worked out. Missouri and Maine would be admitted to the Union simultaneously, thus keeping the balance in the Senate between slave and free states. In the future, slavery would be excluded from all parts of the Louisiana Purchase north of latitude 36' 30", although Missouri, above this latitude, would be allowed entry as a slave state. The South gave up the right to slavery in some territories in order to discredit the 1787 ordinance that acknowledged the right of Congress to determine the status of slavery in the territories. In the future, the North and the South would have to jointly determine the rules governing the status of slavery in the territories. This compromise held for almost three decades, with slave and free states being admitted in lockstep, so that by 1849 there were fifteen free and fifteen slave states in the Union.[34]

The Missouri Compromise of 1820 started falling apart with the acquisition of new territory from Mexico in 1848, the year gold was discovered in California. Whites rushed to California by all available means, elected a legislature, outlawed slavery, and applied to enter the Union as a free State. California had skipped the territorial phase and presented the Union with a fait accompli, while the North and South were squabbling over the Missouri Compromise law of 1820. If the Missouri Compromise line were extended to the Pacific, it would split California in half. Also, if California were admitted as a free state, it would destroy the balance in the Senate between free and slave states. At this time Zachary Taylor, a slaveholder, worrying about his re-election as president, started wavering in his support for the South. He began working closely with Senator William Seward of New York, saying there was no point in quarrelling over territories that could not possibly be won for slavery.[35]

The South was not going to allow California to enter the Union as a free state without a fight. On July 12, 1848, Senator Jefferson Davis urged the territorial government of Oregon, which was north of the Missouri Compromise Line, to permit the introduction of slaves—not because that peculiar institution might strike roots there, but as a fundamental constitutional right. At this point the South was ready to secede from the Union rather than lose its equal status in the Senate. The situation was brought under control with the compromise of 1850, which admitted California to the Union as a free state. New Mexico and Utah were to be organized as territories without specifying whether they were to be free or slave, and a new strict Fugitive slave law was to replace that of 1793.[36]

The South did give the free states a two-vote advantage in the Senate by admitting California into the Union, and it had killed the Missouri Compromise line for good. It could go to any territory in the country with the slaves and fight it out, assisted by the new Fugitive slave law. Slaveholders now had the opportunity of transporting their slave property anywhere without fear of harassment or confiscation. The North thought that the South wanted to kidnap free blacks from the North, which suited the Northerners because they were seeking to rid themselves of their free blacks. The real significance of the Fugitive slave clause was not realized by all politicians, which is why the battle was only delayed until it took place in Kansas—north of the Missouri Compromise line, and by geography and climate considered unsuitable for cotton and slave plantations.[37]

After 1850, the North had an extra free-state advantage in the Senate. The South then directed all its efforts towards admitting a balancing slave state into the Union. Jefferson Davis, who was part of the new Southern leadership, actively began to seek to expand slavery's frontiers into the Caribbean and Latin America. In 1851, Narcisso Lopez, a Cuban adventurer, offered Davis command of a military expedition to liberate Cuba from Spanish rule. Davis refused, believing that command of an expedition was incompatible with his role as United States senator, and recommended that Robert E. Lee serve in his stead. In 1854, Davis became the ruling spirit in a cabal that attempted to force Congress to declare war on Spain on somewhat flimsy grounds so that Cuba might be annexed and carved into slave states.[38]

Instead of giving the South an opportunity to do this, Senator Stephen Douglas worked out a compromise with the passage of the Kansas-Nebraska bill in 1854. With this, the explicit repeal of the Missouri Compromise was conceded by including a provision applying the principles of the 1850 Compromise to the Nebraska territory. This would give the slaveholders an opportunity to test their strength in Nebraska to see if they could turn it into a slave state. The northerners agreed to this compromise for two reasons: First, it would put an end to the possibility of slave states in Cuba. Second, they felt that growing cotton in Nebraska with slaves was unlikely, and they were getting the concession over Cuba without giving up anything of importance. Growing cotton in Nebraska was not, however, the real issue for the slaveholders. They knew that the new territories were necessary for their survival. If the slaves could not grow cotton, they would work in the mines of the new territories. S. D. Moore of Alabama wrote that the South was "excluded from California, not pretendedly even by isothermal lines, or want of employment of slave labor, for in regard to climate and mining purposes the country was admirably adapted to the institution of African slavery."

Had it not been for the anti-slavery agitation, Representative Thomas Clingman told the House in 1850, Southerners would have used slaves in California mines, thus transforming it into a slave state. Even as a free state, California demonstrated the usefulness of slave labor. In 1852, the state legislature passed a mischievous fugitive slave law that could be and was interpreted as allowing slaveholders to bring slaves into the state to work in the mines and then send them home. Similarly, a Texan wrote in 1852 that a Mississippi and Pacific railroad would secure the New Mexico territory for the South by opening the mining districts to slave labor.[39]

The South had to expand, and its leaders knew it. Judge Warner of Georgia declared in the House of Representatives in 1856, "There is not a slaveholder in this House or out of it, but who knows perfectly well that whenever slavery is confined within certain specified limits, its future existence is doomed." Percy L. Rainwater's study of sentiment in Mississippi in the 1850s shows how firmly convinced slaveholders were that the system had to expand or die. W. Burwell of Virginia wrote in 1856 that:

> The South needed no more territory at the moment and faced no immediate danger of a redundant slave population. Yet statesmen like provident farmers, look to the prospective demands of those who rely upon their forethought for protection and employment. Though, therefore, there may be no need of southern territory for many years, yet it is important to provide for its acquisition when needed ....

It was necessary to introduce slavery into new territories to prevent non-slaveholders and poor whites from fleeing the South to seek an alternative way of life.[40]

With the passage of the Kansas-Nebraska bill, William H. Seward made a speech in the Senate: "Come on then, Gentlemen of the Slave States, since there is no escaping your challenge, I accept it in behalf of the cause of freedom. We will engage in competition for the virgin soil of Kansas, and God will give the victory to the side which is stronger in numbers as it is in right." Therefore, instead of being a compromise, the Kansas-Nebraska bill initiated a fight for the control of Kansas. The slaveholders tried to infiltrate Kansas from the adjacent slaveholding counties of Missouri, but were overwhelmed by the spontaneous movement of yeoman farmers from the old Northwest Territory, Kentucky and Tennessee. Therefore, right from the outset, Kansas was a battleground between the slaveholders and non-slaveholders of the South, with the North supporting the yeoman farmers. Many years of intricate and violent conflict followed in which anti-slavery forces usually carried the day and further polarized the battle between North and South.[41]

Northern concerns about the spread of slavery with the Kansas-Nebraska bill gave birth to the Republican or Free Soil Party of Abraham Lincoln. In the election of 1856, James Buchanan, who was completely dominated by the slaveholders in his cabinet and Congress, won the presidency. Thus, everything was not yet lost for the slaveholders; although the Free Soilers were fighting for an all-white Kansas, the president was aiding the slaveholders. However, the slaveholders were losing the battle in Kansas, so they decided to use their trump card while they still had an opportunity. Of the seven justices on the Supreme Court at this time, five, including Roger Taney, the chief justice, were slaveholders. This gave the slaveholders an opportunity to obtain the clear-cut statement of their rights that they had been unable to establish even in the Kansas-Nebraska bill.

In 1856, the Dred Scott decision was pending before the Supreme Court. Dred Scott, a slave who had returned to Missouri (a slave state), was claiming freedom through the courts on the basis of seven years of residence in a free state (Illinois) and a free territory. The issues to be settled were very narrow in scope: whether Scott had a right to sue in a federal court, and whether he had regained his slave status upon returning to Missouri. After Buchanan was elected, he conferred with the Supreme Court justices, who gave a general decision on Dred Scott's case in three weeks. Roger Taney, speaking for the court, declared that blacks—whether slave or free—were not citizens of the United States and therefore could not sue in federal courts. He also declared that Congress had never possessed the constitutional right to pass or to enforce the Missouri Compromise, thus slaveholders could now take their slaves to any state in the Union without interference. The decision alarmed the North, the Republicans in particular. Abraham Lincoln charged that the Dred Scott decision was part of a vast conspiracy involving Douglas, Pierce, Buchanan, and Taney to make slavery national.[42]

In 1858, Lincoln and Douglas held a series of debates while competing for a Senate seat from Illinois. In these debates, Lincoln and the Republicans made clear their position as Free Soilers (favoring slave-free territories). Although Lincoln conceded slavery's legality in slave states and enforcement of the fugitive slave law, he opposed the spread of slavery to new territories. He recognized the real reason slaveholders wanted to push slavery into the territories. During the debates with Douglas, the Clinton Central Transcript summarized Lincoln's view as follows: "But for the sake of millions of the free laborers of the North—for the sake of the poor white man of the South, and for the sake of the eternal prosperity of the Union, he was opposed to slavery extending one inch beyond its present limits."[43]

Even though Lincoln lost the Senate election in 1858, the Republicans' excellent performance in the state and congressional elections alarmed Southern slaveholders. To facilitate a Free Soil territorial policy, the Republicans attempted to pass a Pacific Railroad bill and homestead laws allowing a person to acquire 160 acres of public land simply by settling on the property. Slaveholders blocked these measures when Buchanan vetoed the Homestead Bill after it had passed both houses. Having lost their leverage in the

House of Representatives and the Senate, the presidency was their last hope for survival. President Buchanan tried his best to set the agenda for the slaveholders in his message to Congress. He asked the Northerners to stop attacking slavery, repeal their "unconstitutional and obnoxious" personal liberty laws, obey the fugitive slave law, and join with the South to adopt a constitutional amendment protecting slavery in all territories. Unless Yankees were willing to do these things, said Buchanan, the South would after all "be justified in revolutionary resistance to the Government." As an additional sign of goodwill, Buchanan also advised the North to support his long-standing effort to acquire Cuba.[44]

At this stage the slaveholders realized that losing the presidency in the election of 1860 would end their control over the government of the United States. A Lincoln victory in 1860 would mean the end of slavery's expansion forever. Not only would slaves be prohibited in the new territories, but Lincoln would attract Southern yeoman farmers and poor whites to the territories with homestead laws and freedom from competition with slaves. This would endanger the very survival of Southern slaveholders. If the South stayed in the Union, the Constitution would protect blacks from Lincoln's clutches. The Constitution could not, however, prevent Lincoln from drawing non-slaveholders out of the South. If that happened, only one course of action would remain for the slaveholders: secession.

Here too there was a rub. If the South were to secede from the Union, they would still be left with no new territories for expansion. Secession would only ensure that the white non-slaveholders would be trapped within the boundaries of the South. The long-term plan was for the independent Southern nation to annex Cuba and other Central American countries to obtain more territories for slavery. Secession at least would leave them with the non-slaveholding whites to protect owners from their slaves and to fight for new slave territories, but this meant ensuring the full cooperation of the white non-slaveholders, while keeping them in the dark about these plans. From the 1830s, the slaveholders had suppressed free speech, free press, free assembly, and the free circulation of ideas in the South. The slaveholders in Congress supported the passage of a Gag

Rule to prevent congressional discussion of petitions and memorials relating to slavery.

Between 1836 and 1844, while the rule was in effect, the right of petition was restricted, which led abolitionists to plausibly argue that slave power would even subvert the Constitution to perpetuate slavery. As part of their campaign to control Southern whites, the slaveholders violated the United States postal system. In July 1835, a mob broke into the Charleston post office, seized packages of abolitionist pamphlets, and burned them in the streets. The postmaster general, Amos Kendall, did not condemn the action taken in Charleston. He wrote: "We owe an obligation to the laws, but a higher one to the communities in which we live." A postmaster who refused to distribute "inflammatory papers" would "stand justified before country and all mankind."[45]

In order to insulate the South from outside ideas, Southern newspapers called for purging textbooks used in Southern schools. They also urged the establishment of new colleges in the South in order to keep Southern students out of Northern institutions, meanwhile suggesting that Southern boys refrain from going North for their education. A Professor Hendrick at the University of North Carolina was dismissed because he admitted that he intended to vote for Free Soiler and Republican John C. Fremont in the election of 1856. The *Raleigh Standard* justified such tactics by writing: "If there be Fremont men among us, let them be silenced or required to leave. The expression of Black Republican opinion in our midst is incompatible with our honor and safety as a people."

Northerners residing in the South were suspect merely on the ground of their nativity. Two Northern teachers living in South Carolina were asked to leave town by a local committee, with the town's newspaper justifying the action as follows: "Nothing definite is known of their abolition or insurrectionary sentiments, but being from the North and therefore necessarily imbued with doctrines hostile to our institutions their presence in this section has been obnoxious and at any rate suspicious." Even Southerners were not exempt from coercive action. A college student who was discovered in Tennessee with abolitionist literature was given twenty lashes as a warning. An anti-slavery man in western Virginia in the 1850s was stripped, tied to a tree, and beaten until he agreed to sell his property and leave the state.

Harriet Beecher Stowe's *Uncle Tom's Cabin*, which appeared in 1852, became a best-seller. The last chapter of the book proposed laws to prohibit breaking up slave families and the sale of slave women to brothels and lascivious masters, prohibition of interstate slave trade, repeal of the Fugitive Slave Law of 1850, and revision of state statutes and constitutions to allow sworn slave testimony against whites. This shrewdly thought-out combination highlighted the differences between the Catholic and Protestant slave codes. It explained why American slavery was immoral and differed from all other forms of slavery practiced elsewhere since biblical times.

Uncle Tom's Cabin struck a raw nerve in the South. Despite efforts to ban it, copies sold so fast in Charleston and elsewhere that booksellers could not keep pace with the demand. The vehemence of Southern denunciations of Mrs Stowe's "falsehoods and distortions" was the best gauge of how close they hit home. The *New Orleans Crescent* declared: "There never before was anything so detestable or so monstrous among women as this." The editor of the *Southern Literary Messenger* instructed his book reviewer: "I would have the review as hot as hellfire, blasting and searing the reputation of the vile wretch in petticoats who could write such a volume." Within two years pro-slavery writers had answered *Uncle Tom's Cabin* with at least fifteen novels whose thesis was that black slaves were better off than the white wage slaves of the North.[46]

With the publication of *The Impending Crisis of the South: How to Meet It,* Hinton R. Helper hit the nail on the head. He showed with statistical tables and census data how Southern non-slaveholding whites were the major victims of black slavery. Slavery, with its class divisions between the slaveholding and non-slaveholding whites, was the curse of the South, especially of the non-slaveholding whites. Helper exposed the vulnerability of the slaveholders, urging the non-slaveholders to fight slavery by using their votes and by heading for the free states if necessary, and "to overthrow the entire system of oligarchical despotism that had caused the South to welter in the cesspool of ignorance and degradation .... Now is the time for them to assert their rights and liberties ... and strike for Freedom in the South."[47]

Helper was careful not to allow the Southern slaveholders to level charges of "nigger lover" against him. He tried to beat the slaveholders at their own game by attacking the blacks: "No Slave nor Would-be Slave, No Negro nor Mulatto, No Chinaman nor unnative Indian, No Black nor Bicolored Individual of whatever Name or Nationality" ought to be allowed to "find Domicile any-where within the Boundaries of the United States." Abolitionists hated slavery because of what it did to black men. Helper wanted to end slavery because of what it did to white men; he in fact wanted to get rid of all the blacks by colonizing them in Africa or elsewhere.[48]

Away from the hullabaloo in the South, the Free Soil Republican Party of Abraham Lincoln noted the Southerner Helper's sup-port for its position on free territories reserved for poor white Southerners. Thus in 1859, a Republican committee raised funds to subsidize an abridged edition of Helper's book to be distributed far and wide as a campaign document. The abridgers ensured a spirited Southern reaction by adding such captions as "The Stupid Masses of the South" and "Revolution—Peacefully if we can, Violently if we must." Sixty-eight Republican congressmen endorsed a circular advertising the book. Even in the North it became common knowl-edge that the real issue was the slavery of the silent, white, non-slaveholding majority in the South.[49]

Several Southern states, alarmed by Helper's book, made it a crime to circulate it. The slaveholders knew that the fatal flaw in their plans had been revealed. A Kentucky editor fretted: "The great lever by which the abolitionists hope to extirpate slavery in the States is the aid of non-slaveholding citizens in the South." The *Charleston Mercury* echoed the same concern: "When Republicans organized their Abolition party of southern men the contest for slavery will no longer be one between the North and the South. It will be in the South, between the people of the South."[50]

The non-slaveholder had to be won over, and this called for a program of disinformation. Confederate propagandists found the pro-slavery argument that stressed the despicable condition of the Northern white wage slaves was not sufficient to bolster Southern morale. The non-slaveholders had to be aroused and motivated to fight for the slaveholders by racist appeals to their insecurities and the need for unity to maintain white supremacy. In 1822, a group of Charlestonians sent a memorial to the state legislature asserting that there was "only one principle that can maintain slavery, the 'principle of fear' .... We should always act as if we had an enemy in the very bosom of the state, prepared to rise upon and surprise the whites, whenever an opportunity afforded."[51]

John Brown's raid on a United States' arsenal at Harpers Ferry and his subsequent hanging provided a timely opportunity for the slaveholders' propaganda machine. Later it was found that John Brown had some support from Northern abolitionists, though prominent Republicans such as Lincoln and Seward condemned Brown as a madman and criminal. There had not been the remotest prospect of success for Brown's stated goal of freeing the slaves and it should have been dismissed as a ridiculous aberration.

Southern slaveholders, however, saw the raid as a golden opportunity to prepare the South to implement its plans. There was a revolution in Southern opinion six weeks after Harpers Ferry. James M. Mason of Virginia said in the Senate that "John Brown's invasion was condemned [in the North] only because it failed." A Mississippi legislator warned his constituents, "Mr. Seward and his followers ... have declared war on us." The governor of South Carolina informed the legislature that the entire North was "arrayed against the slaveholding states." The *Richmond Enquirer* stated that "The northern people have aided and abetted this treasonable invasion of a southern state." It was imperative for the slaveholders to connect John Brown with the abolitionists, then connect the abolitionists with the Black Republicans, then the Black Republicans with all the Northern people. They suppressed any denials from the Republicans that they had anything to do with John Brown. They also suppressed the fact that the abolitionists were a tiny minority in the North and opposed by most Northerners.[52]

As a result of the propaganda campaign, South Carolina's *Sumter Watchman* proclaimed: "Never before since the Declaration of Independence has the South been more united in sentiment." The slaveholders needed unity to protect the South: Governor William H. Gist felt that if the South did not "now unite for her defense, southern leaders would deserve the execration of posterity." Robert Toombs declared: "Never permit the Federal government to pass into the traitorous hands of the black Republican party." The Mississippi legislature passed resolutions declaring that the election of a president by a party unprepared to protect slave property would be a cause for the Southern states to meet in conference, where Mississippi would vote for secession. The people of the South could now see "the destiny which awaited them in this Union, under the control of a sectional anti-slavery party in the free states." If Brown had succeeded, "out of the ashes of our fair Republic would have risen another Saint Domingo."[53]

Once John Brown and the abolitionists had been identified with the "Black" Republican Party, as the slaveholders chose to describe it, it was easy to give the impression that the Republican Party and Abraham Lincoln intended to abolish slavery and free the black slaves and make them the equals of Southern whites. This was contrary to Lincoln's often-stated position, which was emphatic in assuring the slaveholders that no Republican had been detected in any attempt to destabilize them. He urged: "We must not interfere with the institution of slavery in the states where it exists because the Constitution forbids it and the general welfare does not require us to do so." He also specifically agreed to enforce the constitutional injunction for the return of fugitive slaves. The slaveholders were not convinced, asking how Lincoln intended to put slavery on the course to ultimate extinction everywhere, without interference in the Southern states. Actually, both the slaveholders and Abraham Lincoln understood each other, and the posturing was only for the benefit of Southern non-slaveholders.[54]

Lincoln always made it clear that he did not believe in the equality of the races under any circumstances. That did not stop the Southern slaveholders from painting Abraham Lincoln's party as one which would free the slaves to be equal of whites at the first available opportunity. A North Carolina editor wrote during the presidential campaign of 1856: "The expression of Black Republican opinions in our midst is incompatible with our honor and safety as a people." A committee of the Virginia legislature put it thus: "The very existence of such a party is an offense to the whole South." A New Orleans editor regarded every Northern vote cast for Lincoln as "a deliberate, cold blooded insult and outrage" to Southern honor. John J. Crittenden, Kentucky's elder statesman, delivered a speech just before the election in which he denounced the "profound fanaticism of Republicans who think it their duty to destroy the white man, in order that the black might be free .... The South has come to the conclusion that if Lincoln be elected ... she could not submit to the consequences, and therefore, to avoid her fate, will secede from the Union."[55]

To ensure sure that the Southern people understood the consequences of a Black Republican president, the slaveholders used the newspapers, churches, and word of mouth to let them know what would happen when the slaves were freed. A writer in a Texas Methodist weekly was certain that "the designs of the abolitionists are ... poison and fire to deluge the South in blood and flame ... and force their fair daughters into the embrace of buck negroes for wives." Baptist minister James Furman said, "Then every negro in South Carolina and every other Southern State will be his own master; nay, more than that, will be the equal of every one of you. If you are tame enough to submit, Abolition preachers will be at hand to consummate the marriage of your daughters to black husbands."

President James Buchanan in his message to Congress noted, because of the Republicans, "many a matron throughout the South retires at night in dread of what may befall herself and children before morning." On the eve of the election, a Mississippian observed that "the minds of the people are aroused to a pitch of excitement probably unparalleled in the history of our country." In Alabama, a supporter of John Bell, presidential candidate for the Constitutional Union Party in 1860, entitled his speech, "The

Election of Lincoln is Sufficient Cause for Secession." Therefore, the slaveholders and non-slaveholders of the South were ready, willing, and able to perform their duty going into that election.[56]

Northern Dilemmas

Why did the North not just allow the South to secede but chose a war in which more Northerners died than Southerners? The fact was that even the North had its class system comprising the wealthy controller-employers, yeoman farmers, and skilled craftsmen with property, white wage slaves without any property, and the black untouchables, who were restricted by segregation to menial jobs. Stability with growth meant certain checks and balances in this class system and therefore, a balance between wage slaves and yeoman farmers, was the North's primary problem.

The modern, diversified Northern economy that developed between 1840 and 1860 was based on white wage slavery and included an important manufacturing sector, a flourishing commercial life, and an expanding range of urban services and activities. Class divisions were bound to become increasingly visible and pronounced with new industrialists, capitalists, and financiers accumulating fortunes rarely seen in earlier times.

A growing urban middle class became an important factor in American society and a rapidly expanding labor force created an increasingly distinct working class. In this period, four million immigrants poured into the North from Europe from many countries and of various religions, but principally from Ireland and Germany. The Germans, who arrived with more money, went into business in western towns.

The penniless Irish Catholics settled in the eastern cities, forming a large, permanent laboring class. Workers had to live in filthy slums in factory towns. A work day extended from twelve to fourteen hours, and the working conditions were unsanitary and dangerous. Skilled male workers earned only about $7 per week while unskilled workers were fortunate to receive $3.50 a week. Women and children earned even less than men. Some states tried to improve the lot of workers by limiting the working day to ten hours as skilled workers sought to form unions. Effective labor resistance was, however, inhibited by the flow of immigrants who were usually willing to work for lower wages than native workers. Because they were so numerous, manufacturers had little difficulty in replacing disgruntled or striking workers with eager immigrants. Ethnic divisions and tensions between natives and immigrants and among the various immigration groups themselves resulted in internal bickering rather than complaints against employers. The result was that the wealthy industrialists with their political and economic power could enforce a system of white wage slavery in the North. The Irish-Catholic wage earners barely survived at the subsistence level.

A significant development was that the fruits of the labor of the wage slaves accrued principally to a tiny population of wealthy capitalists and industrialists, the Northern aristocracy. In Philadelphia, one percent of the population possessed half the wealth. Among the population of the North as a whole, five percent of the families possessed more than fifty percent of the wealth. This was consistent with the historical distribution of wealth in the United States even before the Revolution.

Yeoman farmers were necessary in the Northwest to balance the numerical strength of the wage slaves. The typical citizen of the Northwest was the owner of a reasonably prosperous family farm. The western farm averaged 200 acres and was owned by the family who worked it. The growing worldwide demand for farm products and rising prices made the western farms increasingly prosperous, especially with the purchasing power of the Northeast sustaining them. The latter in turn found a market in the Northwest for manufactured goods. The absence of black slaves encouraged the Northwestern farmer to increase his productivity with machines and better seeds and move west for fertile soils before they became exhausted.

The importance of the yeoman farmers was not lost on the American political scene. Wisconsin, from the moment of its admission to the Union in 1848, permitted alien farmers to become voters as soon as they had declared their intention of seeking citizenship and had resided in the state for a year. To further encourage yeoman farmers to the west, homestead laws were passed and the western states took steps to keep blacks out.

Mitigating the white wage slave's discontent was the hope for mobility, both economic and geographic. Generally, opportunities for working one's way up the economic ladder were limited. A few workers did manage to move from poverty to riches by hard work, ingenuity, and luck—a very small number, but enough to engender hope amongst those who watched them. A much larger number moved at least one notch up the ladder in the course of a lifetime—for example, by becoming a skilled laborer. Such people could envision their children and grandchildren moving up even further. There was, after all, a huge expanse of unsettled land in the west.

To some workers the dream of saving money to move out to the frontier could become a reality, "a safety valve for discontent." For most, however, the expense and expertise required for a move to the agricultural frontier made such a step impossible. Far more frequent was the movement of laborers from one industrial town to another—victims of layoffs seeking better opportunities elsewhere. Their search seldom led to a marked improvement in their circumstances, but the rootlessness of this large segment of the workforce kept them away from any political or economic power.[57]

Another way of limiting the discontent of the white wage slaves was to direct their hatred to the small number of blacks in the North. De Tocqueville remarked that "the prejudice which repels the blacks seems to increase in proportion as they are emancipated." Fanny Kemble wrote of the blacks in the North:

> They are not slaves indeed, but they are pariahs, debarred from every fellowship save with their own despised race, scoured by the lowest white ruffian in your streets, not tolerated even by the foreign menials in your kitchen. They are free certainly, but they are also degraded, rejected, the offscum and the offscouring of the very dregs of your society. All hands are extended to thrust them out, all fingers pointed to their dusky skin, all tongues,

the most vulgar as well as self-styled most refined, have learned to turn the very name of their race into an insult and a reproach.

Olmsted, recorded his conversation with a free black barber on a Red River steamboat, who said that "colored people could associate with whites much more easily and comfortably at the South than at the North, this was one reason he preferred to live at the South." He was kept at a greater distance from white people and more insulted on account of his color in the North than in Louisiana.[58]

Even so, the concerns of the white wage slave had to be addressed. While the employer-controllers had the political power to control the immigration of white wage slaves from Europe, certain numbers were essential to discourage unionization and intensify competition among them so that wage slaves survived only at subsistence levels. The number of blacks had to be minimized, as they were restricted to menial jobs and only served as targets for the hatred of wage slaves. For political stability, the number of yeoman farmers had to exceed the number of white wage slaves. The Southern slaveholders knew that the white wage slaves of the North lived in worse conditions than the black slaves of the South and kept advertising this fact in the pro-slavery argument. For political stability then, the North had to provide new territories for white yeoman farmers, which had to be free from black competition to be attractive.

Yet another dimension to this complex socio-economic relationship lay in the fact that the Northern employer-controllers benefited as much from black slavery as the slaveholders. Perhaps the North derived greater benefit from black slavery than the Southern slaveholders did because Northerners were middlemen or financiers in most of the transactions of the South. The Southern slaveholders owed the North between 200 and 400 million dollars at the time of the Civil War. Indirectly, jobs for the wage slaves also depended on the prosperity of the Southern slave economy. For the South, land in the west was often bought with money borrowed from Northern banks or earned in industries that derived capital funds from the transoceanic traffic in cotton, sugar, and tobacco.

Much of the capital that carried migration westward came either directly or indirectly from the earnings of slavery.[59]

Yet the Northerners would not countenance the black in his society. Representative Henry C. Murphy of New York expressed the North's sentiments: "As long as that degraded race remained in the South, it might be happy and contented." Once Negroes entered the free states, however, they would almost certainly "be objects of contumely and scorn." Under these circumstances, he appealed to the South to retain its Negro population; indeed, he would favor the adoption of severe laws "against any who shall bring the wretched beings to our Free states, there to taint the blood of the whites, or to destroy their own race by vicious courses." The extent of Northern morality was clear: they wanted to continue to receive benefits from the institution of slavery, but did not want any blacks among them.[60]

Another dilemma facing the North was the anti-democratic Constitution that allowed the South to dominate. A president elected by the Southern slaveholders with support from the Northern employer-controllers could thwart the will of a majority of the American people. There was no way now of getting around it without the North increasing its population. The Constitution, anti-democratic though it was, had kept the South in the Union and allowed the North to benefit from its slavery. With tariff walls against imports and control over the shipping and financial institutions, the North was able to make the South depend on it even for its daily bread. On the flip side, it encouraged a struggle for control between the slaveholders and employer-controllers, on one side, and the yeoman farmers and wage earners on the other.

Served with a Constitution rigged in favor of the slaveholders, the yeoman farmers had to find a way of regaining control over the government and territories of America. The options were to support or oppose slavery in the South, support or oppose slavery in the new territories, or support or oppose the entry of blacks into the Northern states. For Northerners, the only disadvantage of slavery in the South lay in the federal ratio clause. Otherwise they supported it. This was evident in the manner the North mobbed, assaulted, and threatened abolitionist lecturers and teachers with tar and feathers in New York, Pennsylvania, Massachusetts, New Hampshire, Connecticut, and other states. One abolitionist named Lovejoy was actually killed by a mob in Illinois as late as 1837. No major political party, including the Republicans, ever called for the abolition of slavery in its election manifesto.[61]

The question of slavery in the territories was another matter. In a zero-sum game, the North knew that the territories could either be opened to the slaveholders or reserved for yeoman farmers only. White yeoman farmers and wage earners would refuse to compete with black slaves. This had been proven by the fact that the working whites refused to go South while the poor whites of the South wanted to move to free territories. There were no advantages to slaves moving into the territories except for slaveholders of the South and Northern politicians who hoped to win elections with the Southern vote. This was amply demonstrated in Kansas, where the fight was between Missouri slaveholders assisted by President Buchanan, and non-slaveholders from Kentucky and Tennessee who were supported by Northern Free Soilers. The battle for the territories was not between the North and the South, but between the slaveholders and non-slaveholders of both regions, because the wage slaves in the North were also exploited by the employers. Although the majority of the people in the North were for free, white-only territories, a minority of politicians sought to confuse the issue by appeals to the principle of popular sovereignty. David Wilmot summed up the issue of keeping slavery out of all new territories so that free labor could flourish there: "The negro race already occupy enough of this fair continent … I would preserve for free white labor a fair country … where the sons of toil, of my own race and own color, can live without the disgrace which association with negro slavery brings upon free labor."[62]

Had it been a moral question, the North would have welcomed blacks, because that was the only practical solution to the Negro problem in the United States. As the slaves in the South lost their value, they could have been freed and gradually absorbed in the North and spread as "untouchables" throughout the country, as eventually happened after the Civil War. The only thing wrong with this plan was that the Northern whites preferred the status quo, benefiting from black slavery without having to inconvenience themselves with more blacks amongst them.

The strategy represented by the Republican Party of Abraham Lincoln, adopted by the North, was agreeable to continuation of slavery in the Southern states as required by the Constitution. It would also agree to enforcement of the fugitive slave law of 1850 so that the South could take back as many blacks as had escaped to the North. They would oppose the spread of slavery to the territories by reserving them for whites only.

Republican Action Plan

The Republicans insisted that they would abide by the Constitution and in return expected the Southern slaveholders to do the same because the Constitution did not give the South the option of secession. Further, the Republicans would oppose the equality between the races and stress democracy: a government of the people, by the people, and for the people instead of government by the slaveholders. The Republican Party put this strategy into operation for the election of 1860. It stressed that slavery in the Southern states was sanctioned by the Constitution and would not be interfered with. The Republicans denounced John Brown's raid as "among the gravest of crimes." Lincoln described it as an absurd adventure that had resulted in nothing noteworthy except Brown's death. The Republicans also distanced themselves from the abolitionists. William Garrison, the founder of *The Liberator,* accused the Republican Party of "white-manism." The Republican platform affirmed the right of each state to control its institutions.[63]

On the territories, the Republican position was that "the normal condition of all the territories of the United States is that of freedom." This was important, contended Lincoln, because if you let slavery into a territory, it could not be subsequently eliminated. "Keep it out until a vote is taken, and a vote in favor of it cannot be got in any population of forty thousand on earth, who have been drawn together by the ordinary motives of emigration and settlement." Lincoln understood and opposed the strategy of the slaveholders in the Dred Scott decision: "What is necessary for the nationalization of slavery? It is simply the next Dred Scott Decision. It is merely for the Supreme Court to decide that no State under the Constitution can exclude it, just as they have already decided that under the Constitution neither Congress nor the territorial legislature can do it." Lincoln wanted to exclude slavery from the territories by federal action and wanted to place the territories legally "in such a condition that white men may find a home ... I am in favor of this not merely for our own people who are born amongst us, but as an outlet for free white people everywhere, the world over."

Thus Lincoln wanted slave-free territories for non-slaveholding whites from the North, the South, and fresh immigrants from Europe. To further the strategy, the Republicans called for homestead laws and funding for a Pacific Coast Railway to encourage whites into the new territories. A southerner explained that such a law "would prove a most efficient ally for Abolition by encouraging and stimulating the settlement of free farms with yankees and foreigners pre-committed to resist the participancy of slaveholders in the public domain."[64]

The Republicans knew that no party advocating the equality of the races could elect a president of the United States. The slaveholders attempted, in a torchlight procession in New York City before the election of 1860, to identify the Republicans with miscegenation and racial equality. The Republican Party then sought to outdo the slaveholders in professions of allegiance to the principles of white supremacy. Senator Lyman Trumbull, an Illinois Republican leader and a close associate of Lincoln, declared: "We, the Republican party are the white man's party. We are for free white men, and for making white labor respectable and honorable, which it can never be when negro slave labor is brought into competition with it." Most Republicans denied any intention of extending political rights to free Negroes and expressed revulsion at the idea of social intercourse with them.[65]

Abraham Lincoln wanted to be a "safe" candidate by opposing black equality and consistently and accurately reflecting the thoughts and prejudices of the white people in the North and South.

Lincoln told a political rally in 1858: "I am not, nor ever have been, in favor of bringing about in any way the social and political equality of the white and black races—that I am not nor ever have been in favor of making voters or jurors of negroes, nor of qualifying them to hold office, nor to intermarry with white people." He claimed that physical differences made political and social equality between Negroes and whites impossible. So long as both races remained in the United States, "there must be the position of superior and inferior, and I as much as any other man am in favor of having the superior position assigned to the white race." Even though he knew it was impractical, Lincoln concluded that colonization of Negroes offered the only hope of resolving the racial problem.[66]

As part of its election strategy, the Republican Party stressed its belief in full democratic participation of all the people. The Southern slaveholders and the Northern employers were demanding that a minority be given the right to control the majority. The non-slaveholders of the North and South represented more than eighty percent of all whites in the United States, while the slaveholders and employers were a minority in power. The Republican Party that fought the elections of 1856 was the first to oppose the extension of slavery in its manifesto. Lincoln summarized the issue of democracy in America in his message to the special session of Congress that met on July 4, 1861, as follows:

> This issue embraces more than the fate of these United States. It presents to the whole family of men the question whether a constitutional republic or democracy—can or cannot maintain its territorial integrity against its own domestic foes. Our popular government has often been called an experiment. It is now for them to demonstrate to the world that those who can carry an election can also suppress a rebellion; that ballots are the rightful and peaceful successors of bullets; and that when ballots have fairly and constitutionally decided, there can be no successful appeal back to bullets; that there can be no successful appeal, except to ballots themselves, at succeeding elections.[67]

Before the election of 1860 the battle lines had been drawn on both sides. Lincoln had warned the Southerners in December 1859 that if the Republicans elected a president, "and therefore you undertake to destroy the Union, it will be our duty to deal with you as old John Brown has been dealt with. We shall try to do our duty." The slaveholders fully understood the significance of a Republican president. The election of Lincoln could end their two generations of control of all levels of the government for the first time. Jefferson Davis said: "No human power can save the Union, all the cotton states will go." One Southern editor wrote: "We spit upon every plan to compromise." Judah Benjamin agreed that "a settlement is totally out of our power to accomplish."[68]

Three issues made secession and Civil War inevitable. The first was the future of the blacks: any plan of emancipation had to be gradual, and once freed, they were to be doomed to be "untouchables" or underlings. This was essential if the system of white wage slavery was to continue. If the blacks were to fill the untouchable slot, they had to be spread throughout the country, both North and South.

The unfair balance that the undemocratic Constitution offered in favor of the wealthy classes was the second major issue. The Republican Party of the majority of white Americans would not only organize the Northern non-slaveholders, but also set in motion a struggle between the white Southern slaveholders and non-slaveholders. This the Southern slaveholders would not allow to occur without a fight, whose winner could amend the Constitution so that it became democratic and the power was transferred from the state to the federal level.

Finally, there was the economic reality of institution of slavery that had been reduced to an issue of money—large sums of between $ 200 and $400 million. This meant that the slaves in the South were mortgaged to bankers in the North. If the Southern slaves were to lose their value or be freed, how were the Southerners going to pay the Northerners? Though the North controlled two-thirds of the banking capital of the country, they were unwilling to forgive the debts of the Southerners. By seceding, the Southerners could in one stroke repudiate their debts to the North and build a tariff wall so that they could trade directly with Europe, exchanging cotton for manufactured goods. This economic truth made the Civil War inevitable. After the war, even if the slaves were forcibly freed without compensation to the slaveholders, the Northern financiers could foreclose on Southern plantations to recover their debts.[69]

For the North then, the Union had to be maintained. Lincoln made known his position in an open letter to the editor of a newspaper with this statement, which bears repeating: "My paramount object in the struggle is to save the Union, and is not either to save or destroy slavery. If I could save the Union without freeing any slave I would do it, and if I could save it by freeing all the slaves I would do it, and if I could save it by freeing some and leaving others alone, I would also do that." It was clear that the Civil War had nothing to do with the morality of slavery or the future of blacks. The *Boston Herald* predicted the evils that would follow for the North if it allowed the South to secede:

> Should the South succeed in carrying out her designs, she will immediately form commercial alliances with European countries who will readily acquiesce in any arrangement which will help English manufacturing at the expense of New England. The first move the South would make would be to impose a heavy tax upon the manufactures of the North, and an export tax upon the cotton used by northern manufacturers. In this way she would seek to cripple the North. The carrying trade, which is now done by American vessels, would be transferred to British ships, which would be a heavy blow aimed at our commerce. It will also seriously affect our shoe trade and the manufacture of ready-made clothing, while it would derange the monetary affairs of the country.[70]

Clearly, the North's economy was interdependent with the South's; therefore, for self-preservation the North could not allow Southern secession. We shall see how the stated positions of both North and South would inevitably lead to war.

Chapter 9

Lincoln's Solution

You cannot fool all the people all the time
Give the Greatest Good to the Greatest Number
Never knew a man who wished to be a slave
—Abraham Lincoln

With the success of the Republican Party, Lincoln won the presidency in November 1860 with a majority of the electoral votes, but only two-fifths of the popular votes. He did not carry a single state in the South. True to its threat, the South decided to secede while the iron was hot. Jefferson Davis later described the South's decision:

> We waited until a sectional President, nominated by a sectional convention, elected by a sectional vote—and that the vote of a minority of the people—was about to be inducted into office, under the warning of his own distinct announcement that the Union could not permanently endure "half slave and half free"; meaning thereby that it could not continue to exist in the condition in which it was formed and its Constitution adopted.[1]

Quick action was necessary before the ardor of the people subsided. For the slaveholders, delay was their worst enemy. By December 1860, in a South Carolina convention composed of those who were ready to stand alone, if necessary, in defense of southern rights, an ordinance of secession was adopted. Within six weeks, six more states followed South Carolina's example. The cotton kingdom was ready to form itself into the Confederate States of America.

Even so, secession had been accomplished after a hard-fought battle against the will of a majority that was unable to stem the emotional tide. Only one of the seceding states submitted its ordinance of secession to popular ratification. Before the end of January 1861, nearly all the congressmen from the Deep South had resigned, and Northern and border states had no opportunity for compromises. Without wasting any time, the South formed a provisional government of the seceded states, elected Jefferson Davis president, and inaugurated him at Montgomery before Lincoln could be inaugurated at Washington.[2]

When Lincoln took the oath of office on March 4, 1861, Virginia and the other states of the upper South had still not left the Union. In his inaugural address, Lincoln was firm on the maintenance of the Union and conciliatory on the matter of slavery. He made it clear that the Constitution was inviolate and that he did not recognize either the right to secede or the independence of the Confederacy.

On the slavery question, he stuck to his refusal to allow expansion of slavery into the territories. He indicated, however, that he would accept a proposal to write a guarantee of slavery into the Constitution and leave slavery alone in the states where it already existed. Specifically, Lincoln noted that there was no need for war or bloodshed, and he promised not to fire the first shot. He also indicated that "the power confided to me will be used to hold, occupy, and possess the property and places belonging to the government because it was registered in heaven," thus drawing the line for the secessionists to cross.[3]

The South had heard it all before; Lincoln was offering only the status quo. Thinking through this, the Southerners knew no realistic compromise could protect their interests better than secession. On April 12 they took up Lincoln's challenge by firing on Fort Sumter. Major Robert Anderson surrendered to the Confederates two days later. The Rebels had ignored the warning of Southerner Alexander Stephens: "Revolutions are much easier started than controlled, and the men who begin them [often] ... themselves become the victims."[4]

America's Bloodiest War

While Lincoln was waiting for the first shot to be fired, other Republican leaders favored decisive action. They warned that the North would not tolerate the abandonment of Sumter. Meanwhile, the differences between Union and Confederate tariff schedules frightened numerous Northern merchants into feeling the need for drastic action. By the end of March many businessmen had reached the point where they felt that anything, even war, was better than the existing indecision, which was fatal to trade. One observer wrote: "It is a singular fact that merchants who, two months ago, were fiercely shouting 'no coercion,' now ask for anything rather than inaction." With the surrender at Fort Sumter, Lincoln proclaimed a blockade of all Southern ports and called for a force of 75,000 volunteers to restore federal authority in the South. The crisis had been transformed into a battle of power: firepower, dollar power, horsepower, manpower, and willpower.[5]

With Lincoln's proclamation the upper Southern states of Virginia, Arkansas, Tennessee, and North Carolina seceded, waiting only for the first shot to be fired. The border states of Kentucky, Maryland, and Missouri straddled the fence, adopting a wait-and-see attitude to determine which side would prevail. At this point there were twenty-three states in the Union with a population of approximately twenty-two million, including half a million blacks, while the eleven Confederate States had a population of about nine million, of whom three and a half million were slaves. The North was in a position to manufacture practically all its war materials while the South had to rely on Europe throughout the war. Although the land area of the Union and Confederate States was about equal, the North had approximately twenty thousand miles of railroads to only ten thousand miles in the South. This proved to be an advantage for the Southerners, who fought a defensive war on their own land, with local support and a more intimate knowledge of their own terrain. Despite the Northern advantage in terms of manpower and material, the war took place in unfamiliar territory, which rendered a quick and decisive result in the North's favor uncertain.

Lincoln knew that his ultimate objective was to preserve the Union, not to destroy the South. Blacks and slavery were not the real issues. Ultimately the South was a part of the Northern economy and represented a part of Northern investment. Lincoln believed that after the war ended, the North and South must coexist as one nation and one people with a common heritage. His goal therefore was to put down the Southern slaveholders' rebellion with the least possible death and destruction in the shortest possible time. He had to act in such a way that no lasting ill feeling or enmity simmered between the two sections. Lincoln knew that the three border states of Maryland, Kentucky, and Missouri could prove crucial in the achievement of his objectives. They encompassed large and resolute secessionist minorities; and as they were riding on the fence, much was at stake in the contest to win their allegiance. These three states would have added forty-five percent to the white population and military manpower of the Confederacy, eighty percent to its manufacturing capacity, and nearly forty percent to its supply of horses and mules. For almost five hundred miles, the Ohio River flowed along the northern border of Kentucky, providing a defensive barrier or an avenue of invasion, depending on which side could control and fortify it. Lincoln reportedly said that while he hoped to have God on his side, he must have Kentucky, and bore the three states in mind when working on strategy.

He had to de-emphasize the slave issue if he was going to get the North's white population to join the war. Some of those who voted for Lincoln and some who had voted for his opponents in the North would have refused to support an anti-slavery war in 1861. Samuel S. Cox, a Democratic Congressman, warned that Ohio's soldiers would no longer fight for the Union "if the result shall be the flight and movement of the black race by millions northward." Archbishop John Hughes added his warning that "We Catholics, and a vast majority of our brave troops in the field, have not the slightest idea of carrying on a war that costs so much blood and treasure just to gratify a clique of Abolitionists." The attitude of the white Northern population was summed up by the war cry, "To the flag we are pledged, all its foes we abhor. And we ain't for the nigger, but we are for the war."[6]

Taking account of the reality of this feeling, the Union policy was to turn away blacks who volunteered to fight in the war. Also, all slaves who tried to escape to the Union lines or were captured were to be returned. On the July 4, 1861, Colonel Pryor of Ohio delivered an address to the people of Virginia in which he repudiated the accusation that the Northern armies were abolitionists:

> I desire to assure you that the relation of master and servant as recognized in your state shall be respected. Your authority over that species of property shall not in the least be interfered with. To this end, I assure you that those under my command have peremptory orders to take up and hold any Negroes found running about the camp without passes from their masters.

Henry Halleck in Missouri in 1862 refused to let fugitive slaves enter his lines. Generals Ambrose Burnside, Don Carlos Buell, Joseph Hooker, George Thomas, Alpheus Williams, and George McClellan himself all warned their soldiers against receiving slaves. They instructed their armies to use force to return fugitives seeking shelter in the Union lines to their Southern masters. Most of them, in fact, permitted owners to remove slaves found within the lines.[7]

Loyal newspapers and Northern politicians, while advocating stringent measures for putting down the rebellion, carefully disclaimed any intention of disturbing the slave institution of the South. The secretary of state informed foreign governments through the diplomatic corps that this was not the purpose of the government. Leading generals, on entering Southern territory, issued proclamations to the same effect. One even promised to put down any slave insurrection "with an iron hand." Blacks were not to be employed as laborers or armed as soldiers. The North avoided the appearance or the desire to change the prevailing status of blacks. Lincoln knew that what blacks thought or what happened to blacks in the long run was inconsequential.

Frederick Douglass summarized the black point of view that the Civil War was begun "in the interests of slavery on both sides. The South was fighting to take slavery out of the Union and the North was fighting to keep it in the Union; the South fighting to get it beyond the limits of the U.S. Constitution and the North fighting for the old guarantees—both despising the Negro, both insulting the Negro." The limitations of Lincoln's argument that "slavery is immoral" were well known to the blacks. As Lincoln refused to advocate repeal of the fugitive slave law, Wendell Phillips went so far as to call him "the Slave Hound of Illinois." H. Ford Douglass, an Illinois Negro leader, recalled that Lincoln once refused to sign a legislative petition asking for repeal of the state law barring Negro testimony in cases involving whites. If blacks dared to send their children to Illinois schools, the Negro leader charged, "Abraham Lincoln would kick them out, in the name of Republicanism and anti-slavery!" What Lincoln and the blacks knew was that he was the lesser evil, and blacks had no better place to turn.[8]

In the fall of 1861, Lincoln asked Congress for a resolution committing it to support state slave emancipation with federal funds. He justified the measure as one that deprived the South of hope of victory. Once the border states started gradual emancipation, the Confederacy would be deprived of the hope that these states would ever join it. He justified the proposal's constitutionality by letting the states decide for themselves. The plan was politically motivated because it involved compensation for the owners, gradualism, and colonization of the emancipated blacks. He hoped the change in the status of blacks would take place with the least social and economic shock. Because the plan was impractical—it extended the period of gradual emancipation to 1900—no border states responded to it nor did Congress pass it. A large section of the public was impatient with peacetime methods that were indirect, costly, and slow, nor had they any desire to obtain the rebels' consent.[9]

With the Union army's defeats in the latter half of 1862, making it clear that the war was going to be much longer and more disagreeable than he had anticipated, Lincoln realized that his policy of not inciting the blacks in the Confederate States and keeping black participation in the war to a minimum was proving costly. Frederick Douglass expressed this conviction: "To fight against slaveholders, without fighting against slavery, is but a half-hearted business, and paralyzes the hand engaged in it .... Fire must be met with water .... War for the destruction of liberty must be met with war for the destruction of slavery." Southerners boasted that slavery was "a tower of strength to the Confederacy" because it enabled the South "to place in the field a force so much larger in proportion to her population than the North." Douglass said: "The very stomach of this rebellion is the negro in the form of a slave. Arrest that hoe in the hands of the negro and you smite the rebellion in the very seat of its life."[10]

Lincoln saw the merit in this line of thinking. He signed the Emancipation Proclamation in September 1862, giving one hundred days notice to the Confederate States. Effective on January 1, 1863, all slaves in the Confederate States not under the control of the Union army were freed, thus encouraging their rebellion by letting them enlist in the Union army. Lincoln did not want to free the slaves in the border states because that would violate the Constitution and encourage them to join the Confederate States. The distinction could be made because the Confederate States were engaged in a domestic insurrection, and therefore the escaped slaves from the Confederate States could be put to work on the Union side as "contraband of war." Northerners who had reservations about the Emancipation Proclamation were told that the action was out of "military necessity." In November 1862, the war department also authorized the creation of an all-black regiment, the First South Carolina Volunteers. It was only in 1863 that the enlistment of black troops began in earnest, and by the end of the war about two hundred thousand blacks from the South had served in the Union army and navy, although they had to serve in segregated units with reduced pay.[11]

In spite of the Emancipation Proclamation, Lincoln did not change his position that colonization of Negroes was the only solution to get rid of blacks. Addressing a Negro delegation in 1862, the president stressed the physical incompatibility of the two races and the fact that "on this broad continent, not a single man of your race is made the equal of a single man of ours." Inasmuch as Americans did not desire the further presence of the Negro population, Lincoln urged black men to look elsewhere: to Liberia, which had had a limited success; or preferably to Central America, where location, natural resources, and climate offered splendid opportunities. To follow through on his plan, Lincoln signed an agreement with Bernard Kock, a charlatan adventurer on December 31, 1862, providing for the settling of five thousand American Negroes on Cow Island at a cost to the government of $50 a head. Kock raised capital in New York for over four hundred Negroes to be shipped to Cow Island, where they were abandoned because of the greed and corruption of Kock and the Haitian officials. When reports of the fiasco filtered back to Washington, Lincoln issued a proclamation on April 16, 1863, canceling his contract with Kock.[12]

Despite the collapse of the Cow Island venture, Lincoln persisted with his purpose. At some early date in 1863, the president approached Lucius E. Chittenden, the Register of the Treasury, with a curious proposal: "It is to remove the whole colored race of the slave States into Texas. If you have any acquaintance who would take that contract, I would like to see him." The Register presented John Bradley, a well-known Vermonter, to Lincoln for discussion. After a two-hour meeting Bradley, overflowing with admiration for the president and enthusiasm for his proposed assignment, said: "The proposition is to remove the whole colored race into Texas, there to establish a republic of their own. The subject has political bearings of which I am no judge, and upon which the President has not yet made up his mind. But I have shown him that it is practicable. I will undertake to remove them all within a year." Although it was too late to implement this plan once the war had started, it would have been the only workable solution to avoid the Civil War. Once blacks had been removed to Texas, they might well have died for lack of food, shelter, and jobs; such extermination would have been the only way of preventing the Civil War.[13]

Things were heating up for the South as well. While Lincoln was planning a slave revolt in the South with his Emancipation Proclamation in September 1862, manpower needs forced the Confederate Congress to raise the upper age limit for conscription from thirty-five to forty-five. This made the heads of many poor families subject to the draft at a time when the summer's drought had devastated food crops. In addition, the Congress added insult to injury by a provision to exempt one white man on every plantation with twenty or more slaves.[14]

By granting a special privilege to a class constituting only five percent of the white population, the "Twenty Negro Law" became as popular in the South as substitution for the draft in the North. Although only a few thousand planters or overseers obtained exemptions under the law, its symbolism was powerful. Many men who deserted from Confederate armies during the winter of 1862–1863 agreed with a Mississippi farmer who went AWOL because he "did not propose to fight for the rich men while they were at home having a good time." Alarmed by what he had heard on a trip home from Richmond, Mississippi's Senator James Phelan wrote to his friend Jefferson Davis on December 9: "Never did a law meet with more universal odium …. Its influence on the poor is calamitous … it has aroused a spirit of rebellion in some places, I am informed, and bodies of men have banded together to resist, whilst in the army it is said it only needs some daring men to raise the standard to develop a revolt.'[15]

From the outset the slaveholders had trouble defining their war aims for the South's non-slaveholders. They could not explicitly claim that defense of slavery was a primary Confederate war aim because this might have proved more divisive than unifying. Rather, they portrayed the South as fighting for liberty and self-government, unmindful of Samuel Johnson's question about an earlier generation of American rebels: "How is it that we hear the loudest yelps for liberty among the drivers of negroes?" A Confederate soldier captured early in the war, whose appearance made it clear that he was not a member of the planter class was asked why he, a non-slaveholder, was fighting to uphold slavery. He replied: "I'm fighting because you're down here." For this soldier, as for many other Southerners, the war was not about slavery. The slaveholders' propaganda campaign sought to persuade them that without slavery there would have been no black Republicans to threaten the South's way of life, no special Southern civilization to defend against Yankee invasion. The fatal weakness of the Confederacy was that a Southern majority who were non-slaveholders thought, many of them unconsciously, that the fruits of defeat would be less bitter than those of success.[16]

Ultimately, Lincoln's strategy of creating discontent among the slaves in the Confederate States and starving the slaveholders into submission proved successful. The Confederate commissary general warned of a subsistence crisis in Southern armies after food riots in July of 1863. In September, a mob at Mobile, crying "bread or blood," looted stores on Dauphine Street. In October, the *Richmond Examiner* declared that civilians were being reduced "to a point of starvation." A government clerk reported the following exchange between a woman and a shopkeeper in Richmond, the former, when asked for $70 for a barrel of flour exclaimed "My God! How can I pay such prices? I have seven children; what shall I do?" "I don't know, madam," the merchant replied, "unless you eat your children."[17]

Jefferson Davis was so desperate to raise new manpower that he induced the Confederate Congress to give freedom to any slave who enlisted in the army. Slavery was dead and the Confederacy dying. On April 2, 1865, Jefferson Davis and the Confederate government fled when Richmond had to be evacuated. Meanwhile, Robert E. Lee was finding it impossible to stage an organized retreat. So complete was the collapse of the Confederacy that supplies could not get to the soldiers, some of whom went for days without rations. Desertions multiplied; for months they had been so numerous that Lee had been unable to spare troops to bring back the runaways. By then men simply fell out on the road west. Grant's pursuing army found something new: rifles abandoned on the roadside.

Instead of fighting another battle that would mean certain annihilation, Lee handed over his sword in surrender to Grant on

April 9, 1865. On April 14, Robert Anderson returned to raise his old flag over Fort Sumter exactly four years after the surrender. On that very day Lincoln went to the theater in Washington where he was shot in the head by John Wilkes Booth. He was dead the following morning.[18]

The Scorecard

In tallying the cost of the Civil War, it was estimated that over 620,000 soldiers lost their lives in four years: 360,000 Yankees and at least 260,000 rebels. Southern civilians who died as a direct or indirect result of the war were conservatively estimated at 50,000. Every six slaves freed cost the life of one soldier, a staggering price. Many wondered whether the liberation of four million slaves was worth the cost. Their freedom was only a side effect of a war that had to be fought to pay for two hundred years of crimes against blacks and whites so that the nation could start over with a clean slate.[19]

In cash terms, the cost was not as easily appraisable. The war expenses of the belligerents amounted to about five billion dollars. The outlay for three years of reconstruction was placed at three billion more. On the other hand, the cost of four million slaves was estimated at two billion dollars. Therefore, the monetary cost of the conflict far exceeded the value of the slaves.

Would it have been better to compensate the slaveholders to free their slaves? Compensation to the slaveholders was a necessary but not a sufficient condition to free the slaves. The real issue was dealing with the free blacks, whom neither the South nor the North wanted. When abolishing slavery after the war, the North hoped that blacks would stay put in the South. Alexander H. Stephens, the Confederate vice-president, addressed the Georgia Legislature on February 22, 1866, calling for a return to orderly government:

> Slavery, as it was called, or the status of the black race, their subordination to the white, upon which all our institutions rested, is abolished forever, not only in Georgia, but throughout the limits of the United States. This

required that the former slaves be given ample and full protection so that they may stand equal before the law, in the possession and enjoyment of all rights of person, liberty and property.[20]

Overall, the supreme outcome of the Civil War was the destruction of the Southern planter aristocracy, which along with the Northern employer-controllers had virtually ruled the United States since the Revolution. It was a class war and a victory for democracy because the Republicans were the first party to represent the yeoman farmers and wage workers who were in a majority in both the North and South. It should be remembered that the North had just over 400,000 aristocratic employers who were rich enough to pay enough income taxes during the Civil War to match the resources of the 385,000 slaveholders of the South. In the election of 1860, the slaveholders of the North and South had separated by splitting their votes. The destruction of the Southern planter aristocracy, including slavery itself, was more complete than the destruction of the clergy and the nobility in the French Revolution.[21]

Before Lincoln's assassination, Congress had passed the Thirteenth Amendment to the Constitution and sent it to the states for ratification. It called for the abolition of slavery but made no provision for the livelihood of blacks. The amendment's primary objective was to remove slavery from the Constitution of the United States. There was no place for the Negro in the Constitution. To get the Constitution ratified, all explicit mention of slavery had been avoided. The slaveholders had, however, successfully included the federal ratio clause and what amounted to a fugitive slave clause in the Constitution.

With the Thirteenth Amendment, the North hoped to neutralize these clauses once and for all, as those clauses of the Constitution had been one of the sore points for the Northerners who did not have any slaves. This was a logical first step. The North also hoped that freeing the slaves, thereby eliminating the only reason for blacks to go North, would encourage ex-slaves to stay in the South. Freeing slaves was not in itself the intention of the Thirteenth Amendment;

it was a side-effect of more important objectives. Starting with the Thirteenth Amendment, political power radically shifted from the state to the federal level. Eleven of the first twelve amendments to the Constitution had limited the powers of the national government; six of the next seven, beginning with the Thirteenth Amendment in 1865, vastly expanded those powers at the expense of the states.

During the first seventy-two years of the republic, from George Washington to Abraham Lincoln, a resident of the southern Confederate States had been president of the United States for forty-nine of those years, more than two-thirds of the time. In Congress, twenty-three of the thirty-six Speakers of the House and twenty-four of the presidents pro tem of the Senate had been Southerners. The Supreme Court always had a Southern majority: twenty of the thirty-five justices had been appointed from the slave states. After the Civil War, a century passed before a resident of an ex-Confederate state was elected president. For half a century, none of the Speakers of the House or presidents pro tem of the Senate came from the South, and only five of twenty-six Supreme Court Justices appointed during that half-century were southerners.[22]

What did the Civil War do for blacks? Their emancipation, in Lincoln's phrase, sent them flying into the economic class system as "a laboring, landless, and homeless class." After two hundred years of experience under the Protestant slavery code, blacks lacked the education, knowledge, community cohesiveness, or capital to become economically independent even if they were given land. With the Fourteenth and Fifteenth Amendments of the Constitution, forced on the Southern states under military occupation, blacks were given certain rights of citizens on paper. Even the three former slave states that had not seceded—Delaware, Maryland, and Kentucky—registered their disapproval of the amendments. The Fourteenth Amendment made three offerings to blacks. It promised them citizenship and equal protection under the law and attempted to confer the vote on black men.

The catch with all Civil Rights laws was that there was no practical way of enforcing them. Even Northern states such as Connecticut, New Jersey, Pennsylvania, Ohio, and others excluded blacks from voting. In 1870, the Fifteenth Amendment was ratified, declaring that the right of citizens to vote should not be denied on account of race, color, or previous condition of servitude. Again, this amendment failed to reckon with the political and juristic ingenuity of the white race.[23]

With the abolition of slavery, the status of blacks would become uniform throughout the Union. With a total population of thirty million, four million of whom were blacks, the trend for the future would be set. As white immigration increased, the proportion of blacks in the total population would decrease. Gradually the dependence on black labor would decrease, and blacks would assume the role of "untouchables" in the economic and social class system of the country. They would be segregated as untouchables in all aspects of living. Blacks would live in separate areas, work at menial jobs, eat in separate areas, have separate bathrooms, and be buried in black cemeteries.

CHAPTER 10
LESSONS OF THE CIVIL WAR

We cannot escape history.
> —Abraham Lincoln

For nothing is ours that another can deprive us of.
> — Thomas Jefferson

"Love not the world," the preacher said,
And winked his eye, and shook his head;
He seized on Tom, and Dick, and Ned,
Cut short their meat, and clothes, and bread,
Yet still loved heavenly union.
> —Frederick Douglass, "The Parody," 1854

Journalist Noah Brooks reported in the *Washington Chronicle* on December 6, 1864:

> On Thursday of last week two ladies from Tennessee came before President Lincoln asking the release of their husbands held as prisoners of war at Johnson's Island. They were put off till Friday, when they came again; and were again put off to Saturday. At each of the interviews one of the ladies urged that her husband was a religious man. On Saturday the President ordered the release of the prisoners and said to this lady: "You say your husband is a religious man; tell him when you meet him, that I say I am not much of a judge of religion, but that, in my opinion,

the religion that sets men to rebel and fight against their government, because, as they think, that government does not sufficiently help some men to eat their bread on the sweat of other men's faces, is not the sort of religion upon which people can get to heaven!"

It is a pointer to some basic lessons of war, a war that is often the result of built-up imbalances in institutions failing to resolve themselves within the rules that govern opposing forces. Not until the war is won can the winner change the rules to reflect the new reality and power structure. Given the set of motivational, socio-economic, geographic, and political factors, amongst which the need to keep America united was the first priority, the free black concept could only find expression in a society into which they could be assimilated as "untouchables" or underlings.

Untouchables as "Separate but Equal"

The Civil War finally settled one issue, the fact that blacks were here to stay. It was not possible to get rid of them after they had served their usefulness. A new set of rules had to be created so that the blacks could live together with the whites in the United States of America. Direct competition between the black and white races had to be avoided, and the white race always had to have a superior status.

The Thirteenth Amendment to the Constitution was the first attempt to define the structure between black-white relationships. Its only purpose was to abolish slavery from the Constitution of the United States by neutralizing the federal ratio clause and the fugitive slave clause. The amendment was passed by Congress on January 31, 1865; and it was ratified and became part of the Constitution in December 1865. But this amendment did not guarantee citizenship and voting rights to blacks. Also in May 1965, Andrew Johnson, the new president, offered amnesty and restitution of property, except slaves, to the rebels who would take an oath of allegiance. Although the blacks would be free, they were not given land or economic restitution for centuries of slavery. They would be only free to work or starve, just like the landless whites.

For the new Congress, which had a three-fourths Republican majority, the next priority was to make sure that the black population would continue to work and live in the South. In the fall of 1865, several Northern states had rejected referendums to amend their constitutions to enfranchise the few black men in those states. The writing was on the wall for all to see. The new Congress knew that they would not be able to change Northern opinion, but they could force their will on the rebel states, which were at their mercy due to losing the Civil War.

To restrict the blacks to the South, it was necessary to show that they had more rights and opportunities in the South than they would ever have in the North. A Freedman's Bureau with white northern agents was created to smooth the transition of returning the land to pardoned planters and establishing conditions for the freed black slaves to return to work. Few blacks had the money and almost none were in a position to buy land. Besides, the whites often refused to sell or rent land to blacks. In order to repair war devastation and plant crops, the Freedman's Bureau cut off rations to able-bodied blacks and forced unemployed blacks to sign farm labor contracts. Ultimately, few blacks attained economic independence, and most ended up working for white landowners who were often their former masters.

The planters often compensated the black workers with a share of the crop. They advanced food, seed, and tools to the black laborers until the crop was harvested, then charged interest for the advanced goods. As most of the workers were illiterate, they ended up owing more to the landlord at the end of the harvest than at the beginning thus had little to show for their labor. The Freedman's Bureau had succeeded in restoring secure and stable labor for the South without changing the economic condition of the black workers.

Black Codes—laws to regulate the new status of blacks—were adopted by the southern states during 1865 and 1866. They authorized the freedman to own property, make contracts including legal marriages, sue and plead in courts, and provide black testimony in cases where blacks were parties. However, the codes excluded blacks from juries, prohibited racial intermarriage, and required segregated public accommodations. The new Congress could not complain because the Northern states had similar provisions.

To restore the blacks to their former status, the Black Codes had provisions related to vagrancy, apprenticeship, labor, and land rights. Vagrancy was defined broadly so that any unemployed black could be fined for vagrancy and hired out to a planter to pay the fine. Freedmen under eighteen without adequate parental support could be bound as apprentices, with former owners given preference. Some states prohibited neighboring employers from enticing laborers with offers of higher wages. Blacks were required to get special licenses to engage in occupations other than as agricultural laborer. Also freedmen were generally prohibited from renting or leasing land outside cities.

The Republican congress was distressed at the speed with which the blacks were being reduced to their former status with the active support of President Andrew Johnson, who had southern sympathies. They decided to provide a Constitutional guarantee of the rights and security of freedmen in the form of the Fourteenth Amendment to the Constitution. This included a definition of all native-born or naturalized persons, including blacks as citizens, thus nullifying the Dred Scott decision. It also prohibited the states from depriving any person of life, liberty, or property, or the equal protection of the laws. Later the Fifteenth Amendment was also passed, which forbade states to deny the right to vote only on grounds of race, color, or previous condition. However, the amendments were vague enough to provide leeway in enforcement and interpretation by the Supreme Court for decades to come.

Now the immediate problem was the ratification of the amendments so that they became part of the Constitution. To achieve this, the Congress made ratification of the Fourteenth and Fifteenth Amendments a condition for admitting the rebel states into Congress. The southern states were powerless outside Congress. So they ratified the amendments to gain entry into Congress by 1870. Once inside Congress, they could always neutralize the Fourteenth and Fifteenth Amendments by not enforcing them and by violence if necessary.

During this forced reconstruction period, the rebel states decided to defend themselves by accommodating the rise of the Ku Klux Klan. Many of the former Confederate soldiers were part of the informal Ku Klux Klan groups who were engaged in guerilla warfare and terrorism. Their objective was the social and economic control of the black population. They specially targeted black schools, which were perceived to be threats to white supremacy. These groups were outside the control of the Southern state governments, even if the governments were controlled by Southern Republican parties and governors. If the Klansmen were apprehended, it was impossible to empanel a jury that would convict, independent of the severity of the crimes.

Eventually the North realized that forced reconstruction would drive all whites into the Democratic Party and intensify Ku Klux Klan terrorism. Also, starting in 1870, the control of southern states shifted to the Democrats. By the time of the election of 1876, forced reconstruction for implementing the Fourteenth and Fifteenth Amendments was nullified by local self-government in most of the southern states. Now the southern states were ready to sanctify the status of the black man as second-class citizens in practice and by law with the help of the Supreme Court.

Once the black man was denied monetary compensation for slavery, he was economically doomed. By 1880 only a fifth of black farm operators owned land. On the average, the black farms were half the size of white farms with worthless land. With segregated schools, about seventy percent of blacks were still illiterate. Fewer than two-fifths of the black children of school age attended schools. By using property qualification tests, literacy tests, poll taxes, and other devices, black voting was effectively eliminated. To restore virtual slavery, the convict lease system was instituted. Ninety percent of the convicts were black as a result of racially motivated law enforcement. The annual death rate of black prisoners reached fifty percent in some states. Frequent lynchings constantly reminded the blacks not to step out of line. Until the year 1900, about a hundred blacks were lynched in the South annually.

During this period the southern states practiced segregation or untouchability informally. In 1889 the Interstate Commerce Commission ruled that railroads must provide equal accommodation for both races. Soon several states passed "Separate but Equal" laws for providing facilities to both the races. In *Plessey v. Ferguson* (1896), the Supreme Court made "Separate but Equal" the law of the land. Now untouchability could be enforced in the North and South to keep blacks out of white facilities. Essentially apartheid laws separated blacks from whites in factories, parks, exits, entrances, toilets, streetcars, jails, hospitals, and even cemeteries—effectively ending all intercourse by day or night and in life or death.

In *Williams v. Mississippi* (1898), the Supreme Court upheld the constitutionality of literacy, property, or tax qualifications for voting purposes, thus effectively eliminating the black vote. By the end of the nineteenth century, the Supreme Court had nullified the Fourteenth and Fifteenth Amendments to the Constitution by narrow interpretation, and made blacks the untouchables or second-class citizens of the United States of America.

At the beginning of the twentieth century, the original goal of keeping blacks in the South was attained as ninety percent of blacks remained in the South. During the World War I, there was a shortage of labor and the blacks started migrating North to meet the labor shortage. In the 1930s, with the depression and unemployment, the whites had to be given first preference in filling available jobs; and many blacks had to return to the South for survival. Again in World War II, there was a severe shortage of labor and blacks migrated to the North. About a million blacks served in the United States armed forces during World War II but only in segregated units.

After the World War II, the United States became a nuclear power and was engaged in a Cold War for supremacy with the Soviet Union. The "separate but equal" laws that basically legislated blacks to untouchable status were proving to be embarrassing to the country because of treatment of black diplomats from Africa and Asia. As a result of political pressure, the Supreme Court reversed itself in *Brown v. Board of Education* (1954), which made untouch-ability illegal. At the next available opportunity, in 1967, President Johnson appointed Thurgood Marshall as the first black Supreme Court justice.

But enforcing equal rights for blacks became the new issue. As the race issue evolved over the next fifty years, the practice of racism and untouchability became more devious. Before the *Brown v. Board of Education*, untouchability was essentially the law of the land. After this decision, blacks and whites were entitled to same treatment and facilities in the eyes of the law. But the burden of proof shifted from the perpetuator to the victim of discrimination. The victim had to prove that he had not only suffered discrimination but also that the victimizer had an intention to cause suffering. Effectively the victim had to be able to read the mind of the person accused of discrimination.

The ultimate result at the turn of the millennium was that racism and untouchability became more transparent. As slaves, blacks could not marry each other, and their food and shelter was guaranteed. Today blacks are free to marry, yet seventy percent of black families are headed by single unwed mothers. This is coupled with the fact that America has one of the largest per capita prison populations, approaching two million, a majority of which are black—even though blacks constitute only twelve percent of the population. Annual surveys in *The New York Times* and *The Wall Street Journal*, which can be pointers to the racist biases of the American majority, concluded that fifty percent of Americans feel that blacks are criminally inclined and lack family values.

The Constitutional Class System

The Civil War revealed the flaws in the constitutional class system, which was based on the have-gots and have-nots of property and savings. It was structured in such a way that the property holders would always control the government even if they were a minority. And because the class system was part and parcel of the Constitution, it has continued to the present day with suitable adjustments for the changing times and circumstances.

The class system of the North, based on white wage slavery, was destined to spread all over the country with suitable adjustments for rectification of some flaws. Although the working class did not have property and savings, they were white, could vote, and were in the majority. Even though the Constitution was written for control by the minority, for long-term stability, the ruling class had to ensure that the middle-class property holders were always a majority and the votes of the working class were ineffective.

Racism was a vital requirement for the stability of the American class system. As the Constitution divided the whites into those who did and those who did not own property, these groups had to be united to forget their differences and concentrate on their common bonds in white supremacy. The rage of the white working class for failing to accumulate savings and property was directed at the black untouchables. Also, as the white working class would share the same facilities with the white middle class, they would aspire to move up the class system in a generation or two. For these reasons, racism has thrived in the American class system to the present.

In America the working class is typically unable to accumulate savings so that they are motivated to work or starve. To control savings, the income of the working class has to be limited so that they earn just enough to pay for food, shelter, and transportation. A reserve unemployed labor force is necessary to offer competition for available jobs and reduce wages to the basic level. Traditionally the reserve unemployed labor force has been created by the ruling class with immigration policy. By also controlling Union activity, a working class that is unable to accumulate property and savings has been part of the class system for almost two centuries.

From the time that slavery was abolished by the Northern states until the depression of 1930, immigration has been controlled to meet the requirements of class system stability. During the depression of the 1930s, there was so much unemployment that immigration was finally stopped. World War II was necessary for the economy to pick up and restore employment to acceptable levels.

After World War II, the creation of the reserve unemployed labor force shifted from immigration to minimum wage laws and trade policy. By adjusting the minimum wage level, which is not applicable to overseas jobs, the jobs could be exported overseas. In this way there would always be an unemployed labor force domestically that serves to limit the earnings of the working class by providing competition for jobs.

The vital lessons learnt from the Civil War, to keep fine-tuning the Constitutional class system, have been so successful that the system has survived with political stability for over 150 years and continues to thrive. The ruling class still controls the government and economy. The middle class still supports the ruling class and enjoys subsidies for housing, education, and healthcare. The working class continues to work without being able to accumulate savings or property. Blacks in general are still identified with the underclass. Racism is alive and kicking, but covertly.

Myth and Reality

The reality about slavery was so shameful and devastating that myths had to be created to restore hope and confidence in the Constitution and government. This process of damage control and controversy has continued until the present day.

A Civil War revealed that the Constitution was not democratic. The most important advantage of a democratic form of government is that ballots can replace bullets. Fair and open elections with a government of the people by the people and for the people ensure that nothing can be gained by Civil Wars because the end result would be the same. The Constitution had created a minority government of the slaveholders and employers, and this character was impossible to correct even though an overwhelming majority opposed it and it violated basic principles of morality and fairness.

Another realization of the Civil War was that despite the lofty words of the Constitution, that all men are created equal, all men were not created equal and therefore are not treated equally. It was not only recognized that blacks were not created equal with whites, but the Constitution was written in such a way that the whites were not created equal either. In fact, it was politically expedient to deny equal opportunity to half the population so that they could not accumulate savings or property or earn living wages for themselves and their families.

The third inescapable conclusion drawn from the Civil War was that the Constitution was a racist document. Not only did the Constitution deny the humanity of the blacks, but it made a mockery of the Bill of Rights even for whites because they were not enforceable in the States. The Dred Scott decision of the Supreme Court had revealed the reality of the Constitution in denying citizenship to the blacks or the rights to life, liberty, or property. Subsequently the Supreme Court would neutralize the Fourteenth and Fifteenth Amendments to the Constitution, creating second-class citizenship for blacks. It was clear that racism was part and parcel of the Constitution and could continue as long as it was necessary.

Starting at the end of the Civil War, the program for creating myths for damage control has continued to the present day. The first myth created by the historians and politicians was that the Civil War was accidental and could not be prevented as its causes were unknown. Even Jefferson Davis, the President of the Confederate States, stated that slavery was not a cause of the Civil War. Historians speculated that the South seceded because they were defending States Rights, a different form of civilization, and a different way of life. Some even blamed the climate differences and political economy of slavery.

Another method of damage control was to keep repeating the Declaration of Independence and the Bill of Rights at every available opportunity. If repeated often enough the mass of people would think that the Declaration of Independence was the guiding principle for the Constitution. They would not realize that the Constitution of the United States is the controlling document, the law of the land, and contradicts many of the principles of the Declaration of Independence. Also the general public will not realize that the Bill of Rights was an eye-wash that could not be enforced in the states where most of the population lived.

The most effective propaganda for damage control was ***the "good* cop, bad cop" myth**. The Northern states were painted as the moral majority who were opposed to slavery and fought the Civil

War to free the slaves. History books were revised to stress the role of the abolitionists and how they helped the slaves to freedom via the underground railroad and highlighted the participation of the blacks in the independence struggle and Civil War. What was not mentioned was that the abolitionists in the North were not more than one percent of the white population, the Northern state constitutions did not want blacks among them, and the North also benefited from black slavery.

As a complementary argument, the Southerners were painted as immoral criminals who did not want to free the slaves as the Northerners had done. The South could be conveniently blamed for all that was evil and indefensible about slavery as they had lost the Civil War. Anger and rage of the black race was diverted from the Constitution to the Confederate Flag, the Ku Klux Klan and "Dixie" songs.

This ideology of damage control has continued to the present day with the objective of diverting attention from the Constitution and the continuing reality of racism. The news media regularly reports on the controversy to remove the Confederate flag from the State Capitol in South Carolina. The National Association for the Advancement of Colored People has announced an economic boycott of the state until the Confederate flag is removed. Similarly the nation's attention was drawn to a march in New York City by the Ku Klux Klan. The matter was resolved by allowing the Klan to proceed with the march, but the Klansmen were forced to remove their hoods in the interests of public safety. Even the Chief Justice of the United States Supreme Court, William H. Rehnquist, was not immune to criticism. He was denounced for singing "Dixie" in public because this was tantamount to an attack on the United States Constitution, which he has sworn to defend.

Politicians and historians even found ways to rationalize the institution of slavery by pointing out the fact that slavery has existed since biblical times, the Romans and Greeks had slaves, and slavery has continued through the centuries. There were many slaveholders who did not respect the marriage bonds of slaves under Catholic slavery. Similarly there were many slaveholders in Protestant

America who tried to keep families together. In the end all kinds of slavery were alike.

In spite of all the myths created, the most telling comment on the immorality of Protestant slavery and the retribution of Civil War takes one back to Colonel George Mason's statement at the Constitutional Convention: "As nations cannot be rewarded or punished in the next world, they must be in this. By an inevitable chain of causes and effects, Providence punishes national sins by national calamities."

EPILOGUE

OBAMA TRUMPS THE CONSTITUTION

In his book *Dreams from My Father,* Barack Obama relates the following experience he had while sitting in the library of Occidental College, where he studied for two years before transferring to Columbia University:

> An Iranian student, an older balding man with a glass eye, was sitting across the table from us and he had noticed Marcus [Obama's black friend] reading a book on the economics of slavery. Although the drift of his eye gave the Iranian a menacing look, he was a friendly and curious man, and eventually he leaned over the table and asked Marcus a question.
>
> "Tell me, please," the man said, "How do you think such a thing as slavery was permitted to last for so many years?"
>
> "White people don't see us as human beings," Marcus said. "Simple as that. Most of 'em still don't."
>
> "Yes, I see. But what I mean to ask is, why didn't black people fight?"
>
> "They did fight. Nat Turner, Denmark Vescey—."
>
> "Slave rebellions," the Iranian interrupted. "Yes, I have read something about them. These were very brave men. But they were so few, you see. Had I been a slave, watching these people do what they did to my wife, my children… well, I would have preferred death. This is what I don't

226

understand—why so many men did not fight at all. Until death, you see?"

Marcus remained silent. His lack of response confused me, but after a pause I took up the attack, asking the Iranian if he knew the names of the untold thousands who had leaped into shark-infested waters before their prison ships had ever reached American ports; asking if, once the ships had landed, he would have still preferred death had he known that revolt might only visit more suffering on women and children. Was the collaboration of some slaves any different than the silence of some Iranians who stood by and did nothing as Savak thugs murdered and tortured opponents of the Shah? How could we judge other men until we had stood in their shoes?

What Obama seemed unaware of at the time was that denial of the humanity of blacks was the fundamental thesis of American Protestant Slavery and was written into the Constitution. A government of the slaveholders, by the slaveholders, and for the slaveholders forever was structured into the Constitution with the slaveholders in charge of the Legislative, Executive, and Judicial branches of government. In any branch of government, a breach contrary to the rule of the slaveholders could easily be mended or restored by the other two branches, often requiring centuries to make any meaningful changes to the Constitution. Therefore, it is not surprising that after two hundred years of a living Constitution with numerous constitutional amendments, a Civil War, Civil Rights legislation, and Supreme Court decisions, many white people still do not see blacks as equal human beings.

It is an established fact that Barack Obama was elected President of the United States of America in November 2008, exactly two hundred years after the 1808 Constitutional ban on the importation of black slaves. Obama had obtained a Constitutional Law Degree from Harvard University and taught Constitutional Law at the University of Chicago for ten years. He was fully informed and understood the Constitution of the United States, how the government had operated for two hundred years through numerous wars and peace times. Obama, as a self-proclaimed "mutt" (the child of a milk-white mother and a pitch-black father), had plenty of personal experience into the thinking and practice of racism in America. It is interesting to see how Obama used his knowledge, his experience, his being at the right place at the right time to capture the Presidency of the United States and trump the slaveholders' Constitution in a "Black Swan" moment in American history.

Racial Bridge

Obama was ideally suited to form a bridge between the white and black races in America. Physically, he would be unequivocally identified as a black man. Obama's maternal grandparents had reluctantly supported their daughter's wedding to his father because she was three months pregnant. After his father divorced his mother and abandoned the family when Obama was two years old, he was brought up by his mother and his stepfather in Indonesia, and then by his white grandparents in Hawaii until he finished high school. Growing up in a white family, white neighborhood, and white schools, Obama came to know, understand, and experience firsthand the white mindset and its prejudices and stereotypes about the black race. Obama became the perfect candidate for the racial bridge with his black body and a white mind. His mother Ann told her son to aim for the White House. If anyone had a shot at being the first black President, she said, it was he.

In his book *Dreams from My Father,* Obama runs down a ledger of slights he encountered during his school days because he was black: "the first boy, in seventh grade, who called me a coon; his tears of surprise … when I gave him a bloody nose …. The tennis pro who told me during a tournament that I shouldn't touch the schedule of matches pinned up to the bulletin board because my color might rub off …. The older woman in my grandparents' apartment building who became agitated when I got on the elevator behind her and ran out to tell the manager that I was following her; her refusal to apologize when she was told that I lived in the building." Obama also related how whites in hotels sometimes assumed he was a valet and handed him car keys to drive their vehicles from the garage. He recalled having difficulty flagging down taxis that would not stop for a black man. Clearly, the black race would identify him as being one of them. The black trestle of the racial bridge was in place, and Obama did not waste effort or resources in obtaining black allegiance or support.

In his book *Audacity of Hope*, Barack relates a racially charged argument between his grandparents that involved a black panhandler who scared his white grandmother. Obama described his grandmother as "a woman who helped raise me, a woman who sacrificed again and again for me, a woman who loves me as much as she loves anything in this world, but a woman who confessed her fear of black men who passed by her on the street, and who on more than one occasion has uttered racial or ethnic stereotypes that made me cringe." From his grandmother's experience, Obama learned "that men who might easily have been my brothers could still inspire their rawest fears."

The stereotypes of the black race in the white mind and in the media were explored in the book *Audacity of Hope*. Obama notes, "The collapse of the two-parent black household is a phenomenon that is occurring at such an alarming rate when compared to the rest of American society that what was once a difference in degree has become a difference in kind, a phenomenon that reflects a casualness toward sex and child-rearing among blacks that renders black children more vulnerable ... and for which there is simply no excuse."

The concept of a black underclass—separate, apart, alien in its behavior and in its values—has also played a central role in modern American politics. Television images of black looters and muggers, and news reports of "welfare queens" who produced babies just to collect a check, made white conservatives argue that what was needed was a stern dose of discipline, more police, more prisons, more personal responsibility, and an end to welfare. For even middle-class black Americans, separation from such stereotypes is never an option—not just because of skin color, but because the white society draws conclusions from the black color, making blacks only as free, only as respected, as the least of us. Statistics reinforce the attitudes of the whites: Seventy percent of black babies are born out of wedlock with the father unknown, and more than a million abandoned black children are waiting for adoption. America has the largest per capita prison population in the world (more than two million prisoners), a majority of which are black.

To overcome these negative statistics and the resulting stereotypes, Obama realized that to win any statewide office or national office, he would have to direct all his abilities to win the hearts and minds of the white people of the United States. To do this, he would first have to acquire impeccable credentials which would provide unquestionable credibility among the whites of every class, age group, financial status, or political party. Then he had to make sure that none of his actions would threaten the beliefs or sensibilities of the whites. Finally, Obama had to keep repeating the theme of Unity as the candidate of the whites and never mention black victimization, prejudice, or suffering, whether real or imagined. Blacks were to be out of sight and out of white minds.

Establishing Credentials: After graduating from Columbia University, Barack Obama was admitted to the Harvard Law School, thus following his Kenyan father who also obtained a postgraduate degree from Harvard University. At the end of his first year, Obama was selected as an editor of the *Harvard Law Review* and became president of the journal in his second year. As far as most whites were concerned, Obama and the other blacks at Harvard were beneficiaries of affirmative action programs and did not deserve to be there. But Obama's election as the first black president of the *Harvard Law Review* established the competence and credibility with whites nationwide because this position is earned on merit, through a fair and transparent competition with fellow classmates who are among the best and brightest students in the nation. The *Harvard Law Review* has been a traditional path to a Supreme Court clerkship, or at the very least, a job with one of the nation's top law firms. Obama's achievement gained national media attention, a write-up in the *New York Times,* and led to a publishing contract and advance for a book about race relations, though it evolved into a personal memoir and was published as *Dreams from My Father.* This established Obama's competence, credibility, and credentials among whites—especially among the corporate, media, and academic elites, as well as legislative and judicial officials. Obama has proven to be an outstanding communicator and mediator who can outperform and out-think the best and brightest whites at their own game and on their terms. This would become indispensable to Obama in communicating and getting a foot in the door with whites and the old boy network of the nation.

Eliminating the Threat: Having assimilated the white man's way of thinking, Obama took action to remove any doubts that might threaten his position. He knew that historically black men who became involved with white women, sometimes by just looking or talking to white women, were often arrested, shot, or lynched. He put white minds to rest by marrying a black woman, Michelle Robinson, a Princeton law graduate and his contact at the law firm in Chicago where he worked as an intern. Typically, the only black faces in Obama's public appearances would be Barack himself, Michelle, and their two daughters.

In this way Obama avoided the pitfalls of black man/white women images that posed a threat to the white psyche as experienced by Democratic candidate Harold Ford, Jr. in the 2006 election for U.S. senator from Tennessee. Ford, a black man, maintained a slight lead in the Senate race against Bob Corker, a white man, until the Republican Party ran a television advertisement. A white woman, played by Johanna Goldsmith, talked about meeting Ford, who was unmarried at that time, at "the playboy party." The ad was denounced by many people, including President Bill Clinton, who called it "a very serious appeal to a racist sentiment." Corker subsequently pulled ahead in the polls and won the Senate seat. Obama, however, applied his personal objectivity of the white mindset to avoid a similar obstacle.

Barack Hussein Obama's father, as suggested by his middle name, was a Muslim, though not a practicing one. His mother Ann was not particularly religious, although she married an Indonesian Muslim after divorcing Barack's father. Obama was raised by his maternal grandparents, who were Christian but rarely attended church. By reading *The Autobiography of Malcolm X*, Obama knew the havoc and disruption the Arabic middle name Hussein could cause in his life and in the mind of the white man. So he was careful to join the church of Reverend Jeremiah Wright when he was a community organizer in Chicago, married Michelle in a church wedding, and had his two daughters baptized. In this way, Obama neutralized the image in the American mind of a closet Muslim related to the hated and executed dictator of Iraq, Saddam Hussein.

For seven years Obama was a member of the Illinois Senate and crafted his image for total acceptance according to the white way of thinking and expectations. He adjusted his dress and food habits, started drinking beer instead of wine, ate doughnuts instead of croissants, and used French yellow mustard instead of Dijon. He took up golf and played poker with white state senators to develop contacts, ignoring black colleagues. Barack made efforts through networking and listening to known white Republicans. White conservatives marveled at his use of language and metaphors that resonated with their core beliefs.

Throughout his election campaign for the U.S. Senate and later for the Presidency, Obama made sure that the public and media had contact and interaction with white men only. His campaigns were designed and executed by Democratic political consultant David Axelrod, media consultant and spokesman Robert Gibbs, and campaign manager David Plouffe—a tight inner circle of three white guys. The only black guys visible were his security guards and personal assistant. Obama even canceled the appearance of Reverend Wright at his Presidential run announcement in Springfield, Illinois. Obama kept Jesse Jackson and Reverend Sharpton, whose images were threatening in white minds, at arm's length and out of sight during his campaign. Obama knew that if white voters got the impression that blacks like Sharpton were influential advisors to him, it would undermine voters' willingness to take a chance on him.

Advancing the Unity Theme: The third strategy for Obama's racial bridge was to adopt the theme of Unity and a common purpose for all Americans. In his keynote address at the Democratic Convention in 2004, he quoted the Declaration of Independence, "We hold these truths to be self-evident, that all men are created equal, that they are endowed by their Creator with certain inalienable rights that among these are life, liberty and the pursuit of happiness." Later he declared: "there is not a liberal America and a conservative America, there is the United States of America. There is not a Black America and a White America and Latino America and Asian America, there's the United States of America." Obama repeatedly highlighted his white family experience and connections: his mother was born in Kansas; her father worked on oil rigs and farms through most of the Depression. The day after Pearl Harbor his grandfather signed up for duty, joined Patton's army, marched across Europe. Back home his grandmother raised a baby and went to work on a bomber assembly line. After the war, his grandparents studied on the G.I. Bill, bought a house through FHA, and later moved west all the way to Hawaii in search of opportunity. He stressed the opportunity for achieving the American Dream available to all Americans.

To reinforce his theme of Unity, Obama was careful not to discuss blacks as being different or as having their own values and experiences. He kept repeating what he knew the white man wanted to hear. If the American dream passed by some Americans, they had only to work harder, be disciplined, concentrate on educational achievement, and assume responsibility for their own behavior. These values applied to all Americans without exception, and Obama himself was a living example of what could be achieved. This message proved largely successful with the predominantly white population of the U.S. as well as a majority of blacks, though some were unimpressed. In at least one instance, Reverend Jesse Jackson, unaware that his microphone was on, whispered to his fellow guest that he was fed up with Barack, "talking down to black people. I wanna cut his nuts off."

Still, Obama rightly assumed that if he could achieve credibility with the white people, the support of the black people would automatically follow because blacks had no alternative, and his black face and family were established realities. Having spent his entire life walking the fine line between races, cultures, religions, and classes, Obama was perfectly suited to plan and implement the racial bridge strategy to win the support and votes of the white people.

Constitutional Electoral System

Getting elected to the Presidency of the United States is a step-by-step process with rules at each step that depend on the Constitution of the United States, the rules of the Democratic and Republican Parties, the legislated rules of each state including the District of Columbia, and the rules controlling their caucuses and primaries. Obama knew that first he had to win the Democratic Party nomination at their convention according to Democratic Party rules. He'd worry about the national contest with the Republican candidate when that situation arose. Obama's intimate knowledge of party and election rules at every step and his careful allocation of time, effort, and resources would be crucial to his election as President of the United States.

Also crucial to his strategy was understanding of the Electoral College process, which is part of the original design of the U. S. Constitution. To change the system requires that Congress pass a Constitutional Amendment. Over the past two hundred years, over 700 proposals have failed in Congress to reform or eliminate the Electoral College. One did pass in 1804—the Twelfth Amendment, which expanded voting rights and designated the popular vote in the states as the vehicle for selecting electors, substantially changed the original process. Each state defines its own rules for selection of the electors and forty-eight states have selected the "winner takes all" basis for awarding electors. The purpose of the electoral system is to discourage third parties in the election process. For example, in 1992 Ross Perot won nineteen percent of the popular vote nationwide; he did not, however, win any electoral votes since he was not particularly strong in any state. In fact, Bill Clinton was elected because the rules divided the votes of the Republican Party, making Ross Perot's votes ineffective.

One of the side effects of the Electoral College and winner-take-all system is to de-link the election result from the popular vote totals of the candidates. The battle over the 2000 election focused on Florida's twenty-five electoral votes. Questions arose in several Florida counties about the accuracy of their election results based on information from polls. Florida is a winner-take-all state, and the election potentially hinged upon the popular vote in a single county in that state. If a recount were to show that Gore had received more popular votes than Bush in Florida, Gore would have received the twenty-five electoral votes and would have won the election. Ultimately George Bush did not win the 2000 popular vote, but had won in the Electoral College. Obama was fully aware that the national election was based on the "winner take all" basis for electors in the Electoral College system and designed his election strategy accordingly.

But before a candidate reached the national stage, he or she had to win the nomination of the party. The rules for the selection of the party candidates in the primaries and the convention are determined by the parties themselves. Initially both the Republican and Democratic Parties mirrored the winner-take-all rules of the national election because each party wanted to pick a candidate who had the best chance and most popular support to win the national election. The rules, however, changed after the disorganized 1968 Democratic Convention, which was a public relations fiasco, with conflicts over delegate seating, public humiliation inside the convention hall, and lawlessness outside the hall. Following the defeat of their presidential candidate, the Democrats started planning ahead to democratize their convention and candidate-selection process. Over a thirty-year period, the rules were changed to proportional representation with equal representation for the many special interest groups within the Democratic Party, appealing especially to young voters and minorities. The Democratic Party selection rules, which awarded candidates their proportion of the votes, were out of sync with the National and Republican Party rules, both of which operate on a winner-take-all basis. As a result the Democratic candidates were at a disadvantage in Presidential elections and conceded more elections to the Republican Party.

During the Democratic Primary season in 2008, Obama designed his election strategy to take full advantage of the Democratic Party rules, which are very complicated and confusing. He focused his resources and strategy on winning the Iowa Caucus, the first state on the Primary calendar. This way he would get the attention of the voters and media and break out of a crowded field of Democratic candidates. After the primaries and caucus in the first four states, the Democrat field was reduced to Obama and Hillary Clinton. Subsequently, all heavily populated states such as California, New York, and New Jersey were won by Hillary Clinton. Operation of the proportional representation rule made it difficult for either of the two leading candidates to get a decisive lead over the other. Even with the proportional delegate rules, Hillary Clinton would have won the nomination had the delegates of Florida and Michigan not been disqualified. Both these states had primaries before the beginning of sanctioned voting under party rules, a violation that led to serious and draconian sanctions from the party. Hillary Clinton had the majority of the votes in both states that were not included in the delegate count, leaving a dark cloud over the Democratic nominating process. Here again Obama was fortunate to be in the right place at the right time, with all stars aligned in his favor. Had the National Presidential election rules been applied to the Democratic nomination with winner-take-all delegates for each state, Hillary Clinton would have eliminated Obama from the Democratic nomination.

Barack Obama had another advantage: his chance of winning the nomination was extremely improbable. All Barack's main rivals in the primaries and debates were white; therefore, they spent much of their time attacking each other, thus self-destructing and undermining the other white candidates in the race. Nobody wanted to risk seeming racist by criticizing the only black candidate; besides, Obama didn't appear to be a threat. Also the Democratic Primary rules allowed the Super Delegates to endorse the candidate of their choice. Because of past rivalries with Hillary Clinton and proper deference shown by Obama, Senator Kennedy, Caroline Kennedy, Senator Kerry, Senator Edwards, and Vice President Gore publicly endorsed Obama before the Super Tuesday voting in the larger states. Obama also received 80 to 90 percent among the black voters and the young new voters as the first black candidate. At the Democratic Convention, Hillary Clinton nominated Barack Obama as the party candidate by acclamation because the Super Delegates claimed, "We live by the rules and we die by the rules." The improbable nomination of Barack Obama became a reality because unforeseen rules and events including proportional representation of delegates, the Super Delegate factor, allocation of delegates from Michigan and Florida, and manipulation of other rules by the campaign managers.

Internet Money, Race, and Votes

The Constitution of the United States was originally structured in such a way that only the very rich could be elected to the Senate or to the Presidency. At the 1787 Constitutional Convention, it was suggested that a candidate for the Presidency have a net worth of $100,000 (equivalent to $10 million in twenty-first–century dollars). Even though this limitation was not adopted, only a plantation slaveholder or persons with extraordinary means and resources could campaign and win a majority of the votes in a state. Although most viable presidential candidates are wealthy, such as the two Bushes, the U.S. has also elected presidents who did not come from family wealth, such as Ronald Reagan and Bill Clinton.

It has been a different story with black candidates for our nation's highest offices until the Presidential election of 2008. In modern times, blacks rarely have been elected to the United States Senate (in fact, currently no blacks serve in the Senate). In 2004, Barack Obama became the only black Senator even though blacks constituted twelve percent of the U.S. population. At the same time, thirteen senators were Jewish, a group that constitutes only two per-cent of the national population. Barack Obama noted in *Audacity of Hope* that he would need $5 million to wage a statewide campaign in Illinois just for the Democratic Senate Primary and another $15 million for the general election. Obama also noted that money is a necessary condition but not a sufficient condition for election to the Senate. The Republican incumbent, Peter Fitzgerald, had spent $19 million of his personal wealth to win this senate seat the previous time around.

In the 2004 Democratic Primary for the senate seat, Obama's opponent was Blair Hull, a wealthy Goldman Sachs partner who had a net worth of over a half-billion dollars, and as a self-financing candidate spent ten times the resources available to Obama. Obama won the primary when Mr. Hull's campaign imploded with allega-tions that he'd had some ugly run-ins with an ex-wife.

Then Obama was selected to deliver the keynote address at the Democratic National Convention—seventeen minutes of unfil-tered, uninterrupted airtime on national television that provided unprecedented recognition, credibility, publicity, and support from all the voters in Illinois. Meanwhile, the Illinois Republican Party chose Alan Keyes, a black former presidential candidate as Obama's opponent, even though he had never lived in Illinois and proved so fierce and unyielding in his positions that even conservative Republicans were scared of him. Obama's election as the Senator from Illinois looked like a fluke, and some reporters would declare him the luckiest politician in the entire fifty states.

Barack Obama's election as the Senator from Illinois gave him visibility and a platform for entering the Democratic Presidential nomination sweepstakes in 2007. He organized his campaign by harnessing the Internet community energy through social net-working sites such as Facebook, and developed a website where people could connect with neighborhood groups, volunteer, donate money, and read the latest news from his campaign. Although Obama's campaign war chest exceeded the $230 million raised by Hillary Clinton, he would have lost the Democratic nomination were it not for the proportional representation rules. However, the

Internet community organization efforts were essential in winning the Democratic nomination for the Presidency by bringing out the voters.

In the national election, Obama amassed and spent more than twice the amount by his rival, Republican John McCain. McCain accepted $84 million in taxpayer money through the public financing system. Obama became the first presidential candidate to decline public financing and to raise far more than any other candidate through thirteen million e-mail donations. Overall, Obama raised $745 million during his marathon campaign and still had $30 million in the bank after the election. Record-breaking fundraising through the Internet was crucial to his winning the Presidency even though it was based on winner-take-all Electoral College rules. The Founding Fathers who wrote the Constitution could not have dreamed of the organizing and fundraising capabilities of the Internet, which Obama employed successfully to outwit the rules of the slaveholders.

Black Swan 2008

A "Black Swan" event is a high-impact, hard-to-predict, and rare event that is beyond the realm of normal expectations in history, science, finance, or technology. The election of President Barack Obama was a "Black Swan" event in American history. It was an event outside the realm of regular expectations because nothing in the past can convincingly point to its possibility and extreme impact. After the fact, a rare chain of events in American History and in the Constitution of the United States has been identified which allowed this 2008 "Black Swan" event to occur.

Barack Obama was the first President of the United States born to a white mother and a black father in a hospital whose parentage was recorded and verifiable. Throughout American history, most mulattos were born to a black mother and white father, and the white father of the child was "unknown" to the law. For example, in the absence of DNA testing, Thomas Jefferson could deny he fathered five children with his slave Sally Hemings. Usually, when a mulatto was born to a white mother, the baby was abandoned, aborted, or killed to prevent shaming the white family. In Barack Obama's case, his birth certificate and photographs with his white mother and white grandparents were frequently used in the election campaign to dispel any doubts about his citizenship and white mother.

Barack Obama was the first black man to be elected as President of the *Harvard Law Review*. This provided unprecedented credibility, visibility, access, and experience for his entry in the political process. He was also the first black to deliver the keynote address at the Democratic National Convention, nominating John Kerry as the Presidential Candidate in 2004. He was selected because Kerry was also a fellow Harvard graduate and was impressed with Obama's extraordinary communication skills. Obama, focusing on the theme of Unity in his keynote speech, delivered beyond the expectations and would gain national recognition and exposure. As a result of this sequence of events, Obama would win the election to become the first black male U.S. Senator representing the State of Illinois. Both his Democratic and Republican opponents, though self-funded multi-millionaires, self-destructed in personal scandals, making way for Obama.

Obama's entry into the Senate coincided with the defeat of long-time Democratic leader Senator Daschle. Obama took advantage of the situation by having Daschle's very experienced staff members transferred to his office. Over the next two years, Obama developed alliances with fellow Senators in a deferential nonthreatening manner, showing proper respect for their senior status. During the debates for the Democratic Presidential nomination, the white candidates attacked each other, leaving alone the long-shot candidate and only black, Barack Obama, to avoid any hint of racism and to steer clear of antagonizing the black voters.

Obama was the first candidate for the Democratic Presidential nomination who had a black face but a white mindset, having grown up in a white household. His campaign strategy—to concentrate his time, resources, and image to win the white caucus in Iowa, the first Primary state—proved successful when he became the first black to win in Iowa, ahead of Hillary Clinton and John Edwards.

Propelled by the Internet, Barack Obama was the first presidential candidate to effectively use it as a fundraising and organizational tool. His supporters created 35,000 groups to bring out the vote during primaries. He raised a record-breaking $600 million in contributions from more than three million people during the primaries and the national presidential contest.

Obama was the first democratic presidential candidate to win the nomination based on the proportional representation rules of the Democratic Party, even though Hillary Clinton obtained more delegates based on the winner-take-all rules. Again he was aided by the chance disqualification of the delegates from Michigan and Florida. Therefore, he became the first black presidential nominee of the Democratic or any other major party.

There were several firsts in the 2008 election campaign. The Republican Party nominated John McCain and Sarah Palin to oppose Obama in the national election. This was the first time in more than half a century that a sitting president or vice-president was not running for the Presidency, a fact that left the presidency "up for grabs." Also, for the first time in American history, both major parties in the Presidential election chose sitting U.S. Senators as their nominees. However, the age difference between presidential candidates Obama and McCain was the largest in American history—giving the younger Obama a boost. Furthermore, the inexperience of Sarah Palin, the Republican Party's first female nominee for Vice-President, worked in Obama's favor because her nomination undercut any arguments about his own lack of executive experience.

By chance during this election, America was engaged in two unpopular wars in Afghanistan and Iraq. The American casualties and costs for these wars exceeded the deaths and financial losses of 9/11. Obama had opposed these wars while McCain had supported them. Obama also successfully tied McCain with the actions of George Bush and positioned himself as the candidate for change.

Just before the election of 2008, the United States suffered a once-in-a-lifetime financial crisis since the Great Depression of 1930. The housing bubble burst, resulting in failure of major banks and brokerage houses, causing the stock market to plunge. Obama was able to blame George Bush and the Republican Party with failed policies, fraud, and record unemployment while promising change. It is well known that the status of the economy two months before an election is a dominant factor in determining the outcome of the election.

Barack Obama was the first Democratic Presidential nominee to refuse public funds and still raise more private money. In contrast, McCain accepted $84 million in taxpayer money through the public financing system. When all was said and done, Obama raised and spent twice the resources of McCain and had $30 million to spare after the election. This juggernaut of fund raising from small, repeat donations through the Internet proved decisive in the election of 2008.

The election of Barack Obama as the first black President of the United States of America in 2008 was a rare "Black Swan" event beyond the realm of expectations from the United States Constitution and history. Blacks were denied their humanity with American Protestant Slavery and in the Constitution of the United States. As acknowledged by Barack Obama himself, many whites do not see blacks or treat them as humans even today. Obama was able to overcome these hurdles with a coming-together of chance events such as Democratic Party primary rules, maturing of the Internet for organizing and fund raising, a "Black Swan" financial crisis, a "Black Swan" 9/11 attack on the United States leading to never-ending wars, and many other unpredictable events. This combination of factors ultimately led to Obama's election as Senator from Illinois and then as "Black Swan" President of the United States of America.

NOTES

Chapter 1 - The Moral Setting

1. Emanuel Hertz, *The Hidden Lincoln* (New York: The Viking Press, 1938).

2. Paul M. Angle (ed.), *Herndon's Life of Lincoln* (New York, 1930); *New York Herald*, 27 February 1861.

3. Douglas Southall Freeman, *R.E. Lee: A Biography* (New York, 1935).

4. Robert W. Johannsen (ed.), *The Lincoln-Douglas Debates of 1858* (New York, 1965).

5. Richard Hall (ed.), *Acts Passed in the Island of Barbados from 1643 to 1762 Inclusive* (London, 1764).

6. John Codman Hurd, *Law of Freedom and Bondage, I.*

7. *Le Code Noir, ou, edit du roy, servant de reglement pour le gouvernement & l'adminstration de la justice, police, discipline & le commerce des esclaves negres, dans la province & colonie de la Louisianne Donne a Versailles au mois de mars, 1724* (Paris, 1728).

8. Henry Charles Lea, *A History of the Spanish Inquisition* (New York, 1906).

9. Roy P. Basler, *Collected Works*, VIII.

10. I. Wiley Bell, *The Road to Appomattox* (Memphis, 1956).

11. Basler, *Collected Works* II.

12. Charles A. and Mary R. Beard, *The Rise of American Civilization*, vols. 1 & 2 (New York, 1927).

13. J. C. Furnas, *Goodbye to Uncle Tom* (New York, 1956); Thomas Jefferson, *Notes on the State of Virginia* (Boston, 1829).

Chapter 2 - The Economic Class System

1. Charles A. and Mary R. Beard, *The Rise of American Civilization* (New York, 1927); *Selection from the Letters and Speeches of the Hon. James H. Hammond of South Carolina* (New York, 1866); *Letters on Slavery: The Pro-Slavery Argument* (Philadelphia, 1853), pp. 119–35.

2. William Goodell. *The American Slave Code* (New York, 1853).

3. Olmsted, *Seaboard Slave States.*

4. Le Code Noir, Articles 40–4; *Natchez Courier and Journal*, 1 January 1836; *Alexandria Red River Whig*, 25 April 1840.

5. Acts of the First Legislature, 1853; Hardesty V. Sukey, *Wormley* (1855) Catterall, Helen C., *Judicial Cases*.

6. *Le Code Noir*, Articles 20–1.

7. Joseph C.G. Kennedy, *Population of the United States in 1860: Compiled from the Original Returns of the Eighth Census* (Washington, 1864).

8. Arthur Styron, *The Cast-Iron Man* (New York, 1935).

9. Ibid.

10. Achille Loria, *The Economic Synthesis*, tr. M. Eden Paul (London, 1914).

11. W. F. Caraven, *White, Red, and Black: The Seventeenth Century Virginian* (Charlottesville, Va., 1971).

12. *Farmers Journal II* (1853).

13. *A Century of Population Growth from the First Census of the United States to the Twelfth, 1790–1900* (Washington, D.C., 1909); *Negro Population* in the United States, 1790-1915 (Washington D.C., 1918).

14. Hinton Rowan Helper, *The Impending Crisis of the South* (1858).

15. Olmsted, *Seaboard Slave States*.

16. Helper, *the Impending Crisis of the South* (1858).

17. Edward Needles, *Ten Years' Progress; or, A Comparison of the State and Conditions of the Colored People in the City and County of Philadelphia from 1837 to 1847* (Philadelphia, 1849); Robert Ernst, "The Economic Status of New York City Negroes."

18. Beard, *The Rise of American Civilization* (New York, 1927).

Chapter 3 - Law and Order

1. Carl Schurz, *Henry Clay* (Boston, 1887).

2. Richard Halled, *Acts Passed in the Island of Barbados from 1643 to 1762 Inclusive* (London, 1764).

3. Cooper and McCord, *Statutes at Large of South Carolina* VII.

4. Charles Pettigrew to Ebenezer Pettigrew, 1802, Pettigrew Family Papers; Catterall (ed.), *Judicial Cases*, II.

5. Guion Griffis Johnson, *Ante-Bellum North Carolina*; J. Winston Coleman, *Slavery Times in Kentucky*; Phillips (ed.), *Plantation and Frontier*, II.

6. *Southern Banner* (Athens, Ga.) 14 June 1860.

7.   J. E. Cutler, *Lynch Law* (New York, 1905).

8.   *Alexandria (La.) Red River Republican*, 8 January 1848; Harrison Anthony Trexler, *Slavery in Missouri*.

9.   James B. Sellers, *Slavery in Alabama*.

10.   John S. Bassett, *Slavery in North Carolina*; Douglas, *My Bondage*.

11.   Douglas, *My Bondage*; Charles S. Sydnor, *Slavery in Mississippi*.

12.   Hinton Rowan Helper, *Impending Crisis of the South* (1859).

13.   *The Wellsburg (Va.) Herald*, 1856.

14.   *Le Code Noir* (Paris, 1742) Articles 32–5.

15.   Acts of the First Territorial Legislature, 1806, 150–90.

16.   *Donaldsonville Vigilant*, 6 July 1850; Clinton, *American Patriot*, 24 January 1855; *Baton Rouge Gazette*, 12 March 1831.

17.   Acts of the Seventh Legislature 1826; Acts of Thirteenth Legislature 1837; Acts of the Seventeenth Legislature 1845; Acts of the Second Legislature 1855.

18.   James Stuart, *Three Years in North America, I*; Acts of the Third Legislature, 1857; Samford (ed.), *Police Jury Code of the Parish of East Feliciana*.

19.   Acts of the Third Legislature 1857; "Penitentiary Report" Legislative Documents 1856; "Annual Report of the Attorney General," Legislative Documents, 1858.

20.   Acts of the First Territorial Legislature, 1806: Inquest Record, Concordia Parish, undated, copy by Doris V. Casper, Department of Archives, Louisiana State University.

21.   *Le Code Noir*, Articles 12–14; Acts of the First Territorial Legislature, 1806; Acts of the First Legislature 1814; Acts of the Second Session of the Thirteenth Legislature of the State of Louisiana 1837–38.

22.   Clark, State Records, XXIII; *Newborn Journal* 11 April 1855.

23.   Clark, State Records, XXIV.

24.   *The Revised Statutes of the State of North Carolina 1836–7*, (Raleigh, 1837).

25.   Laws, 1831–5; Clark, *State Records XXIII; Raleigh Register*, 6 April 1807.

26.   Laws 1823–31; *Raleigh Register*, 12 April 1836.

27.   George Wilson Pierson, *Tocqueville and Beaumont in America* (New York, 1938).

28.   Isaac Chandler, *A Summary View of America* (London, 1824).

29. *"Free Negroism; or Results of Emancipation in the North and the West India Islands"* (New York, 1862); *Journal of the Senate of Pennsylvania 1836–7, Session I.*

30. Frances Anne Kemble, *Journal* (London, 1863); Frederick Douglass, *My Bondage.*

31. Letter to Hugh Brown of Robeson County, 26 June 1821, Neill Brown papers.

32. *Le Code Noir*, Article 3, Baudier, *Catholic Church in Louisiana.*

33. Thomas Hamilton, *Men and Manners in America II*; Roger Baudier, *Catholic Church in Louisiana.*

34. Hephzibah Church Books, 17 July 1814, 20 November 1819.

35. Herbert Aptheker, *American Negro Slave Revolts* (New York, 1943); Joseph C. Carroll, *Slave Insurrection in the United States, 1800-1865* (Boston, 1938).

Chapter 4 - Family Values

1. Merrill D. Peterson, *Jeffersonian Image* (New York, 1960).

2. William W. Crosskey, *Politics and the Constitution* (Chicago, 1953); James T. Callender in the *Richmond Recorder*, 1 September 1802; Isaac Jefferson, *Memoirs of a Monticello Slave* (Charlottesville, 1951).

3. Thomas Jefferson, *Notes* (ed. Penden).

4. W. W. Hening, *The Statutes at Large: Being a Collection of All the Laws of Virginia* (Richmond, Va., 1809–23); George Washington Williams, *History of the Negro Race in America*, I.

5. Thomas R. R. Cobb, *An Inquiry into the Law of Slavery in the United States of America* (Philadelphia, 1858).

6. Frazier V. Spear, Catterall, *Judicial Cases*, I; *"State* vs. *Samuel* (a slave)"; Catterall, *Judicial Cases*, II.

7. Roger Baudier, *The Catholic Church in Louisiana* (New Orleans, 1939); Robin, *Voyages dans Louisiane*, III.

8. Comite Plantation Diary, 1857, Kilbourne Papers; Police Jury Minutes, Lafayette Parish, I; *Opelousas Courier*, 7 January 1854.

9. Index to *Spanish Judicial Records*, L.H.Q., VI (1923); VI (1923); XV (1932).

10. *Le Code Noir*, Articles 40–4; *Vidalia Concordia Intelligencer*, 29 December 1849.

11. Coleman, *Slavery Times in Kentucky.*

12. J. C. Furnas, *Goodbye to Uncle Tom*, (New York, 1956).

13. *Massie Slave Book.*

14. *American Cotton Planter and Soil of the South* II; Rachel O'Conner to David Weeks, Weeks Collection.

15. Catterall (ed.), *Judicial Cases*, II.

16. Catterall (ed.), *Judicial Cases*, I.

17. Milledgeville Southern Recorder, 7 January 1851.

18. Catterall (ed), *Judicial Cases*, II; Bills Diary, entry for 7 January 1860.

19. Kemble, *Journal.*

20. *American Cotton Planter and Soil of the South* I (1857); Rachel O'Conner to A.T. Conrad, 12 April 1835, Weeks Collection.

21. Olmsted, *Back Country*; *Massie Slave Book*; Catterall (ed), *Judicial Cases*, II,III.

22. Catterall (ed.), *Judicial Cases*, III.

23. Susan Dabney Smedes, *Memorials*; Frederick Law Olmsted, *Seaboard.*

24. Furnas, *Goodbye to Uncle Tom* (1956).

25. *Massie Slave Book*; Kemble, *Journal*; Coleman, *Slavery Times in Kentucky.*

26. Catterall (ed.), *Judicial Cases*, I.

27. Olmsted, *Seaboard*; James H. Johnston, *Miscegenation in the Ante-Bellum South*; *Southern Agriculturist*, VIII (1835).

28. Furnas, *Goodbye to Uncle Tom* (1956).

29. Frederick Douglass, *Narrative of the Life.*

30. Catterall (ed) *Judicial Cases*, II.

31. Ben Ames Williams (ed.), *A Diary from Dixie* (Boston 1949); Olmsted, *Seaboard.*

32. Olmsted, *Seaboard.*

33. *New Orleans Picayune*, 9 September 1851; Johnson, *Ante-Bellum North Carolina*; James Hugo Johnston, *Race Relations in Virginia.*

34. *Borden* vs. *Borden*, 14. N. C.; *Scroggins* vs. *Scroggins*, 14 N. C.

35. Andrew Adgate Lipscomb and Albert E. Bergh, *Writings of Jefferson*, I; Jefferson, *Notes* (ed. Penden).

36. Joanne Grant, *Black Protest: History, Documents and Analysis from 1619 to the Present* (Fawcett World Library, New York, 1968).

37. *National Intelligencer* (Washington, D.C.), 19 January 1833; Herbert G. Gutman, *The Black Family in Slavery and Freedom 1750–1925* (Vintage Books, New York, 1976).

Chapter 5 - Human Rights

1. Douglas Southall Freeman, *George Washington: A Biography* (New York, 1948–57) III; Worthington Chauncey Ford (ed.), *The Writings of George Washington*, XII (New York, 1892–9); Paul Leland Haworth, *George Washington, Country Gentleman* (Indianapolis, 1925).

2. Helen Tunnicliff Catterall (ed.), *Judicial Cases Concerning American Slavery* and the Negro, II (Washington, D.C., 1929).

3. Harriet Beecher Stowe, *Uncle Tom's Cabin* (Boston, 1852).

4. *Southern Planter*, XII (1852); *Southern Cultivator*, VIII (1850); *Farmers Register*, I (1834).

5. Olmsted, *Seaboard*.

6. Frederick Douglass, *My Bondage and My Freedom*.

7. J. Hepburn, "The American Defence of the Christian Golden Rule" (N.P., 1715); Coleman, *Slavery Times in Kentucky*; Olmsted, *Back Country*.

8. Mark Twain, *Tom Sawyer*; Duncan Clinch Heyward, *Seed from Madagascar*; Frederick Douglass, *Narrative of the Life*.

9. Thomas Jefferson, *Notes on the State of Virginia*; Charles Mackay, *Life and Liberty in America* (1859).

10. Frederick Douglass, *Narrative of the Life*; Furnas, *Goodbye to Uncle Tom* (1956).

11. Frederick Douglass, *Narrative of the Life*.

12. Olmsted, *Plantation and Frontier*, I.

13. Furnas, *Goodbye to Uncle Tom* (1956).

14. Olmsted, *Seaboard*; *Farmers Register* V; Sydnor, *Slavery in Mississippi*.

15. Furnas, *Goodbye to Uncle Tom*, 1956.

16. Frederic Bancroft, *Slave Trading in the Old South* (Baltimore, 1931); Coleman, *Slavery Times in Kentucky*.

17. Furnas, *Goodbye to Uncle Tom* (1956).

18. Bancroft, *Slave Trading*.

19. Olmsted, *Back Country*; Sydnor, *Slavery in Mississippi*; Hammond Diary, entry for 26 February 1838.

20. Catterall (ed.), *Judicial Cases* I, II and III.

21. Ulrich B. Phillips, *American Negro Slavery* (1918).

22. Nathan Irvin Huggins, *Black Odyssey* (New York, 1977).

23. Benjamin Drew, *The Refugee*.

24. Olmsted, *Seaboard.*

25. Drew, *The Refugee.*

26. Olmsted, *Back Country*; Henson, *Story*; Douglass, *My Bondage*; Marston, Diary, 1825.

27. Ingraham (ed.), *Sunny South*; Steward, *Twenty-Two Years a Slave.*

28. Douglass, *My Bondage*; Sitterson, *Sugar Country.*

29. Sir Charles Lyell, *Travels in North America in the Years 1841–2,*, I (New York, 1845).

30. Kemble, *Journal.*

31. *Southern Cultivator*, XII (1854); Drew, *The Refugee*; Kemble, *Journal*; Douglas, *My Bondage.*

32. Joseph Holt Ingraham, *South West* II; Kemble, *Journal.*

33. Emerson, *Journal*, 1841.

34. Harding-Jackson papers , 1850; Kemble, *Journal.*

35. Hundky, *Social Relations*; Olmsted, *Seaboard*; Douglass, *My Bondage.*

36. Ulrich B. Phillips, *Life and Labor in the Old South* (Boston, 1929).

37. Kenneth M. Stampp, *The Peculiar Institution* (New York, 1956).

38. *Southern Cultivator* XVI (1858).

39. *De Bow's Review* IX (1850); James B. Sellers, *Slavery in Alabama* (University, Alabama, 1950).

40. *Southern Cultivator* XII (1854).

41. Phillips, *American Negro Slavery.*

42. *American Farmer*, VII (1852).

43. *American Cotton Planter and Soil of the South*, III (1859).

44. *Charleston Courier*, 1857; *Southern Agriculturist* II (1829).

45. Pettigrew Family papers (1849).

46. Daniel Webster, Letter to Rev Mr. Furness dated 15 February 1850; William MacDonald, *Documentary Source Book of American History* (New York: Macmillan, 1914).

Chapter 6 - Civil Rights

1. William Chambers, *Things as They Are in America* (London, 1854); Max Farrand (ed.), *Records*, III; Carl Brent Swisher, *Roger B. Taney* (New York, 1935).

2.   Herbert Friedenwald, *The Declaration of Independence* (New York, 1904).

3.   Ibid.

4.   Peter Force (ed.), American Archives fourth series, III.

5.   Benjamin Quarles, *The Negro in the American Revolution* (Chapel Hill, 1961).

6.   *George Washington and the Negro* (Washington, 1932).

7.   David Dunham Wallace, *The Life of Henry Laurens* (G. P. Putnam's Sons, New York, 1915).

8.   Benjamin Quarles, *The Negro in the American Revolution* (Chapel Hill, 1961).

9.   Max Farrand (ed.), *The Records of the Federal Convention* (New Haven, 1911).

10.   James Madison, *Alexander Hamilton and John Jay: The Federalist Papers*, No. 42 (New Rochelle, 1965).

11.   Farrand, *Records* I.

12.   *Constitution of the United States*, Articles, I, Section 9.

13.   Ulrich B. Phillips, *American Negro Slavery.*

14.   House Document 107, 15th Congress, 1820.

15.   Constitution of the United States, Clause 3, Section 2 of Articles, IV.

16.   Farrand, *Records*, III.

17.   Annals, 2nd Congress, 2nd Session, 1793.

18.   Campbell, *Slave Catchers.*

19.   Annals, 1st Congress, 2nd Session 1790.

20.   F. G. Franklin, *Legislative History of Naturalization*, 1776–95; William Chambers, *American Slavery and Color* (London, 1857).

21.   John Bassett Moore (ed.), *The Works of James Buchanan* (Philadelphia, 1908); *Official Opinions*, X.

22.   Annual Reports of the American Anti-slavery Society 1858 (New York, 1859).

23.   Ibid., 1857.

24.   *Official Opinions*, I and II.

25.   Gerald M. Capers, *John C. Calhoun—Opportunist* (Gainesville, 1960).

26.   *Le Code Noir*, Articles 34, 44, 53–4 ; Records of the Superior Council, L.H. Q., II (1919).

27. Parish Records of Louisiana, No. 45, St. Charles Parish, Series I; Helen Catterall, *Judicial Cases Concerning American Slavery and the Negro*, III.

28. Acts of the First Legislature, 1853.

29. Acts of the First Session of the First Legislature, 1846.

30. Catterall, *Judicial Cases*, III.

31. Baucry Family Account Books, II, Louisiana State University Archives; Dumont, *Memoires sur la Louisiane*, II.

32. Records of the Superior Council, L.H.Q. IV (1921); Surrey, *Commerce of Louisiana*; Gayarre, *History of Louisiana*, I.

33. Baudier, *Catholic Church in Louisiana*; *Le Code Noir*, Articles 20–1; Rowland (ed.), *Claiborne Letter Books*, II.

34. *Acts Passed by First Legislature of the Territory of Orleans, 1807* (New Orleans, 1807); *Acts of the Ninth Legislature of the State of Louisiana, 1830* (New Orleans, 1830); *Acts of the Second Session of the Fourth Legislature of the State of Louisiana, 1859* (Baton Rouge, 1859).

35. George M. Stroud, *A Sketch of the Laws Relating to Slavery in the Several States of the United States of America* (Philadelphia, 1856).

36. Shepherd (comp.), *Statutes Va.*, I; Augustin S. Clayton (comp.), *A Compilation of Laws of the State of Georgia 1800*; Russell, *Free Negro in Virginia*.

37. Hurd, *Law of Freedom and Bondage*, II; *Laws Passed by the General Assembly 1825–1830* (Raleigh, 1844); Green et al., V. Lane et al., 43 NC.

38. *Raleigh Register*, 6 October 1801; *Raleigh Register*, 27 August 1827; *Fayetteville Observer*, 30 July 1855.

39. Clark (ed.), *State Records of NC*, XXIV; Shepherd (comp.), *Statutes Va.*, I; Clayton (comp.), *Laws of Georgia*.

40. Shepherd (comp.), *Statutes Virginia*, II; Clayton (comp.), *Laws of Georgia*.

41. *Plantation and Frontier*, II.

42. *Texas Supreme Court Reports* XXIV; *North Carolina Supreme Court Reports* LX.

43. J. H. Russell, *The Free Negro in Virginia*; Orville Taylor, *Negro Slavery in Arkansas* (Durham, N.C., 1958); *Baltimore American*, January 1860.

44. Clement Eaton, *Freedom of Thought* (1940; rev. ed., New York, 1964); North Carolina (NC) Laws 1823–31.

45. *NC Laws* 1823–31.

46. NC Legislative Papers for 1857 Laws Passed by General Assembly, 1860–1 (Raleigh, 1862).

47. Stephen Beauregard Weeks, *History of Negro Suffrage*.

48. Annals of Congress, 4th Congress, 2nd Session.

49. Charles Francis Adams (ed.), *The Works of John Adams* (Boston, 1856).

50. *Indiana Constitutional Debates of 1850*, I.

51. *Illinois Constitutional Debates of 1847* (Springfield, 1919).

52. Ibid., *Indiana Constitutional Debates of 1850*.

53. Catterall (ed.), *Judicial Cases*, V; Emma Lou Thornbrough, *The Negro in Indiana* (Indianapolis, 1957).

54. *Journal of the Senate of the State of Ohio*, 36 General Assembly, I Session.

55. Salmon P. Chase (ed.), *The Statutes of Ohio and of the North West Territory* (Cincinnati, 1833).

56. Edward Raymond Turner, *Negro in Pennsylvania*; Pierson, *Tocqueville and Beaumont in America*.

57. *Oregon Constitutional Debates of 1857*.

58. Catterall (ed.), *Judicial Cases*, V; *Ohio State Journal*, 24 February 1849.

59. Turner, *Negro in Pennsylvania*; Joseph Sturge, *A Visit to the United States in 1841* (London, 1842).

60. William F. Worner, "The Columbia Race Riots" *Lancaster County Historical Society Papers*, XXVI (1922).

61. *New England Magazine* II (1832); Abdy, *Journal of a Residence and Tour*, III.

62. Mackay, *Life and Liberty in America*, II.

63. *Coloured American*, 28 July 1838.

64. Robert H. Collyer, *Lights and Shadows of American Life* (Boston, 1836); Ernst, *Immigrant Life in New York City*.

65. William Chambers, *American Slavery and Color*; Charles K. Whipple, *Relations of Anti-Slavery to Religion* (Anti-Slavery Tracts No.19, New York).

Chapter 7 - Educational Opportunity

1. Letter to John Waring, Philadelphia, 17 December 1763; Labaree, *Franklin*, X.

2. *Narrative of the Life of Frederick Douglass, written by Himself* (Boston, 1845).

3. W. W. Hening, *Statutes at Large*, vol. i.; Special Report of the US Commissioner of Education, 1871.

4. Samuel Ashe, *History of North Carolina*, vol.i. (Greensboro, 1908).

5. Rev. William Meade, *Four Sermons of Reverend Bacon* (Maryland, 1749); Colyer Meriwether, *Education in South Carolina* (Washington, 1889).

6. Meriwether, *Education in South Carolina*; McCrady, *South Carolina* etc.

7. Weeks, *Southern Quakers*

8. Hening, *Statutes at Large*, vol. xvi; Levi Coffin, *Reminiscences,* (Cincinnati, 1880).

9. Joshua Coffin, *Slave Insurrections.*

10. *City Gazette and Commercial Daily Advertiser,* Charleston, South Carolina, 21 August 1822.

11. Joseph Tate, *Digest of the Laws of Virginia*; Poindexter, *Revised Code of the Laws of Mississippi.*

12. Dawson, *A Compilation of the Laws of the State of Georgia, etc., Laws of Virginia, 1830–1831.*

13. William Sidney Drewry, *Insurrections in Virginia.*

14. A. Hutchinson, *Code of Mississippi*; *Laws of Delaware, 1832*; *Acts of Florida, 1846.*

15. C. C. Clay, *Digest of the Laws of the State of Alabama*; Special Report of the U.S. Commissioner of Education, 1871.

16. H. Cobb, *Digest of the Laws of Georgia*; Prince, *Digest of the Laws of Georgia*; *Laws of South Carolina, 1834.*

17. John S. Bassett, *Slavery in North Carolina.*

18. *Laws of the State of Missouri, 1847.*

19. DeBow, *The Industrial Resources of the Southern and Western States,* vol. i.

20. Coffin, *Slave Insurrections*; William Goodell, *Slave Code.*

21. Baird, *Collections, etc.*

22. Fee, *Antislavery Manual*; Jay, *An Inquiry, etc.*

23. *Code Noir, 1724*; *Jesuit Relations*, vol. V.

24. *Laws of Louisiana.*

25. Henry Adams Bullard and Thomas Curry, *A New Digest of the Statute Laws of the State of Louisiana.*

26. *Daily National Intelligencer,* 29 August 1818; *Special Report of the US Commissioner of Education, 1871.*

27.   *Special Report of the US Commissioner of Education*, 1871.

28.   Samuel J. May, *Some Recollections of Our Anti-Slavery Conflict* (Boston, 1869).

29.   Jay, *An Inquiry*, etc.

30.   *African Repository* (entitled) "Education in Liberia."

31.   Samuel Clarke, *The Condition of the Free People of Color* (1859); Du Bois and Dill, *The Negro American Artisan*.

32.   *The Liberator*, 13 June 1835.

33.   Monroe, *Cyclopaedia of Education*, vol. iv; *The Liberator*, 9 July 1831.

34.   Monroe, *Cyclopaedia of Education*, vol. iv; Douglass, *Life and Times*.

35.   Stroud and Brightly, *Purdon's Digest of the Laws of Pennsylvania*, Wickersham, *History of Education in Pennsylvania*. (Lancaster, Pa., 1886)

36.   Samuel Sidwell Randall, *History of Common School System of New York* (New York, 1851); Thomas B. Stockwell, *History of Education in Rhode Island* (Providence, 1876).

37.   Eliza Wigham, *The Anti-slavery Cause in America*.

38.   *Laws of Ohio*, vol. xxiii; Hickok, *The Negro in Ohio*.

39.   Richard Gause Boone, *History of Education in Indiana* (New York, 1892).

40.   Ibid.

41.   Thorpe, *Federal and State Constitutions; Constitution of Illinois*.

42.   *Special Report of the US Commissioner of Education*, 1871; *Journal of the Constitutional Convention of the State of Iowa*, 1857.

43.   Chambers, *Things as They Are in America*.

44.   Rosenberg (ed.), *American System*.

45.   Allan Nevins, *Ordeal of the Union*, 1947.

46.   Hinton Rowan Helper, *The Impending Crisis*.

47.   Ibid.

Chapter 8- The Reckoning

1.   Margaret Mitchell, *Gone with the Wind* (Macmillan Publishing Company).

2.   Jefferson Davis, *The Rise and Fall of the Confederate Government* (New York, 1958).

3.   Thomas Hart Benton, *Abridgement of the Debates of Congress...*, XIII (New York, 1860).

4.   Winthrop D. Jordan, *American Attitudes over the Negro, White over Black* (Chapel Hill, N.C., 1968).

5.   Russel B. Nye, *Fettered Freedom: Civil Liberties and the Slavery Controversy, 1830–1860* (East Lansing, Michigan, 1949).

6.   Edward Channing, *A History of the United States, 1905–1925*, 6 vols., VI (New York).

7.   Benjamin Quarles, *Lincoln and the Negro* (New York, 1962).

8.   Glover Moore, *The Missouri Controversy, 1819–1821* (Lexington, Kentucky, 1953).

9.   Jesse T. Carpenter, *The South as a Conscious Minority, 1789–1861* (New York, 1930).

10.   Charles A. and Mary R. Beard, *The Rise of American Civilization*, 2 vols. (New York, 1927).

11.   Robert R. Russel, *Economic Aspects of Southern Sectionalism, 1840–1861* (Urbana, Illinois, 1924).

12.   Eugene D. Genovese, *The Political Economy of Slavery* (New York, 1961).

13.   Kenneth M. Stampp, *The Causes of the Civil War* (Englewood Cliffs, N. J., 1959).

14.   Paul M. Angle, *Lincoln 1854–1861, Collected Works*, III.

15.   Kenneth M. Stampp, *The Imperiled Union* (New York, 1980).

16.   Ulrich B. Phillips, *American Negro Slavery* (1918).

17.   Wesley, *Negro Labor in the United States.*

18.   *Savannah Republican*, 26 May 1851; *Charleston Courier*, 12 December 1840.

19.   Kenneth M. Stampp, *The Peculiar Institution* (New York, 1956).

20.   Charles Grier Sellers (ed.), *The Southerner as American*; Angle, *Created Equal.*

21.   Eugene D. Genovese, *The Political Economy of Slavery* (New York, 1961).

22.   John Hope Franklin, *The Free Negro in North Carolina* (New York, 1943).

23.   Orville Taylor, *Negro Slavery in Louisiana*; Jackson, *Mississippian*, 12 January 1858.

24.   *Austin Texas State Gazette*, 26 June; 18 December 1858.

25.   Roy P. Basler (ed.), *Works* II.

26.   Avery Craven, *The Coming of the Civil War* (Chicago, 1942).

27.   Basler, *Thomas Jefferson to John Holmes, Works* II, 22 April 1820.

28.   Olmsted, *Seaboard Slave States; Southern Cultivator*, XVI, 1858.

29.   Charles Francis Adams (ed.), *The Work of John Adams*, II.

30.   *De Bow's Review*, XXV, 1858.

31.   Gavin Diary, entry for 4 July 1856.

32.   Samuel Eliot Morison, *The Oxford History of the American People* II.

33.   Donald L. Robinson, *Slavery in the Structure of American Politics* (New York, 1971).

34.   Glover Moore, *The Missouri Controversy 1819–1821*.

35.   Hugh Brogan, *The Penguin History of the United States of America*.

36.   Charles Dudley Rhodes, *History*, I (New York, 1910).

37.   Stanley W. Campbell, *The Slave Catchers* (Chapel Hill, 1968).

38.   Rhodes, *History*, II.

39.   *De Bow Review*, XXVIII, May 1860; Clingman, *Speeches*, 22 January 1850; Delihah L. Beasley, "Slavery in California," *DeBow Review*, XIII, July 1852.

40.   George M. Weston, *The Progress of Slavery in the United States*, (Washington D.C., 1857); Nevins, *Emergence of Lincoln*, I.

41.   *Congressional Globe*, 33 Congress, I Session.

42.   Basler, *Works*, II.

43.   Basler, *Works*, II.

44.   Nevins, *Emergence* I; Richardson, *Messages and Papers*, V.

45.   Russel B. Nye, *Fettered Freedom* (East Lansing, Mich., 1949).

46.   C. Vann Woodward (ed.), *Mary Chestnut's Civil War* (New Haven, 1981).

47.   Hinton R. Helper, *The Impending Crisis of the South: How to Meet It* (New York, 1860).

48.   Hugh C. Bailey, *Abolitionist-Racist: Hinton Rowan Helper* (University of Alabama, 1965).

49.   Edward Channing, *A History of the United States, 1905–1925*, VI, 6 vols. (New York).

50.   *Kentucky Statesman*, 5 October 1860; *Charleston Mercury*, 11 October 1860; Dumond (ed.), *Southern Editorials*.

51.   William J. Cooper, Jr. *The South and the Politics of Slavery, 1828–1856*.

52. Villard, Brown, and Harold S. Schultz, *Nationalism and Sectionalism in South Carolina, 1852–1860*.

53. Nevins, *Emergence II*, 24 December 1859; Henry D. Caper, *The Life and Times of C. G. Memminger* (Richmond, 1893); *Congressional Globe*, 36 Congress, I Session.

54. Paul M. Angle, *Created Equal*.

55. W. F. Craven, *Growth of Southern Nationalism*; Oswald Garrison Villard, *John Brown*; Mering, *The Constitutional Union Campaign of 1860*.

56. Reynolds, *Editors Make War*; Richardson, *Messages and Papers*, V; *Natchez Free Trader*, 2 November 1860.

57. Hugh Brogan, *The Penguin History of the United States of America* (New York, 1985).

58. Frederick Law Olmsted, *Back Country*; Kemble, *Journal*.

59. Donald L. Robinson, *Slavery in the Structure of American Politics* (New York, 1971).

60. *Congressional Globe*, 30 Congress, I Session, Appendix.

61. Jefferson Davis, *The Rise and Fall of the Confederate Government* (New York, 1958).

62. *Congressional Globe*, 29 Congress, 2 Session, Appendix.

63. *A Political Textbook for 1860*, (Tribune Press, New York, 1860).

64. Basler (ed.), *Works of Lincoln*, II; Nevins, *Ordeal*, II.

65. Francis P. Blair, Jr., *The Destiny of the Races of this Continent*, (Washington, DC, 1859).

66. Basler (ed.), *Collected Works of Abraham Lincoln*, II, III.

67. Richardson (ed.), *Messages and Papers of the Presidents*, VI.

68. Basler (ed.), *Complete Works of Abraham Lincoln*, III; Reynolds, *Editors Make War*; Barlow Papers, Henry E. Huntington Library, 1860.

69. Algie M. Simons, *Class Struggles in America* (Chicago, 1906).

70. *Boston Herald*, 12 November 1860.

Chapter 9 - Lincoln's Solution

1. Henry Wilson, *History of the Rise and Fall of the Slave Power in America, 1872–1877* (Boston).

2. Avery Craven, *The Coming of the Civil War*.

3. Roy P. Basler (ed.), *Complete Works of Abraham Lincoln*, III.

4.   Ulrich B. Phillips (ed.), *The Correspondence of Robert Toombs, Alexander H. Stephens and Howell Cobb* (Washington, 1913).

5.   *New York Courier and Enquirer*, 14 December 1860; *New York World*, 22 March 1861.

6.   Benjamin J. Blied, "Catholics and the Civil War," *Congressional Globe*, 37 Congress, 2 Session, Appendix, Milwaukee, 1945.

7.   John Hope Franklin, *From Slavery to Freedom* (New York, 1947).

8.   James M. McPherson, *The Negro's Civil War* (New York, 1965).

9.   Isaac N. Arnold, *The History of Abraham Lincoln and the Overthrow of Slavery*, Chicago, 1866; Roy P. Basler (ed.), *Abraham Lincoln: His Speeches and Writings* (Cleveland, 1946).

10. *Douglass' Monthly*, September–May 1861; *Montgomery Advertiser*, 6 November 1861; *Douglass' Monthly*, July 1861.

11. John Hope Franklin, *From Slavery to Freedom* (New York, 1947).

12. Basler (ed.), *Collected Works of Abraham Lincoln*, III, IV.

13. Hume, *Abolitionists*, quoting L. E. Chittenden, *Recollections of President Lincoln*.

14. Armstead Robinson, *Bitter Fruits of Bondage: Slavery's Demise and the Collapse of the Confederacy, 1861–1865* (Charlottesville, Va., 1942).

15. James M. McPherson, *Battle Cry of Freedom* (New York, 1988).

16. Shelby Foote, *Civil War*, I.

17. Emory M. Thomas, *Confederate Nation*; Jones, *War Clerk's Diary* (Miers).

18. Hugh Brogan, *The Penguin History of the United States of America* (London, 1985).

19. Thomas J. Pressly, *Americans Interpret Their Civil War* (Princeton, 1954).

20. Cleveland, *Stephens*.

21. Charles A. and Mary R. Beard, *The Rise of American Civilization*, 2 vols. (New York, 1927).

22. James M. McPherson, *Battle Cry of Freedom* (New York, 1988).

23. Charles A. and Mary R. Beard, *The Rise of American Civilization*, 2 vols. (New York, 1927).

BIBLIOGRAPHY

Abdy, Edward Strutt. *Journal of a Residence and Tour in the United States of North* America (London, 1835).

Adams, Charles Francis. (ed.) *The Works of John Adams* (Boston, 1856).

Adler, Mortimer J. *We Hold These Truths* (New York, 1987).

Ahlstrom, Sidney E. *A Religious History of the American People* (New Haven, 1972).

Angle, Paul M. *Created Equal?* (Chicago, 1958).

Angle, Paul M. (ed.) *Herndon's Life of Lincoln* (New York, 1930).

Angle, Paul M. (ed.) *Lincoln, 1954–1861, Collected Works, III* (Chicago, 1991).

Apthekar, Herbert. *American Negro Slave Revolts: Nat Turner, Denmark Vesey, Gabriel, and others* (1943; reprint, New York, 1969).

Arnold, Isaac N. *The History of Abraham Lincoln and the Overthrow of Slavery* (Chicago, 1866).

Ashe, Samuel. *History of North Carolina* (Greensboro, 1908).

Bailey, Hugh C. *Abolitionist–Racist, Hinton Rowan Helper* (University of Alabama, 1965).

Bancroft, Frederic. *Slave-Trading in the Old South* (Baltimore, 1931).

Basler, Roy P. (ed.) *Abraham Lincoln: His Speeches and Writings* (Cleveland, 1946).

Basler, Roy P. (ed.) *The Collected Works of Abraham Lincoln, 8 vols.* (New Brunswick, 1953).

Bassett, John S. *Slavery in the State of North Carolina* (New York, 1912).

Baudier, Roger. *The Catholic Church in Louisiana* (New Orleans, 1939).

Beard, Charles A. *An Economic Interpretation of the Constitution of the United States* (New York, 1986).

Beasley, Delilah L. *Slavery in California* (reprint, Westport, CT, 1969).

Beard, Charles A. and Beard, Mary R. *The Rise of American Civilization, 2 vols.* (New York, 1927).

Benton, Thomas Hart. *Abridgement of the Debates of Congress* (New York, 1860).

Berlin, Ira. *Many Thousand Gone; The First Two Centuries of Slavery in North America* (New York, 1998).

Berlin, Ira. *Slaves Without Masters: The Free Negro in the Antebellum South* (New York, 1974).

Berlin, Ira and Hoffman (eds.) *Slavery and Freedom in the Age of the American Revolution* (Charlottesville, 1983).

Blair, Francis P. Jr. *The Destiny of the Races of this Continent* (Washington D.C., 1859).

Blied, Benjamin J. *Catholics and the Civil War* (Milwaukee, 1945).

Block, W. R. *The Character of American History* (New York, 1960).

Boles, John H. (ed.) *Masters and Slaves in the House of the Lord: Race and Religion in the American South, 1740–1870* (Lexington, Ky., 1988).

Boone, Richard Gause. *History of Education in Indiana* (New York, 1892).

Brackett, Jeffrey R. *The Negro in Maryland* (North Stratford, N.H., 1977).

Breeden, James O., (ed.) *Advice among Masters: The Ideal in Slave Management in the Old South* (Westport, Conn., 1980).

Brogan, Hugh. *The Penguin History of the United States of America* (New York, 1985).

Bullard, Henry Adams and Thomas Curry. *A New Digest of the Statute Laws of the State of Louisiana* (New Orleans, 1836).

California Legislature Assembly. *Constitution of the United States* (Sacramento, CA, 1989).

Campbell, Stanley W. *The Slave Catchers* (Chapel Hill, 1968).

Capers, Gerald M. *John C. Calhoun-Opportunist* (Gainesville, 1960).

Carpenter, Jesse T. *The South as a Conscious Minority 1789–1861* (New York, 1930).

Carroll, Joseph C. *Slave Insurrection in the United States 1800–1865* (Boston, unknown).

Cash, W. J. *The Mind of the South* (New York, 1941).

Catterall, Helen Tunnicliff (ed.). *Judicial Cases Concerning American Slavery and the Negro* (Washington D. C., 1929).

Chambers, William. *American Slavery and Color* (London, 1857).

Chambers, William. *Things as They Are in America* (London, 1854).

Chandler, Isaac. *A Summary View of America* (London, 1824).

Channing, Edward. *A History of the United States, 6 vols.* (1905–1925, New York).

Chase, Salmon P. (ed.) *The Statutes of Ohio and of the North West Territory* (Cincinnati, 1833).

Clarke, Samuel. *The Condition of the Free People of Color* (City unknown, 1859).

Clay, C. C. *Digest of the Laws of the State of Alabama* (Tuskaloosa, 1843).

Cobb, Howell. *Digest of the Laws of Georgia* (Washington D.C., 1846).

Cobb, Thomas R. R. *An Inquiry into the Law of Slavery in the United States of America* (Philadelphia, 1858).

Coffin, Levi. *Reminiscences of Levi Coffin* (Cincinnati, 1880).

Cole, Arthur C. *The Irrepressible Conflict: 1850–1865* (1934; reprint, Chicago, 1971).

Coleman, J. Winston. *Slavery Times in Kentucky* (Chapel Hill, N.C., 1940).

Collyer, Robert H. *Lights and Shadows of American Life* (Boston, 1836).

Cooper, William J., Jr., *The South and the Politics of Slavery, 1826–1856* (Baton Rouge, 1982).

Cooper, Thomas, and David J. McCord. *Statutes at Large of South Carolina VII* (Baltimore, 1968).

Craven, Avery O. *Growth of Southern Nationalism 1848–1861* (Baton Rouge, La., 1953).

Craven, Avery. *The Coming of the Civil War* (Chicago, 1942).

Craven, W. F. *White, Red and Black: The Seventeenth Century Virginian* (Charlottesville, VA, 1971).

Crosskey, William W. *Politics and the Constitution* (Chicago, 1953).

Cuomo, Mario M. and Harold Holzer. *Lincoln on Democracy* (New York, 1990).

Curry, Leonard P. *The Free Black in Urban America, 1800–1850: The Shadow of a Dream* (Chicago, 1981).

Cutler, J. E. *Lynch Law* (New York, 1905).

Current, Richard N., T. Harry Williams, Frank Freidel, and Alan Brinkley. *American History—A Survey* (New York, 1987).

Davis, David Brion. *The Problem of Slavery in the Age of Revolution* (Ithaca, N.Y., 1975).

Davis, Jefferson. *The Rise and Fall of the Confederate Government* (New York, 1958).

Degler, Carl N. *Neither Black Nor White* (New York, 1971).

Degler, Carl N. *Out of Our Past: The Forces That Shaped* (New York, 1959).

Douglass, Frederick H. *My Bondage and My Freedom* (reprint North Stratford, NH, 1968).

Douglass, Frederick. *Narrative of the Life of Frederick Douglass* (Boston, 1845).

Douglass, Frederick. *The Life and Times of Frederick Douglass* (1892; reprint, New York, 1969).

Drew, Benjamin. *A North-Side View of Slavery. The Refugee* (New York, 1968 reprint 1856 ed.).

Drewry, William Sidney. *Slave Insurrections in Virginia 1830–1865* (Washington, 1900).

Du Bois, W. E. Burghardt. *The Souls of Black Folk* (New York, 1970).

Du Bois, W. E. B. *John Brown* (1919; reprint New York, 1972).

Duncan, John M. *Travels through Part of the United States and Canada in 1818 and 1819* (New York, 1823).

Eaton, Clement. *The Freedom-of-Thought Struggle in the Old South* (1940; rev. ed., New York, 1964).

Edwards, Franklin (ed.) *E. Franklin Frazier on Race Relations* (Chicago, IL, 1968).

Elkins, Stanley M. *Slavery—A Problem in American Institutional and Intellectual Life* (Chicago, Il., 1959).

Ernst, Robert. *The Economic Status of New York City Negroes* (Port Washington, N.Y., 1949).

Ernst, Robert. *Immigrant Life in New York City 1825–1863* (Port Washington, N.Y., 1965 c1949).

Farrand, Max (ed.) *The Records of the Federal Convention* (New Haven, 1911).

Fee, John Gregg. *An Antislavery Manual* (New York, 1969).

Fehrenbacher, Don E. *Prelude to Greatness: Lincoln in the 1850's* (Stanford, Ca., 1962).

Fehrenbacher, Don E. *The Dred Scott Case: Its Significance in American Law and Politics* (New York, 1978).

Finch, John A. *Travels in the United States of America and Canada* (London, 1833).

Fogel, Robert William. *Without Consent or Contract: The Rise and Fall of American Slavery* (New York, 1989).

Foner, Eric. *Free Soil, Free Labor, Free Men: The Ideology of the Republican Party Before the Civil War* (New York, 1970).

Foner, Eric. *Nat Turner* (Englewood Cliffs, N.J., 1971).

Foner, Eric. *Politics and Ideology in the Age of the Civil War* (New York, 1980).

Foner, Eric. *Tom Paine and Revolutionary America* (New York, 1976).

Foner, Philip S. *Business & Slavery: The New York Merchants and the Irrepressible Conflict* (1941; reprint, New York, 1968).

Foote, Shelby. *The Civil War I* (New York, 1958–74).

Force, Peter. *American Archives* (Washington, 1837–53).

Ford, Worthington Chauncey (ed.) *The Writings of George Washington* (New York, 1892–1899).

France Laws. *Le Code Noir, Ou, Edit du Roy* (Paris, 1728).

Franklin, Frank George. *Legislative History of Naturalization in the United States* (New York, 1969).

Franklin, John Hope. *The Free Negro in North Carolina 1790–1860* (New York, 1943).

Franklin, John Hope. *From Slavery to Freedom* (New York, 1947).

Frazier, E. Franklin. *The Negro Family in the United States* (Chicago, Il., 1939).

Fredrickson, George M. *The Black Image in the White Mind: The Debate on Afro-American Character and Destiny, 1817–1914* (New York, 1971).

Freeman, Douglas Southall. *George Washington, a Bibliography* (New York, 1948-1957)

Freeman, Douglas Southall, R. E. Lee. *R. E. Lee: A Bibliography* (New York, 1935).

Friedenwald, Herbert. *The Declaration of Independence* (New York, 1904).

Furnas, J. C. *Goodbye to Uncle Tom* (New York, 1956).

Galenson, David W. *White Servitude in Colonial America: An Economic Analysis* (Cambridge, Eng., 1981).

Genovese, Eugene D. *From Rebellion to Revolution: Afro-American Slave Revolts in the Making of the Modern World* (Baton Rouge, 1979).

Genovese, Eugene D. *The Political Economy of Slavery: Studies in the Economy and Society of the Slave South* (New York, 1965).

Genovese, Eugene D. *Roll, Jordan, Roll: The World the Slaves Made* (New York, 1974).

Genovese, Eugene D. *The World the Slave Holders Made: Two Essays in Interpretation* (New York, 1969).

Goodell, William. *The American Slave Code* (New York, 1853).

Grant, Joanne. *Black Protest: History, Documents and Analysis from 1619 to the Present* (New York, 1968).

Gunnar, Myrdal. *An American Dilemma* (New York, 1944).

Gutman, Herbert G. *The Black Family in Slavery and Freedom 1750–1925* (New York, 1976).

Hall, Richard (ed.) *Acts Passed in the Island of Barbados from 1643 to 1762 Inclusive* (London, 1764).

Hamilton, Thomas. *Men and Manners in America II* (New York, 1968 reprint 1843 ed.).

Hammond, James Henry. *"Letters on Slavery," The Pro-Slavery Argument* (Philadelphia, 1953).

Hammond, James Henry. *Selection from the Letters and Speeches of the Hon. James H. Hammond of South Carolina* (New York, 1866).

Haworth, Paul Leland. *George Washington, Country Gentleman* (Indianapolis, 1925).

Helper, Hinton Rowan. *The Impending Crisis of the South—How to Meet It* (Cambridge, Mass., 1968).

Hening, W. W. *The Statutes at Large: Being a Collection of All the Laws of Virginia* (Richmond, VA, 1809–23).

Hepburn, J. *The American Defense of the Christian Golden Rule* (N.P., 1715).

Hertz, Emanuel. *The Hidden Lincoln* (New York, 1938).

Heyward, Duncan Clinch. *Seed from Madagascar* (Chapel Hill, 1937).

Hickok, Charles Thomas. *The Negro in Ohio, 1802–1870* (New York, 1975 reprint 1896 ed.).

Huggins, Nathan Irvin. *Black Odyssey—The Afro-American Ordeal in Slavery* (New York, 1977).

Hurd, John Codman. *Law of Freedom and Bondage in the United States* (Boston, 1858–1862).

Hutchinson, A. *Code of Mississippi* (Jackson, Mississippi, 1848).

Ingraham, Joseph Holt. *The South West* (New York, 1835).

Ingraham, Joseph Holt. *The Sunny South* (Philadelphia, 1860).

Jacobs, Paul and Saul Landau, with Eve Pell. *To Serve the Devil* (New York, 1971).

Jefferson, Isaac. *Memoirs of a Monitcello Slave* (Charlottesville, 1951).

Jefferson, Thomas. *Notes on the State of Virginia* (Boston, 1829).

Johannsen, Robert W. (ed.) *The Lincoln-Douglas Debates of 1858* (New York, 1965).

Johnson, Guion Griffis. *Ante-Bellum North Carolina; a Social History* (Chapel Hill, 1937).

Johnston, James Hugo. *Race Relations in Virginia & Miscegenation in the South, 1776–1860* (Amherst, Mass., 1970).

Jordan, Winthrop D. *American Attitudes over the Negro, White over Black* (Chapel Hill, 1968).

Kemble, Frances Anne. *Journal* (London, 1863).

Kolchin, Peter. *Unfree Labor: American Slavery and Russian Serfdom* (Cambridge, Mass., 1987).

Kennedy, Joseph C.G. *Population of the United States in 1860* (Washington, D.C., 1864).

Labaree, Leonard Woods. *Mr. Franklin* (New Haven, 1956).

Lea, Henry Charles. *A History of the Spanish Inquisition* (New York, 1906).

Lerner, Max. *America as a Civilization* (New York, 1957).

Levine, Bruce. *Half Slave and Half Free: The Roots of Civil War* (New York, 1992).

Lindrop, Edmund. *The Bill of Rights and Landmark Cases* (New York, 1989).

Lipscomb, Andrew Adgate and Albert E. Bergh. *The Writings of Thomas Jefferson* (Washington D.C., 1903–04).

Loria, Achille. *The Economic Synthesis, M. Eden Paul tr.* (London, 1914).

Litwack, Leon F. *Been in the Storm So Long: The Aftermath of Slavery* (New York, 1979).

Litwack, Leon F. *North of Slavery: The Negro in the Free States, 1790–1860* (Chicago, 1961).

Lyell, Charles, Sir. *Travels in North America in the Years 1841-2* (New York, 1845).

MacDonald, William. *Documentary Source Book of American History* (New York, 1914).

Mackay, Charles. *Life and Liberty in America* (London, 1859).

Madison, James and Hamilton, Alexander and Jay, John. *The Federalist Papers* (New Rochelle, 1965).

Malone, Dumas. *Jefferson and His Time, 6 vols.* (Boston, 1948–77).

May, Samuel J. *Some Recollections of Our Antislavery Conflict* (Boston, 1869).

McDonald, Forrest. *We the People* (New York, 1958).

McPherson, James M. *Battle Cry of Freedom the Civil War Era* (New York, 1980).

McPherson, James M. *The Negro's Civil War: How American Negroes Felt and Acted during the War for the Union* (1965; reprint, Urbana, Il., 1982).

McPherson, James M. *Ordered by Fire: The Civil War and Reconstruction* (New York, 1982).

Meade, Rev. William. *Four Sermons of Reverend Bacon* (Maryland, 1749).

Meltzer, Milton,(ed.) *A History of the American Negro, Vol. 1: 1619–1865* (New York, 1965).

Meriwether, Colyer. *Education in South Carolina* (Washington, 1889).

Mitchell, Margaret. *Gone with the Wind* (New York, 1936).

Moore, Barrington, Jr. *Social Origins of Dictatorship and Democracy* (Boston, MA. 1966).

Moore, George Henry. *Notes on the History of Slavery in Massachusetts* (New York, 1866).

Moore, Glover. *The Missouri Controversy 1819–1821* (Lexington, Ky, 1953).

Moore, John Bassett (ed.) *The Works of James Buchanan* (Philadelphia, 1908).

Morison, Samuel Eliot. *The Oxford History of the American People* (New York, 1972).

Morris, Robert. *Course of Peonage in a Slave State* (Boston, 1852).

Needles, Edward. *Ten Year's Progress; or, A Comparison of the State and Conditions of the Colored People in the City and County of Philadelphia from 1837 to 1847* (Philadelphia, 1849).

Nevins, Allan. *Ordeal of the Union, 2 vols.* (New York, 1947).

Nye, Russel B. *Fettered Freedom: Civil Liberties and the Slavery Controversy 1830–1860* (East Lansing, Mich., 1949).

Oakes, James. *The Ruling Race: A History of American Slaveholders* (New York, 1982).

Oakes, James. *Slavery and Freedom: An Interpretation of the Old South* (New York, 1990).

Oates, Stephen B. *The Fires of Jubilee: Nat Turner's Fierce Rebellion* (New York, 1975).

Oates, Stephen B. *To Purge This Land with Blood: A Biography of John Brown* (Amherst, Mass., 1984).

Oates, Stephen B. *With Malice toward None: The Life of Abraham Lincoln* (New York, 1977).

Olmsted, Frederick Law. *Journey in the Back Country* (New York, 1860).

Olmsted, Frederick Law. *Journey through the Seaboard Slave States* (New York, 1856).

Olmsted, Frederick Law. *Plantation and Frontier* (Austin, 1978; reprint 1857 ed.).

Parish, Peter J. *The American Civil War* (New York, 1975).

Passkoff, Paul F. and Wilson, Daniel J. *The Cause of the South: Selections from De Bow's Review, 1846-1867* (Baton Rouge, 1982).

Pessen, Edward. *Riches, Class and Power before the Civil War* (Lexington, Mass., 1973).

Peterson, Merrill D. *The Jefferson Image in the American Mind* (New York, 1960).

Phillips, Ulrich B. *American Negro Slavery: A Survey of the Supply, Employment and Control of Negro Labor as Determined by the Plantation Regime* (1918; reprint, Baton Rouge, 1966).

Phillips, Ulrich B. *The Correspondence of Robert Toombs, Alexander H. Stephens and Howell Cobb* (Washington, 1913).

Phillips, Ulrich B. *Life and Labor in the Old South* (Boston, 1929).

Phillips, Ulrich Bonnel. *Plantation and Frontier Documents I* (Cleveland, 1909).

Pierson, George Wilson. *Tocqueville and Beaumont in America* (New York, 1938).

Poindexter, George. *Revised Code of the Laws of Mississippi* (Washington City, 1808).

Pole, J. R. *The American Constitution For and Against* (New York, 1987).

Potter, David M. and Fehrenbacher, Don E., (ed.), *The Impending Crisis: 1848-1861* (New York, 1976).

Potter, David M. *Lincoln and His Party in the Secession Crisis* (revised; New York, 1962).

Pressly, Thomas J. *Americans Interpret Their Civil War* (Princeton, 1954).

Quarles, Benjamin. *The Negro in the American Revolution* (Chapel Hill, 1961).

Quarles, Benjamin. *Lincoln and the Negro* (New York, 1962).

Randall, J. G. *The Civil War and Reconstruction* (Boston, Mass., 1961).

Randall, Samuel Sidwell. *History of Common School Systems of New York* (New York, 1851).

Rhodes, Charles Dudley. *History of the Cavalry of the Army of the Potomac* (Kansas City, Missouri, 1900).

Rice, Hooke. *American Catholic Opinion in the Slavery Controversy* (1944; Gloucester, Mass., 1964).

Rice, C. Duncan. *The Rise and Fall of Black Slavery* (New York, 1942).

Robinson, Armstead L. *Bitter Fruits of Bondage: Slavery's Demise and the Collapse of the Confederacy, 1861–1865* (Charlottesville, Va., 1991).

Robinson, Donald L. *Slavery in the Structure of American Politics 1765–1820* (Fort Worth, Texas, 1971).

Rosenberg, Nathan (ed.). *The American System of Manufacturers* (Edinburgh, 1969).

Russell, J. H. *The Free Negro in Virginia 1619–1865* (reprint, Baltimore, 1912).

Russell, Robert R. *Economic Aspects of Southern Sectionalism 1840–1861* (Urbana, Il., 1924).

Schultz, Harold Seessel. *Nationalism and Sectionalism in South Caroline 1852–1860* (Durham, N. C., 1950).

Schurz, Carl. *Henry Clay* (Boston, 1887).

Sellers, Charles Grier. *The Southerner as American* (Chapel Hill, 1960).

Sellers, James B. *Slavery in Alabama* (Alabama, 1950).

Simons, Algie M. *Class Struggles in America* (Chicago, 1906).

Sitterson, Joseph Carlyle. *Sugar Country, the Cane Sugar Industry in the South,* (Lexington, Ky., 1953).

Smedes, Susan Dabney. *Memorials of a Southern Planter* (New York, 1965).

Stampp, Kenneth M. *America in 1857: A Nation on the Brink* (New York, 1990).

Stampp, Kenneth. *And the War Came: The North and the Secession Crisis, 1860–61* (1950; reprint, Chicago, 1964).

Stampp, Kenneth M. (ed.) *The Causes of the Civil War* (1959; rev. ed. Englewood Cliffs, N. J., 1975).

Stampp, Kenneth M. *The Imperiled Union* (New York, 1980).

Stampp, Kenneth M. *The Peculiar Institution* (New York, 1965).

Steward, Austin. *Twenty-Two Years a Slave, and Forty Years a Freeman* (Canandaigua, N. Y., 1867).

Stockwell, Thomas B. *History of Education Rhode Island* (Providence, 1876).

Stowe, Harriet Beecher. *Uncle Tom's Cabin* (New York, 1983).

Stroud George M. *A Sketch of the Laws Relating to Slavery in the Several States of the United States of America* (Philadelphia, 1856).

Stuart, James. *Three Years in North America* (Edinburgh, 1833).

Sturge, Joseph. *A Visit to the United States in 1841* (London, 1842).

Styron, Arthur. *The Cast-Iron Man* (New York, 1935).

Swisher, Carl Brent. *Roger B. Taney* (New York, 1935).

Sydnor, Charles S. *Slavery in Mississippi* (Baton Rouge, 1966).

Tannenbaum, Frank. *Slave and Citizen* (New York, 1946).

Tate, Joseph. *A Digest of the Laws of Virginia* (Richmond, Va., 1823).

Taylor, Joe Gray. *Negro Slavery in Louisiana* (Baton Rouge, 1963).

Taylor, Orville. *Negro Slavery in Arkansas* (Durham, N.C., 1958).

Thomas, Emory M. *The Confederate Nation: 1861–1865* (New York, 1979).

Thornbrough, Emma Lou. *The Negro in Indiana* (Indianapolis, 1957).

Tocqueville, Alexis de. *Democracy in America, 2 vols.* (1835–40; reprint, New York, 1945).

Trexler, Harrison Anthony. *Slavery in Missouri* (Baltimore, 1914).

Turner, Edward Raymond. *The Negro in Pennsylvania* (Washington, 1911).

Tushnet, Mark V. *The American Law of Slavery, 1810–1860: Considerations of Humanity and Interest* (Princeton, 1981).

Twain, Mark. *Tom Sawyer* (New York, 1903).

Villard, Oswald Garrison. *John Brown* (New York, 1943).

Weeks, Stephen Beauregard. *The History of Negro Suffrage in the South* (Boston, 1894).

Weston, George M. *The Progress of Slavery in the United States* (Washington D.C., 1857).

Weyl, Nathaniel and Marina, William. *American Statesman on Slavery and the Negro* (Arlington, Va., 1971).

Whipple, Charles K. *Relations of Anti-Slavery to Religion* (Anti-Slavery Tracts No.19, New York, 1856).

Wickersham. *History of Education in Pennsylvania* (Lancaster, Penn., 1886).

Wigham, Eliza. *The Anti-Slavery Cause in America and Its Martyrs* (London, 1863).

Wiley, Bell I. *The Road to Appomattox* (Memphis, 1956).

Williams, Ben Ames (ed.) *A Diary from Dixie* (Boston, 1945).

Williams, George Washington. *History of the Negro Race in America, I* (New York, 1885).

Wilson, Henry. *History of the Rise and Fall of the Slave Power in America, 3 vols.* (1872–77; reprint, New York, 1969).

Wish, Harvey, (ed.) *Slavery in the South* (New York, 1964).

Woodson, C. G. *The Education of the Negro Prior to 1861* (New York, 1915).

Woodward, C. Vann (ed.) *Mary Chestnut's Civil War* (New Haven, 1981).

Warner, William F. "*The Columbia Race Riots*" (Lancaster County Historical Society Papers, 1922).

Wright, James Martin. *The Free Negro in Maryland* (New York, 1921).

Wright, John S. *Lincoln and the Politics of Slavery* (Reno, N.Y., 1970).

Author Biography

Paul Kalra is a Systems Analyst with a background in economics and marketing. He obtained a B.Tech from the Indian Institute of Technology in Kharagpur, India; an M.S.E.E in Control Systems from the Illinois Institute of Technology in Chicago; and a MBA from the University of Pittsburgh. As an immigrant from India who grew up where the caste system originated, he is in a unique position to provide insight into the political, economic, and cultural characteristics of the class system and its applications in the American landscape. His passion for American History led to his twenty-year quest to find answers to the Civil War and American slavery dilemma. *From Slave to Untouchable* provides his well-researched and insightful answers to commonsense questions for laymen. Mr. Kalra also authored *The American Class System: Divide and Rule* and is a member of Toastmasters and Bay Area Speakers Service.

Breinigsville, PA USA
05 April 2011
259160BV00004B/1/P